Samsung Galaxy Tab® S2 NOOK®

FOR DUMMIES®

A Wiley Brand

by Corey Sandler

Samsung Galaxy Tab® S2 NOOK® For Dummies®

Published by: **John Wiley & Sons, Inc.,** 111 River Street, Hoboken, NJ 07030-5774, `www.wiley.com`

Copyright © 2016 by John Wiley & Sons, Inc., Hoboken, New Jersey

Published simultaneously in Canada

For general information on our other products and services, please contact our Customer Care Department within the U.S. at 877-762-2974, outside the U.S. at 317-572-3993, or fax 317-572-4002. For technical support, please visit `www.wiley.com/techsupport`.

Wiley publishes in a variety of print and electronic formats and by print-on-demand. Some material included with standard print versions of this book may not be included in e-books or in print-on-demand. If this book refers to media such as a CD or DVD that is not included in the version you purchased, you may download this material at `http://booksupport.wiley.com`. For more information about Wiley products, visit `www.wiley.com`.

Library of Congress Control Number: 2015956628

ISBN 978-1-119-17111-9 (pbk); ISBN 978-1-119-17112-6 (ebk); ISBN 978-1-119-17108-9 (ebk)

Manufactured in the United States of America

10 9 8 7 6 5 4 3 2 1

Contents at a Glance

Table of Contents

Introduction

*I*n the beginning was the book, and it was good. There were books carved into stone and books inscribed on papyrus and eventually books made on printing presses in sizes small, medium, and large.

We skip forward to modern times and the invention of the computer, which began in sizes extra large (the first models were the size of houses, with snapping switches and whirring reels of tape). Eventually computers got smaller and more personal.

Then we entered the time of the tablet and the age of the smartphone, each of which are handheld computers. The first tablets were pretty good as a way to display electronic books, and some basic computer tasks including email and Internet access. The first smartphones connected to cellphone systems for telephony and had tiny screens that could be used to connect to the Internet and display fragments of pages of books.

And now . . . almost everything has converged.

Smartphones have gotten larger and smarter; the biggest of them are nick-named a bit awkwardly as *phablets*: phone tablets. You can make and receive calls, read eBooks and newspapers, and watch TV and movies on the go.

At the same time, tablets have gotten smarter and quicker and thinner and lighter. And using a wireless connection, you can even make phone calls from a tablet.

Today's buyers, then, have a choice between a relatively large phone or a relatively small tablet.

The full name of the device we're gathered to explore is the Samsung Galaxy Tab S2 NOOK. It's very much a member of the Samsung Galaxy Tab family, but please don't ask me to explain Samsung's very strange naming conven-tions. We simply don't have the time. Suffice it to say, the Galaxy Tab 4 was followed by the Galaxy Tab S, which begat the Galaxy Tab S2. (For what it's worth, Henry Ford's Model T was followed by the Ford Model A. Go figure.)

The final word in the nomenclature is NOOK, and here's what that means: The Samsung Galaxy Tab S2 NOOK comes predisposed to install the full suite of NOOK apps. They aren't there when you first turn on the device, but you're offered the chance to set up an account with Barnes & Noble and receive all the digital reading tools that come with that free membership.

For the record, you don't have to install the NOOK apps on your new tablet, in which case you'll be the puzzled owner of a Samsung Galaxy Tab S2 NOOK without NOOK features. There's nothing illegal or immoral about that configuration, but if that's your goal, you might as well purchase (at the same price) the tablet directly from Samsung or from an electronics dealer. Going the other way, though, if you happen to purchase a Samsung Galaxy Tab S2, you can always add the NOOK apps, which are freely available by going on the Internet to the Barnes & Noble, NOOK, or Google Play website and installing them on your tablet.

The Samsung Galaxy Tab S2 NOOK is one of the most advanced models on the market with a truly spectacular full-color screen, an advanced set of radios, an improved camera and video recorder (one each on the front and back), a built-in GPS system for maps and direction finding, and full permission for users to add specialized programs *(apps)* that are available from Barnes & Noble, Samsung, Google, and even (perish the thought) from Amazon.

The price, alas, has risen from bargain-basement levels, but buyers will be getting a no-excuses tablet. Depending on the way you want to look at it, the Samsung Galaxy Tab S2 NOOK is either one of the most advanced electronic readers yet made, or Barnes & Noble has added its NOOK software to perhaps the most advanced tablet on the market.

About This Book

I've been writing books about computers and tablets all the way back to the birth of the industry. And as good as the new Samsung Galaxy Tab S2 NOOK tablet is, they have continued a long tradition in computer manufacturing: The skimpy little instruction booklet that comes with it (all of 14 pages of minimal detail) is best used as a coaster beneath your cup of coffee (placed at a safe distance from the tablet, please). The online manual isn't much better.

That's just the way it is. Myself, I'm not complaining: I've made a nice living for a long time filling in the gaping blanks between. Herewith, then, the keys to the Galaxy.

You can read this book from front to back, if you wish. Or you can jump to a section that deals with whatever questions you have. Each of the parts deals with a particular task or function, and each chapter covers a specific topic.

My goal, as always, is to present *news you can use* and skip over as much unnecessary bafflegab as possible. When I feel it necessary to go a bit into technological detail, you'll find those sections nicely fenced off; enter if you want, or keep the barn door latched. We're in this together, and I've done my best to make the book easy to read and understand (and even entertaining in places).

I call the tablet by its first name when it seems appropriate, and in other places I call it the *Tab S2 NOOK*. And in places where the hardware isn't the issue, I might even just call it *the NOOK* or *the tablet*.

Like other books in the constantly expanding *For Dummies* universe, you'll be directed to do things by numbered steps. Sometimes you'll be advised to *choose* a menu item, and then to *tap* a command. It's all quite touchy-feely, I promise.

Foolish Assumptions

The first and most important assumption I make for all of my books of this sort is this: **You, dear reader, are an intelligent, capable, and curious person who wants to know how to *use*** what seems at first glance to be a very complex technical device.

Put another way, you're not looking to build a Samsung Galaxy Tab S2 NOOK from spare parts recovered from your kitchen junk drawer, and you have no interest whatsoever in writing your own software to make the hardware sing and dance.

And the second assumption is this: **You already own, or are seriously considering buying, a Tab S2 NOOK.**

And because we're nearly a decade into the Time of the Tablet, I suspect that **you have seen a tablet** and probably made at least a few swipes at one. Because of this, I skip the "Isn't it amazing?" part and get right to the point: They keep getting better and better.

Although it isn't essential, I also assume that **you have your own desktop or laptop computer or have access to one.** It doesn't matter whether it be a Windows or Macintosh design. And I also assume that you have a Wi-Fi wireless computer network you can use at home or at work or in a public library or other place you can use.

The Tab S2 NOOK needs a Wi-Fi connection for you to register and configure it, and then reach the Internet for all purposes, including stocking the tablet with books and music and video and games.

Another assumption is that **you're aware of the relatively new world of apps.** It's short for *application,* which is another word for a software program. On a desktop or laptop computer, software has become larger and more complex year by year. But in the reduced world of the tablet, there's a different concept: small and specialized.

Icons Used in This Book

This icon is there to tell you when danger — or at least serious problems — lie ahead. If you don't heed this information, you might damage your tablet or yourself or you might lose really important information.

This icon is there to remind you of something. This information tells you how to do something you'll often need.

This icon tells you of useful tips and suggestions to get the most from your new tablet. This information might save you time or money. Or better — both.

You probably don't need to know this stuff, but aren't you a little bit curious? Go ahead, try a few. There are no pop quizzes in this book.

Beyond the Book

I've written a lot of extra content that you won't find in this book. Links to the articles are on the parts pages. Go online to find the following:

- **Make a profile for each person who uses your tablet at**

  www.dummies.com/extras/samsunggalaxytabS2nook

- **If you can't automatically connect to an established email server, try Samsung's recommendations at**

  www.dummies.com/extras/samsunggalaxytabS2nook

✒ **Get the best pictures possible from the camera with help from**

       `www.dummies.com/extras/samsunggalaxytabS2nook`

✒ **Take certain points into consideration before buying an app**

       `www.dummies.com/extras/samsunggalaxytabS2nook`

✒ **Find out about ten fun or helpful — and free — apps at**

       `www.dummies.com/extras/samsunggalaxytabS2nook`

✒ **The Cheat Sheet for this book is at**

       `www.dummies.com/cheatsheet/samsunggalaxytabS2nook`

✒ **Updates to this book, if we have any, are at**

       `www.dummies.com/extras/samsunggalaxytabS2nook`

Where to Go from Here

You go from here to the first part and the sections that lie behind. You could start by reading the copyright and trademark page, or read the names of all the fine people at Wiley who helped transform my keyboard taps into the book you're holding. But perhaps you'd like to save that for an epilogue. Go forth and explore Samsung Galaxy Tab S2 NOOK and the device itself; they're meant for each other.

Part I
Meeting the Samsung Galaxy Tab S2 NOOK

Visit www.dummies.com for more great *Dummies* content online.

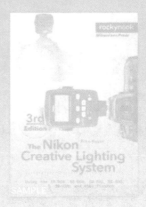

Corey's NOOK Library

In this part . . .

 Explore the Tab S2 NOOK parts.

 Turn it on and set it up it for first use.

 Read about how to use the touchscreen.

 Tap and talk to the keyboard.

TypeMail

My KNOX

Word

Excel

PowerPoint

Microsoft Apps

Settings

Clock

Current Read

NOOK Shop

NOOK Search

NOOK Home

Chrome

Apps

1

Another Galactic Leap
for the NOOK

In This Chapter

▷ Turning it on, turning it off

▷ Flying off into Airplane Mode

▷ Locking and unlocking the door to your tablet

▷ Adding more memory on a microSD card

"*A* rose is a rose is a rose," wrote Gertrude Stein. I take her point: A tablet is a tablet is a tablet.

A small thin box frames a flat plastic screen that sits above some tiny processor and memory chips and a battery and we call it — in its dozens of brands — a tablet. That little box today can hold and display nearly all the world's books, magazines, and newspapers. It can sing, show videos, take pictures, make movies, determine its location from an orbiting satellite, connect to the Internet, and send and receive emails and messages.

So I said a tablet is a tablet, but you could also say the same about cars. Yet you know there's a vast difference between a Ferrari LaFerrari and a Nissan Versa.

With this version of the NOOK, Barnes and Noble has leap-frogged from a very basic model to one with nearly all the bells and whistles you could ever want. This tablet is more of a tablet than a basic tablet. Got that, Rose?

Just about the only thing the Samsung Galaxy Tab S2 NOOK lacks is a decent instruction manual. And that's why I wrote this book.

Cozying Up to Your NOOK

To download books or email or to browse the web with a Tab S2 NOOK, you need access to the Internet. You'll probably use the tablet's built-in Wi-Fi to connect to a system plugged into the Internet. See Figure 1-1.

Battery level

Wi-Fi signal strength   Time

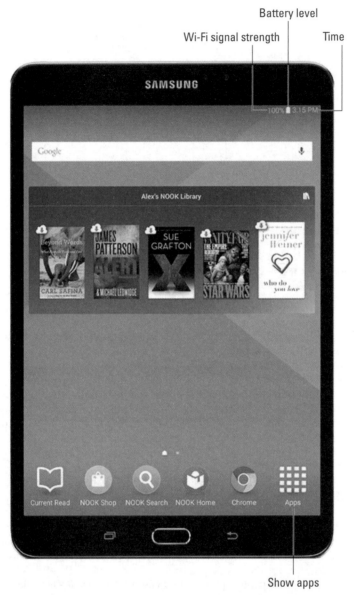

Show apps

Photo courtesy of Barnes & Noble, Inc.

Figure 1-1: Wi-Fi signal strength, battery level, and time are in the upper right. The icon in the lower right displays apps.

When you purchase your Tab S2 NOOK, it comes in an unpretentious cardboard box about the size of a thick paperback book. (Remember those?)

The box is there mostly to protect the tablet on its long and complicated journey from the factory to a warehouse and from there to a store and into your hands. Within the box: the Galaxy Tab S2 NOOK and a few little necessities:

✔ **A USB cable:** This cable carries data to and from your tablet when you connect the tablet to a laptop or personal computer. Use the same USB cable to recharge the internal battery.

✔ **A battery charger:** When you're ready, plug it into an AC wall socket and attach the larger connector of the USB cable to it. Then plug the smaller connector to the Galaxy Tab S2 NOOK. See Figure 1-2.

Figure 1-2: The AC adapter plugs into a wall socket; the larger end of the USB cable attaches to the charger.

✔ **Two business-card-sized booklets:** One is called the *Health & Safety and Warranty Guide,* and it advises you to not drop the tablet on your toe, and how if you do Samsung isn't going to pay for the repair to your tablet or your toe. The other booklet, all 14 pages of it (plus two blanks), is called the *Samsung Galaxy Tab S2 NOOK Quick Start Guide.* It's certainly quick, but not much of a start.

Keep the box, along with the warranty information and your receipt. If you ever need to return the tablet to the seller, send it in for service, or ship it to someone else, the original box is ready.

Sooner or later, you should remove the protective plastic sheet that sits atop the LCD screen. It works well to protect the device in transit, but it will interfere with using the touchscreen and collect dirt. Put it back in the box as a treasured memento.

Nothing like Moses's

What's a *tablet?* Way back in ancient times, about 2007 or so, we came to behold the first electronic reading devices, which were single-purpose handheld devices that used something called eInk to draw text on a nearly white background. A few years later the two devices came together in the first successful tablets, which were thin, flat, multipurpose computers that used touchscreens instead of keyboards and memory chips instead of spinning hard drives. You can still buy an eInk reader, but it isn't much use for anything but reading. The future seems to lie in faster and more colorful tablets with LCD screens.

Charging the Battery

The Samsung Galaxy Tab S2 NOOK comes with a built-in (and non-removable) rechargeable battery. Your battery probably still has some power in it from testing at the factory. (Mine arrived about half full.)

Although you can use the tablet without a full charge, or use it while it's in the process of charging, *don't use it immediately after you get it.*

Why would you want to fully charge the battery before first use?

- ✔ **You want to make sure that the battery, the charger, and the tablet itself are each working properly.**

- ✔ **Bringing the battery to full charge may help it last longer.** That is, if you properly condition it with a full charge before using it first. See Figure 1-3.

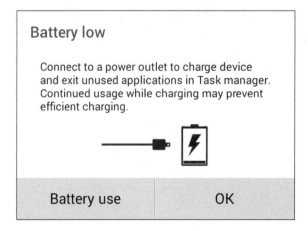

Figure 1-3: The tablet beeps and warns you when the battery level drops to only a few minutes of usable power, and the screen gets dim.

After the battery's fully charged for the first time, you can use your tablet. But don't be in a rush to top off the battery: Let it drain down to nearly empty, then recharge it fully. Do this for the first three or four cycles.

Recharge the battery when it's at 15 or 20 percent of capacity; it's generally not a good idea to let it go all the way to 0. In fact, the NOOK is smart enough to turn itself off *before* it reaches completely empty.

✔ **When you first turn on the tablet, you have to register the device at lots of places.** You have to sign in to a Wi-Fi system and sign in with Samsung, Google, and a few apps makers. And if you want to use the NOOK facilities, you need to sign in and create a Barnes & Noble account or register using an existing account you may already have.

Be sure to install any software updates.

Don't start the registration and update process with an insufficient battery charge. If the tablet were to turn off, you might have to reset all the operating system elements and apps when you begin again.

And so, here's how to give your tablet its first full charge:

1. **Attach the larger end of the USB cable to the charger.**

   The cable only fits one way. Pay attention to the white positioning bar inside the charger and its corresponding bar inside the cable. Don't force the two positioning bars against each other.

2. **Attach the USB cable to the Samsung Galaxy Tab S2 NOOK.**

   The smaller connector on the cable connects to the port on the bottom of your tablet. The side of the cable that has the three-forked USB symbol will be facing you as you're looking at the front of the tablet. Again, don't force the plug in the wrong way. See Figure 1-4.

3. **Plug the charger into a wall outlet.**

   Go for a walk, mow the lawn, read a book printed on dead trees, bake a cake. A nearly empty battery can take as long as four hours to recharge.

For the first three or four times you use your tablet, I recommend draining the battery to nearly empty and then fully recharging it.

You can check on charging by pressing the Home key on the tablet. Unplug the charger when it reaches 100%.

You can also recharge your Tab S2 NOOK by connecting the USB cable to a USB port on a PC or laptop, although this is a relatively slow process that can take six or more hours for a full refill. I consider the USB charging option as an emergency backup only.

Figure 1-4: The smaller end of the USB cable plugs into the bottom of the tablet, slightly off-center to the right of the Home button.

Putting the Tab S2 NOOK on the Table

Begin with a physical examination. No need for a stethoscope or rubber gloves. Place your Tab S2 NOOK on a desk or table in front of you with the tablet lying on its back, with its top facing away from you. See Figure 1-5 for a guided tour.

The front

The front is home to several items of note, the most significant one being the screen:

- A Samsung logo, in case you need to be reminded who made it
- A light sensor, which can automatically adjust screen brightness and contrast depending on the light levels indoors or outdoors
- The front-facing camera lens to take a selfie or a picture of yourself with someone else (an "ussie"?)
- The LCD color touchscreen
- Three keys at the bottom (shown in Figure 1-6) left to right:
  - *Recent.* Tap it to display apps you used recently, or hold it for a second to show Home screen options.
  - *Home and Finger Scanner.* Press this key to go to the Home screen. The same key can read your fingerprint (which you can use instead of a password to get into your tablet); you have to set up this option, and I show you how soon.
  - *Back.* Touch to return to the previous screen or option, or to close a dialog box, menu, or keyboard.

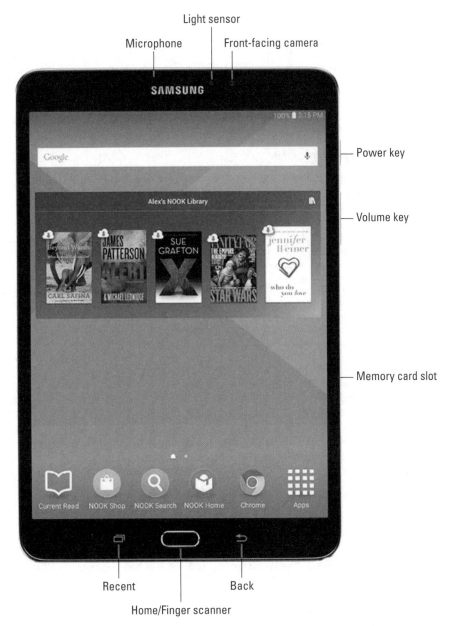

Figure 1-5: A map to the external parts on the front of the Samsung Galaxy Tab S2 NOOK.

The left side

Move along. There's nothing to see here, folks. Really. Nothing. The left side of the Galaxy Tab S2 NOOK serves no purpose other than to give you somewhere to place your fingers when you hold the tablet.

Figure 1-6: The keys just below the screen are Recent, Home, and Back.

The right side

The right side is where you'll find several essential keys, a pinhole, and a slot. From top to bottom on the right side, they are:

- **Power.** Press and hold it for a second or two to turn on your tablet. Press it briefly and release to lock the tablet or wake it from sleep. Press and hold it to turn the device off or restart it, or to put the tablet into Airplane Mode.

- **Volume.** When the Home screen is displayed, press one end or the other of this rocker key to adjust the volume. When you're playing music, any adjustments you make here affect only music volume. Either way, you know how they work, I'm sure: + means louder and – means quieter, all the way down to mute.

- **Memory card slot.** This tiny opening can accept a little sliver of microSD or microSDHC card that holds information in addition to your tablet's built-in memory. The card can be as large as 128GB, and if that huge amount of real estate isn't enough, you can simply remove it and install a new card.

The advanced Tab S2 NOOK also works with USB On-The-Go devices, including flash memory sticks and other accessories. I expect to eventually expand my NOOK by using flash memory that I can also use as a quick means of transport between the tablet and a computer.

The top side

A handsome, shiny near-twin to the left side, the top side has just a tiny little pinhole. Despite what Samsung and Barnes & Noble show in their manuals, this little pinhole is the entryway to the microphone.

Hidden behind a tiny hole, it picks up sound for videos, video conferences, and your voice for Internet (not cellular) phone calls. If you plan to use the microphone, make sure neither the protective case you use, nor your hand, blocks the opening.

The bottom

Way down here is the place where your tablet gets its power and outputs a bit of sound.

Flying your NOOK to the moon

Okay, maybe not the moon, but perhaps you'd like to take your NOOK to Europe or another part of the world that uses a different electrical voltage. (The United States, Canada, Japan, and a handful of other countries provide power between 100 and 120 volts, while most of the rest of the world pumps out 220 or 230 volts and require a plug of a different shape.)

Not a problem for your Samsung Galaxy Tab S2 NOOK or Galaxy Tab 4 NOOK. The power

adapter can work with incoming AC power in the range from 100 all the way to 240 volts. But you need a plug adapter to take the flat rectangular plugs and make them work in other shapes. All you need is the physical adapter — a plug into a different plug device — and *not an electrical transformer.* You can research plug adapters on the Internet; prices should be between a cup of coffee and a pizza.

- You'll find not one but two tiny speakers on the bottom, producing something close to stereo sound (although you shouldn't expect bone-rattling high fidelity). The speakers are used for music, voice, and system notifications. As with the microphone, make sure that the speakers aren't covered, or else the sound will be muffled.

- The second opening from the left is the all-important USB charger/accessory port. Here's where you attach the USB cable that comes with your tablet. That cable, in turn, attaches to the AC adapter, allowing you to recharge the internal battery. You can disconnect that same cable from the AC adapter, then connect the cable to a PC or laptop to transfer or sync music or files.

  Samsung promises that you can use this same port for accessories (not included in original purchase). What kind of accessories? Perhaps an external keyboard or an external memory storage device like a USB flash key.

- The third opening from the left is the headset jack, which works with a standard 3.5mm connector for earbuds or connects to an external sound system.

The headset jack works well with earbuds or headphones, but you can also output audio from your Tab S2 NOOK to stereo systems with advanced controls and large speakers. For example, my car has a 3.5mm input jack for its radio; I bought a cable with a 3.5mm plug on each end (called a *male-to-male cable*) to use my NOOK as a music player for files I loaded onto the tablet.

The back

The tablet's back gives the tablet something to hold up the front. To see it, turn your tablet over so that the front is facing down. Although you don't have to baby your device, for safety's sake put a cloth or a magazine under the screen.

Figure 1-7 points out the two items of note are on the back (plus some more advertising). Here's what you find:

Figure 1-7: The back of the tablet has the rear-facing camera and connectors for certain types of tablet cases.

✔ The rear-facing camera. The lens, above the advertising for Samsung, is part of your tablet's main camera, for taking photos or videos while you watch the LCD on the other side.

✔ A pair of Simple Clickers. These little anchoring points are used to attach certain designs of (unincluded) protective or special-purpose covers for your tablet. One Samsung accessory adds a physical keyboard for attachment to a larger 9.7-inch LCD screen.

Turning On, Turning Off, Going to Sleep

The high-tech battery in your Tab S2 NOOK can hold its charge for several weeks when it's young and fresh, and the tablet is off. When you turn it on, the battery should provide power for somewhere between six and ten hours.

You can make the battery last longer by reducing the screen brightness and by turning off Wi-Fi and Bluetooth radios and the GPS receiver when you don't need them.

Powering on

I've already told you how to use the Power key to turn on your Samsung Galaxy Tab S2 NOOK: Press and hold the key for two seconds (*one Mississippi, two Mississippi*).

If this is the first time you've given life to your tablet, you're can't use it for reading or viewing or Internetting until you complete a few setup steps. The initial setup can take anywhere from 10 to 30 minutes, depending on how much detail you want to get into.

You should charge your tablet's battery before your first use, both for the health of the battery and to avoid the possibility of running out of power while the setup process is under way.

On the other hand, if you've already set up the device, turning it on brings you to either of two places:

✔ The Home screen (for an unsecured tablet)

✔ The Lock screen (if you require all users to enter a protective pattern, password, or PIN, or a swipe of the Home button to scan your fingerprint)

I recommend using one or another form of security to protect your tablet. The fingerprint or a very complex password is your best line of defense. Studies have shown that the most common passwords on millions of computers are *123456* and *password*. Why even bother? Remember that you'll likely be storing personal data, photos, and logins that may keep records of your credit card or banking information.

Use a password that's difficult and illogical. How about 16Friskie66laserBeam? Don't ask me what it means, but it *does* have meaning to me, and I can remember it. And no, I'll never use that password again, but it is of the sort I like.

Powering off

Press the Power switch for about two seconds while the device is running. A message asks if you really, really want to do that; tap Power Off to confirm.

Off is off. No alarms will ring, no email will be collected, no music will play.

Why would you want to completely turn off the NOOK tablet?

- ✔ You're on an airplane preparing for takeoff or landing and the flight attendant is glaring at you.
- ✔ You're in a hospital room with sensitive medical equipment (and doctors).
- ✔ You want to put your tablet on the shelf for a month while you sit down with a yellow legal pad to write your own Great American (or Canadian) Novel.
- ✔ Your battery is very low and you want to fully recharge it as quickly as possible. Attach the microUSB connector to the tablet and the full-size USB connector to an AC adapter that's plugged into the wall.

Going to sleep/Locking the tablet

The third option is to put your tablet to sleep, which in electronic terms is *not* the same thing we mean when Fido is headed to the vet for the last time. Putting a tablet to *sleep* means that the LCD screen and most of its internal circuitry are turned off, and just a small amount of power is provided to the system — enough to allow the device to return from the vet, I mean from sleep, at the push of a button. If you put a fully charged NOOK into Sleep Mode, it should hold its charge for several days.

The other way to look at Sleep Mode is as "Lock Mode," which is a way to block access to the tablet to unauthorized fingers and eyes without fully turning it off.

By default, the tablet automatically goes to sleep after the inactivity period. You get to set that amount of time.

Here's how to put the NOOK tablet to sleep: Briefly touch the Power/Lock key. Don't hold it and count river names.

While the tablet's asleep, the following functions are still awake:

- Email will still be received, *if the Wi-Fi radio is turned on.* You can turn off the Wi-Fi from Settings, or put the tablet into Airplane Mode to reduce power consumption.

- If your tablet is playing music, that will continue.

- Any alarms or timers you've set will remain active. (I discuss alarms in Chapter 14.)

To wake up a sleeping NOOK, briefly press the Power/Lock key. If you have to enter a pattern, password, fingerprint, or PIN, you'll go to the Unlock screen; otherwise, you'll go directly to the Home screen or the last page you were on.

Setting the sleep timeout

Your tablet goes to sleep all by itself if you don't do anything for a while. Why would you want this to happen? It'll save battery power and serve as some protection if someone lays paws on your NOOK without your permission.

Here's how to customize the sleep control:

1. **From the Home screen, tap the Apps icon, and then tap the Settings (gear) icon.**

2. **Choose Display.**

3. **Tap Screen Timeout.**

4. **Choose a timeout value from the list.**

   I prefer 5 minutes; the standard value is 30 seconds. You can set the sleep timeout in a range from 15 seconds to 10 minutes.

5. **Press the Home key to return to the Home screen.**

   For most users, a safe amount of time is between 2 and 10 minutes.

   You can manually lock the screen by briefly pressing the Power/Lock key on the right side of the tablet.

Locking Things Down

Please allow me to ask a few questions:

- Will you ever loan your tablet to someone else?

- Will anyone (family, friends, acquaintances, or perfect strangers) ever have access to your tablet when you're not around? Almost certainly.

- Can you imagine that your tablet might someday (perish the thought) be lost or stolen?

Preparing the tablet for lockdown

The Galaxy Tab S2 NOOK, as delivered, uses the very basic one-finger left-to-right unlock pattern, which is essentially an open door. Anyone picking up your tablet can figure that one out.

The swipe (or the choice of None for the Lock screen) offers no security for your tablet contents. You do have other options:

✔ **Pattern.** A gesture you create by drawing on your screen. This option gives you a medium level of security, which is better than a mere swipe.

The screen displays nine dots in a three-by-three pattern. Set a pattern by tapping any one dot; keep your finger on the screen as you move to other dots on the screen. Don't use an obvious pattern like a box or a line. The pattern lock can start at any dot. See Figure 1-8.

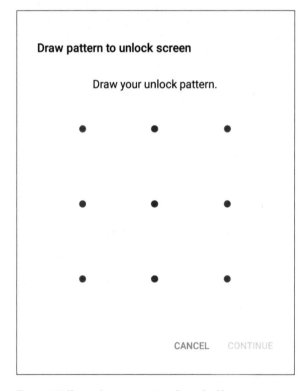

Draw pattern to unlock screen

Draw your unlock pattern.

●   ●   ●

●   ●   ●

●   ●   ●

CANCEL   CONTINUE

Figure 1-8: If you choose a pattern for unlocking, you can start at any of the nine dots and finish wherever you'd like; try something not very obvious.

My favorite type of password is a phone number or address that has no direct connection to you but that you can recall from memory. An old phone number of a distant relative? The street address of the post office in the town you lived in three jobs ago? Oh, and don't write it down on a sticky note and slap it to the bottom of the tablet.

✓ **PIN.** Enter a code number to unlock the tablet, with as many as 16 digits. A four-digit PIN offers 10,000 possible combinations, which makes this a medium- to high-security option . . . unless you choose something simplistic like 1234 or 0000. I often use all ten digits of a phone number that I know well but that isn't in any way directly connected to me. Got a favorite pizza place?

✓ **Password.** Use a complex word, preferably with a mixture of upper- and lowercase letters and a number or two, of as many as 16 characters. Something like 23aArdvarK for a high level of security.

✓ **Fingerprint.** Require the device to recognize your fingerprint for a high level of security. On the Tab S2 NOOK, the Home key has a fingerprint reader.

Registering a fingerprint

The electronic fingerprint reader in the Home key can identify certain unique — or at least rare — characteristics of the markings on the end of one of your fingers. It's not a perfect system, but you can experiment with friends and family, especially siblings. Here's your chance to blame everything on your brother or sister if their fingerprints prove similar enough to fool the reading device.

You can register as many as four fingerprints, and a password will also be recorded as an alternative means of entry to the tablet.

1. **From the Home screen, tap the Apps icon and then the Settings (gear) icon.**

2. **Tap Lock Screen and Security, and then tap Fingerprints.**

3. **Choose an option:**

   - To add a fingerprint, tap Add Fingerprint and follow the instructions. You have to apply and reapply your finger (I use my thumb) about ten times so that the system has a number of samples.

   - To rename a fingerprint, touch and hold the fingerprint and then tap Rename.

   - To delete a fingerprint, touch and hold the fingerprint on the screen and then tap Remove.

To change the backup password for your fingerprints, do this:

1. **From the Home screen, tap the Apps icon, and then tap the Settings (gear) icon.**

2. **Tap Lock screen and Security, and then tap Fingerprints.**

3. **Tap Change Backup Password.**

4. **Enter a new password.**

Fingerprints can also give you access to your Samsung account and certain online accounts. You'll find an option for those settings in the same Lock Screen and Security section.

Customizing your unlock scheme

While you're choosing a pattern, password, or PIN unlocking scheme, you're offered other ways to customize how your tablet greets you. Here are the options:

- **Clock Widget.** You can choose a clock size for your Home screens and decide whether you want to see the current date.

- **Personal Message.** You can put in, "Greetings, earthlings. I come in peace." Or anything else. Keep it clean, people.

- **Owner Information.** You can list your name and other information on the Lock screen, in hopes that a good Samaritan would return it. Tap Owner Information; then tap Show Owner Info on Lock Screen to enable or disable the option. Touch in the text field and type.

My owner information message has my name, email address, and *REWARD FOR RETURN*. I've never had to test whether the promise of a reward will entice someone to return my tablet, because I'm a pretty careful guy. I figure it can't hurt.

- **Lock Automatically.** Say how quickly to lock the screen after the screen automatically turns off.

- **Lock Instantly with Power/Lock Key.** Use this option to enable the Lock screen when the Power/Lock key is pressed. If you don't enable this option, the screen dims or brightens when the Power/Lock key is briefly pressed, but won't lock.

Depending on which lockdown method you select, you'll see one of these options:

- **Make Pattern Visible.** If you choose the pattern, this option lets you see the traces of your pattern as you draw it.

✔ **Make Passwords Visible.** If you choose to use the password, this option lets you see the characters as you type; they appear onscreen briefly and then disappear.

✔ **Make PIN Visible.** If you choose the PIN, this option lets you see the numbers as you enter them; they appear onscreen briefly and then disappear.

Making the pattern, password, or PIN visible may help you make sure you've put it in correctly, but I don't recommend displaying the unlock information if you use your tablet in a public place. Prying eyes are all around us.

Jetting into Airplane Mode

Although many scientists and some pilots say it's much ado about nothing, most airlines require passengers to turn off all electronic devices during takeoff and landing.

Today nearly every passenger has a phone and a tablet, and once on a 12-hour trans-Pacific flight, the annoying kid sitting across the row from me had a radio-controlled robot that beeped and whirred and said something from time to time. The theory is that all of these devices could somehow interfere with an airplane's essential navigational and control systems if they were transmitting radio signals. Little by little, the airlines and government agencies have been relaxing most of the regulations. In fact, some airlines have begun offering Wi-Fi broadcasts of in-flight movies that can be viewed on tablets, laptops, and phones.

In any case, your nifty NOOK has a setting called Airplane Mode. It disables Wi-Fi and Bluetooth radios but lets you read eBooks and play videos and music. You have two quick and easy ways to turn off the transmitting portion of the radios but leave other functions enabled.

The appy way to Airplane Mode:

1. **From the Home screen, tap the Apps icon, and then tap the Settings (gear) icon.**

2. **Tap Airplane Mode and then tap Off (or On to restore its function).**

When Airplane Mode is on, a small airplane icon is at the top of the screen, next to the battery power percentage.

The power way to Airplane Mode:

1. **Press and hold the Power key to display the Device Options menu.**

2. **Tap Airplane Mode.**

Putting More on a microSD Card

Your Galaxy S2 NOOK comes with 32GB of internal memory, which is a lot of space, but a good portion of that memory is devoted to the Android operating system and to various apps, including the NOOK app. You can, though, easily expand the amount of storage space in your tablet by plugging in a fingernail-sized microSD memory card.

There are enough kinds of *secure digital (SD)* cards to confuse even the experts. There are SD, miniSD, and microSD sizes, and then there are SD, SDHC (high capacity), and SDXC (extended capacity).

Here's what you need to know about SD cards:

- *Do* buy a microSD or microSDHC card. They are physically the same; the microSDHC specification, though, allows for larger amounts of memory and you might as well go big.

- *Don't* buy an SD or miniSD card. They are too large to fit in the tiny slot on the tablet.

- *Don't* pay extra for a microSDXC card. That's more speed than the tablet needs or can handle. No X factor needed.

I recommend buying a microSDHC card of at least 32GB, of class 6 speed; the maximum memory card size that can be used by the advanced Samsung Galaxy Tab S2 NOOK is 128GB, which is a huge amount of space. Make sure it's made by a recognized name brand: Kingston, Lexar, Samsung, Sandisk, Toshiba, or Transcend.

Installing a microSDHC card

The kind designers at Samsung have made sure you don't need a postgraduate degree in engineering to install a memory card. You can get to the card slot without removing the back cover, although with the ultra-thin and lightweight Tab S2 NOOK model you do need to make use of a tiny little tool to open the tray on the side of the tablet that holds the memory card. The tool is basically a little pin that fits into a pinhole on the side of the tablet to release the tray. (If you misplace the tool — easy to do — you can do it yourself with a sturdy pin or a thin paper clip.)

Just take your time, be careful, and follow these instructions to install a memory card:

1. **Turn off the device.**

   Technically this isn't required, but it is a good practice anytime you're working with electrical devices.

2. **Place your NOOK face up on a well-lit, clean, level surface.**

   The Samsung logo should be at the top of the device.

   Make sure no cups of coffee, soda, water, molten iron, or anything else can spill onto your tablet.

3. **Find the small, soft, plastic memory tray about two-thirds of the way down the right side of the tablet.**

4. **Carefully insert the removal tool into the pinhole beside the tray and push gently until the tray extends from the tablet.**

   The tray doesn't completely detach; a flexible band attaches to the internals of the tablet.

5. **Hold the memory card with the printed logo facing up toward you. Carefully place it in the tray.**

   The gold electrical contacts face down, toward the back of the device. The small triangle faces toward the Galaxy Tab S2 NOOK.

   Place the card carefully; it only fits in the correct orientation with its gold electrical contacts facing the tablet. If the memory card looks about twice as large as the opening, you've got the wrong card. Only micros need apply.

6. **Gently push the tray into place.**

   When a memory card's installed in the tablet, it's automatically mounted and ready for use. *Mounting* means the tablet has electronically recognized the card and it's ready for use.

Mounting or unmounting the memory card

When you install an optional memory card, it is automatically mounted (electronically recognized by the device) and prepared for use. However, if you choose to remove the card from the tablet, you should unmount the card using the operating system.

Unmounting the card helps prevent damage to the data stored on the card, especially if you remove the memory while the system is powered on.

If you unmount a card but do not physically remove it from the tablet, you will need to instruct the system to mount it again in order for it to be available to you for use.

Here's how to unmount a card:

1. **From the Home screen, tap the Apps icon, and then tap the Settings (gear) icon.**

2. **Tap Storage, and then tap Unmount SD Card.**

3. **Use the tiny removal tool and press the pin into the pinhole on the side of the tablet to release the tray and offer access to the card.**

If you need to manually mount a card, do this:

1. **From the Home screen, tap the Apps icon, and then tap the Settings (gear) icon.**

2. **Tap Storage, and then tap Mount SD Card.**

When you install an optional memory card in your device, the card memory displays as Total Space and Available Space.

Formatting a microSDHC card

When you buy a new microSDHC, it should come *formatted* (a process that electronically indexes its memory so that the computer inside your tablet knows where to store or retrieve information). In that case, it's ready to use.

If you insert an unformatted microSDHC card, the Galaxy Tab S2 NOOK will alert you. No biggie. To format a microSD memory card when the system asks, follow these steps:

1. **Tap the Format Now icon.**

   You're asked if you are sure. Sure you're sure!

2. **Tap Format Now.**

You can manually reformat a memory card, which is a way to clear its contents. Stop and check: Is there anything on the card that you want to keep? If so, make copies of that data in the internal memory of the tablet, or drag and drop the files onto a personal computer or other device connected to your Tab S2 NOOK. Formatting a microSDHC card *permanently deletes all data and apps* on it.

Here's how to manually format (or reformat) a memory card:

1. **From the Home screen, tap the Apps icon, and then tap the Settings (gear) icon.**

2. **Tap Storage and then tap Format SD Card.**

3. **Follow the onscreen instructions.**

If you want to completely wipe the contents of the card, manually format it. You might be clearing the card to give it to someone else, or perhaps installing a used card from another device or another person. Or perhaps you want to remove all traces of the actual plans for Doc Brown's flux capacitor for the *Back to the Future* time machine. I've had to do that many times. Each time I return from a trip to revisit some of the scenes of my childhood.

Formatting a microSDHC card permanently *deletes all data* and any apps that are stored on it. Yes, I'm aware that there are some service bureaus that *may* be able to recover data from a formatted or erased card, but I would hate to see you have to rely on that less-than-certain option.

2

Laying Hands on the Screen

In This Chapter

▶ Gesturing on your touchscreen

▶ Working with menus

▶ Opening more than one window

Some of us are old enough to remember the ultimate expression of the *mechanical* calculator, a desktop device that seemed to have a dedicated button for every possible command. It looked a little like the keyboard of a gigantic pipe organ, with enough controls for four operators,

But that was then. Today, the design of tablets and smartphones has gone entirely the other direction: there are only three control buttons on the front and two on the side of the Samsung Galaxy Tab S2 NOOK. Instead, we use our fingers to swipe, tap, draw, and issue other commands or enter information.

This chapter looks at touching the touchscreen. The next chapter covers tapping (and swiping and talking to) the keyboard.

 Like any piece of advanced electronics, your NOOK could be damaged if it touches a high-voltage device or a strong magnetic field. Don't leave it on top of a powered-on TV or a microwave oven, and don't play static-electricity games with socks on a carpet.

Keying In on the Basics

Your tablet has two physical keys on its right side: Power/Lock and Volume. Three keys sit below the LCD screen. That's it. Less is more. Minimalism surpasses complexity.

Table 2-1 lists their names and functions. The location is based on holding the tablet in *portrait* mode (taller than wide) with the word Samsung at the top.

Table 2-1		Galaxy Tab S2 NOOK Keys	
Icon	*Name*	*Location*	*Actions*
n/a	Power/Lock key	Top of the right side of tablet	Press and hold to turn tablet on.
			Press and hold to turn tablet off, or to put in Airplane Mode.
			Press and release to put the tablet to sleep.
			Press and release to wake the tablet from sleep.
n/a	Volume key	Right side of tablet, below Power/Lock key	Press + to increase volume.
			Press – to decrease volume.
[icon]	Recent key	Left of center on front of tablet, below screen	Tap to display recent apps; jump to one by touching its name or icon.
			Touch and hold to display Home screen options.
[icon]	Home key/ Fingerprint reader	Center on front of tablet, below screen	Press to go to the Home screen.
			The Home key handles the Fingerprint security feature.
 [icon]	Back key	Right of center on front of tablet, below screen	Tap to return to the previous screen or option, or to close a dialog box, menu, or the keyboard.

Gesturing at Your Touchscreen

The glass front of the Samsung Galaxy Tab S2 NOOK is pretty tough, but it is *not* invulnerable. If you back a truck over the tablet, it'll probably break. If you put it in a cement mixer with a load of gravel, it'll eventually scratch. Don't try to control it with a sharp object like a pen or a chisel or a pocket knife; you *can* use a soft-ended plastic stylus, although this particular model isn't specifically designed for that implement. Touch its screen as you would anyone or anything about which you care dearly. Play nicely, in other words.

You have a number of ways to communicate with a touchscreen, with variations depending on the app or control panel:

- **Tap:** To open an application, select an item from a menu, approve a command shown as an onscreen button, or to enter a character from the onscreen keyboard, touch or tap an object or icon on the screen.

- **Touch and hold:** Keep your finger on whatever you've touched to make a menu appear. Another use: to select an item to move or drag to another location. Another name for *touch and hold* is a *long press.*

- **Double-tap:** Touch an item on the screen twice in quick succession. A double-tap zooms in on an image; do it again to zoom back out.

- **Swipe:** Touch your finger on an item and drag it to another spot. Depending on the situation, you can swipe left or right, or up or down. Some apps might call this a *slide.* You can swipe to unlock your device, or to scroll through available options on the Home or other screens of the tablet.

- **Scroll:** Touch a blank part of the screen — a place without an icon or command — and move your finger left or right. Some people slide gently and easily (their finger, that is), while others like to flick as if they were clearing a crumb from the table and onto the floor. (I'm not endorsing, just explaining.)

- **Drag:** You can touch and hold to move an item, icon, *thumbnail* (tiny picture), or other element. Don't lift your finger from the screen before the item is comfortably in its new place.

- **Spread:** This is a two-finger maneuver. Touch the screen with two fingers and move them away from each other to zoom in on or enlarge an image.

- **Pinch:** Touch the screen with two fingers and move them toward each other to zoom out from or reduce an image (the opposite of a spread).

- **Rotate:** Place two fingers on the screen — perhaps your thumb and forefinger — and twist them as if you were turning a dial. If the app supports this gesture, the image rotates on the screen.

> ✔ **Sweep:** Pass or sweep your whole hand across the whole screen, just lightly touching its surface. In some situations this captures a screenshot.
>
> ✔ **Cover:** Cover the screen with the palm of your hand to pause the playback of a video or music file.

Setting Up Screen Orientation

A book is usually printed in *portrait* orientation (taller than wide) and a computer monitor is usually *landscape* (wider than tall). One of the beauties of a tablet is that you can usually have it either way. Some applications — games and some video web pages like YouTube — are locked into one orientation or another, but others allow you to choose.

The Tab S2 NOOK uses a screen with a 4:3 ratio, closer to the proportions of a full-sized book than to a widescreen TV. For many readers, that's a very comfortable sight, and it is one of the reasons Barnes & Noble extended its line of NOOK devices to the S2.

Your Tab S2 NOOK can figure out if you have rotated the screen one way or another. If you have enabled Screen Rotation, it will rotate the image.

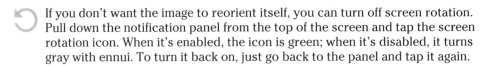

If you don't want the image to reorient itself, you can turn off screen rotation. Pull down the notification panel from the top of the screen and tap the screen rotation icon. When it's enabled, the icon is green; when it's disabled, it turns gray with ennui. To turn it back on, just go back to the panel and tap it again.

Starting at Home Base

Home is where the heart is. Home sweet home. Home base. It's where nearly all good things get their start. And, at least on the Samsung Galaxy Tab S2 NOOK, you can always return home.

The Home screen is the first thing you'll see once your tablet is up and running, and it's where you'll go when you close an app. Here you will find the icons to tap for apps, including the NOOK library and eReader, and where you find your email and the web browser for the Internet.

Everyone's Home screen starts out looking the same, but you customize it.

The first thing I do on any tablet, smartphone, or computer is put my own *wallpaper* behind the home screen. I do this because it makes me feel at home. The wallpaper you see in Figure 2-1 is a photo of the sun rising over lower Manhattan, taken from the bridge of a cruise ship headed for the dock.

The wallpaper on my lock screen is an image of sled dogs summering on an island in the Canadian Arctic. You can see larger versions in the collection of photos on my website at www.coreysandler.com.

You can add *secondary* Home screens by pressing and holding on any Home screen. When the menu appears, choose Page. Scroll left or right to see more Home screens.

Wallpapering your Home screen

Here's how to install your personal wallpaper on your Home screen:

1. **From the main or any secondary Home screen, tap the Apps icon and then the Settings gear.**

2. **Tap Wallpaper.**

3. **Tap Home Screen, Lock Screen, or Home and Lock Screens.**

   That means you can apply an image to Home, or Lock, or both. Or you can add different images to Home and Lock by going through the process twice and making different selections.

You can use one of the provided images as your wallpaper, or you can select an image you have taken with the tablet's camera or loaded onto your device from another source. Those personal images can be found in the Gallery.

Crawl space: Bottom of the Home screen

Let me take you on a tour of the parts of the Home screen, starting at the bottom and working your way up. You can see Figure 2-1 for an illustration.

At the very bottom of the Home screen is a set of app shortcuts, which you can customize to include the apps you visit most often, or the ones you want to be quickest and easiest to find. In the standard setup there's room for five app shortcuts plus the Apps icon that leads to the full list.

At the far right end of the customizable shortcuts is one permanent shortcut: the Apps icon. Touch the Apps icon to see the full suite of preinstalled apps, as well as any others you may have installed. You can get to your settings from here as well.

Throughout this book, for simplicity's sake, I have advised you to get to the Settings (gear) icon by going to any Home screen and tapping the Apps icon; from there you can find Settings. You can get to Settings several other ways, including pulling down the Notification panel on most screens. You'll also find the Settings gear on certain other panels. All the Settings icons take you to the same place.

Search bar   Nook Library widget

Customizable apps   You're home!
shortcuts
                    Tap to see all
                    your apps

Figure 2-1: The Home screen offers up apps. Here, I'm adding an image as wallpaper.

You probably won't be able to see all the apps on one screen. Scroll or flick left or right to see more. As long as you're just lightly touching the screen, and not pointing with conviction at a particular icon, you can scroll easily. Start any app by tapping its icon here (or tap its shortcut on the Home screen). Either method brings you to the same end: *appyness*.

Home screen indicator

Just above the Apps list, between the third and fourth app, you'll see a few tiny icons. If you see a very small symbol of a *home,* then this tells you that you are working on the main Home screen. If instead you see a smaller box shape, you're on one of several available secondary Home screens.

Swipe on the Home screen left or right to go through the various available screens. You can customize your system to place all of your Internet-related apps on one screen, for example, and all your tools on another. Or if your mind works this way, put them in alphabetical order from A to Z, or Z to A. And send me a note if you work backwards; I think I'd like to understand that form of logic.

If you don't see the app you want to open, scroll left or right. If you don't see the app at all, you can add it to one of the Home screens. On the Apps screen, press and hold the icon you want; a *copy* of the icon appears on the main Home screen (or a secondary Home screen if that was open when you went to the apps list). Press and hold on the shortcut and drag it left or right and then release it when it's on the Home screen you want as its resting place.

App folders

Moving up above the Home screen indicators is space for as many as five rows of app folders, which you can create and organize any which way you want. You can place copies of icons for everything related to one project or to one type of work in a folder and then tap that folder to go quickly to the appropriate apps.

Placing an app in a folder doesn't remove it from the full list of apps that are displayed when you tap the apps list. You can have multiple shortcuts that lead to the same place.

Midscreen: A word from our sponsors

In the standard layout for the Samsung Galaxy Tab S2 NOOK, the centerpiece of the Home screen is grabbed by a set of icons and a bookshelf for our sponsor, Barnes & Noble, and the NOOK Store. Collectively, they're known as the NOOK Library widget.

This is the most direct way to go to a book, magazine, video, or other item you have downloaded from the NOOK Store. You'll also see occasional messages or special offers from B&N. See Figure 2-2.

The standard setup has the NOOK Library right there in the middle of the screen, which makes sense for some people — especially those who think of their device as an eReader. But you don't have to give up so much real estate to the NOOK Library; you can touch and hold on it and then slide it to one of the secondary Home screens. You can also slide it to the top of the screen.

Tap to see more of your titles

Figure 2-2: As delivered, your tablet will give the NOOK Library prime real estate on the main Home screen, but you can move or delete it.

If you wish, you can remove the NOOK library from the Home screen, period. Press and hold it and then drag it to the trash can. Removing the NOOK library from the Home screen *doesn't* remove NOOK capabilities from your tablet. You can still open NOOK apps individually or from the Apps menu.

To NOOK or not

The Samsung Galaxy Tab S2 and the Samsung Galaxy Tab S2 NOOK are the same hardware and as delivered include the same set of basic operating system and apps.

As I have already noted, when you first turn on the version with NOOK in its name, the device is going to ask you if you want to install the NOOK app, and if you do it will add the library, store, and e-reader facilities that are part of that offering.

I expect that nearly everyone who buys the Galaxy Tab S2 NOOK will indeed install the NOOK software. However, it isn't required. And also, if you don't install the NOOK software when you're first setting up, you can always go back and add it at a later time.

Here's what you can do with the NOOK Library as it appears on your Home screen. Chapter 9 explains more:

- Tap the cover of any item to open it. If it's a book, the NOOK eReader opens. If it's a video, it will get ready to play. If the item has a small downward arrow in the corner of its image, it's waiting for you to download it. (You need a Wi-Fi connection to the Internet to download items.)

  Tapping the icon takes you to the most recently opened book, magazine, catalog, or other piece of reading material in your NOOK Library. It'll go to the last page you were reading before you did something else on your tablet.

- Tap the arrow at the end of the shelf to see other items in your collection.

- Tap the books icon at the right end of the shelf to open a more fulsome display of all the titles in your Library.

  The NOOK Book icon won't take you to a book you downloaded from Google's Play Store, or from your local library, or another source. This is for NOOK uses only.

The upper reaches of Home screen

The standard setup for the upper part of the Home screen includes space for widgets that can do things like tell you the time and date and current weather conditions and forecast.

And then you have the status bar, which runs across the top of the screen.

Our other sponsor

The Samsung Galaxy Tab S2 NOOK tablet uses the Android operating system, which is developed and distributed by Google. (The two most common operating systems for tablets are Android and Apple's OS. A small percentage of tablet devices use a version of Microsoft Windows and an even tinier slice employ other operating systems.)

As I explain in this book's introduction, we're fully into the Age of Convergence, meaning that more and more of the electronic devices we use share common operating systems and apps and even physical components. For Samsung users,

that makes for an easy transition between smartphones and tablets, and also makes it easy for the devices themselves to communicate and exchange data and settings.

And so the other standard widget that gets premier placement on a Home screen is a Google search bar. That makes it very easy to quickly search the Google compendium of websites, provided your tablet has an active Internet connection. You can, however, remove the Google search bar and replace it with another widget, or leave the space empty.

Notification bar and panel

At the left side of the status bar is a place of notification icons, which tell you when your tablet has received new emails or messages, notifications from the system or from Samsung, Google, or another supplier of apps, or information for apps you have. For example, if Samsung wants to provide an update or an upgrade to the operating system or to system software, you may see a message here asking you to authorize download and installation.

If you see a notification icon, you can delve deeper by pulling down the notification panel. Swipe down from the top of the screen with one finger (not two). Tap Email to go to the Email app, tap Screenshot to go to the Gallery and see the image, and so on. See Figure 2-3.

Here are some of the most common notifications:

- **New email has arrived.** If you are using the full-featured email client in your tablet, *and* if your tablet has recently been connected to the Internet, you'll see an icon of the back of an envelope with an @ sign on it. Open the email app to read your messages.

- **New Gmail has arrived.** An envelope with a large M on it means that mail has arrived in the Gmail app, a service offered by Google. (Why they didn't put a G on the envelope is beyond my understanding.)

- **Download is in progress.** A large down-facing arrow tells you that the download of a file or an app is currently underway.

- **Upload is in progress.** A large upward-facing arrow indicates that a file is being sent to a site on the Internet.

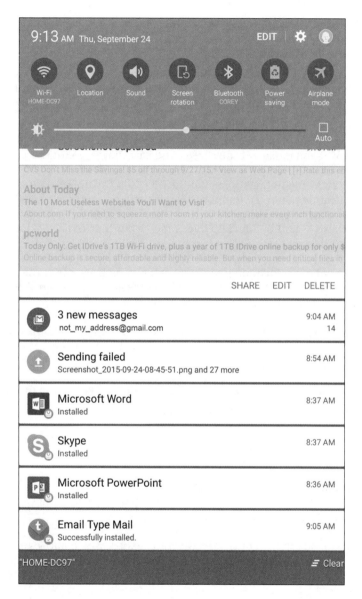

Figure 2-3: The notification panel recaps recent actions.

    ✓ **Location service is active.** A compass-like symbol, a circle with a point
      at its bottom, tells you that the tablet's GPS system is turned on. This
      allows apps to show your location on a map, display nearby points of
      interest, or provide turn-by-turn directions.

- ✔ **Google Play Updates are available.** A suitcase icon with a right-facing arrow tells you that updates to apps you obtained from the Google Play Store are available.

- ✔ **Google Play updates are complete.** Updates or installation of apps from Google are done. (If you use a different source for your apps, the website may push its own notification onto your tablet.)

- ✔ **Keyboard is in use.** A little icon of a keyboard tells you that the tablet is expecting input from the onscreen keyboard, which you would also know if you looked at the screen and saw the keyboard there.

To clear away the notifications, tap the blue X in the upper-right corner of the notification panel. To temporarily put them out of the way, roll the panel back up to from where it came or press the Back key; the notifications will still be there — and building up over time — but there's always tomorrow to deal with them.

Speaking of the notification panel, you can customize some of the apps or controls that appear there and adjust brightness of the screen and how loud the beeps, squawks, voices, and music are. Here's how:

1. **Swipe down from the top of the screen to display the notification panel.**

2. **Tap the Settings (gear) icon.**

3. **If it isn't already selected, tap the Devices tab at the top of the screen.**

4. **On the left panel, tap the notification panel.**

5. **Change the settings on the right side of the screen.**

Status icons

As if owning a Samsung Galaxy Tab S2 NOOK weren't enough of a symbol of how far you've come, you can always sidle up to perfect strangers and ask if they would like to see your status bar.

 At the right side of the status bar are status icons, which show you important information such as the signal strength for a Wi-Fi connection, a readout of the battery charge (either graphically or as a percentage), and other hardware notices.

At the right corner of the status bar is the current time. You can customize that, too: Adjust the date and time, select a different time zone, use the 24-hour or military clock format, or change the date format.

1. **Swipe down from the top of the screen to show the notification panel.**

2. **Tap the Settings (gear) icon.**

3. **If it isn't already selected, tap the General tab at the top.**

4. **On the left panel, locate the Device Manager section and then tap Date and Time.**

5. **Change the settings on the right side of the screen.**

Battery life

Way back when I was in college, I knew a guy named Bob who seemed to survive entirely on a diet of pork rinds. Your Tab S2 NOOK is much more sophisticated: It sups only on electrons.

You can see how much power remains in the internal battery by looking at the can-shaped icon next to the time. If it's full, your tablet is full of power. If it's almost empty and looking a little red, recharge it. (If you're using the tablet while it's plugged into its recharger, you'll see a black lightning bolt within the battery icon, telling you that the juice is flowing in.)

Don't let the battery die back to nothingness. That can damage the battery. Also, don't try to replace the internal battery. It should last a few years. Contact Barnes & Noble or Samsung directly if the tablet needs a battery transplant.

Wi-Fi connection

Although you'll use the reading and other apps without an Internet connection, most of the time you'll want to be in communication by Wi-Fi. The icon's presence (a pie wedge with curved plates plus a set of arrows) means the Wi-Fi system is active and connected. If the arrows are moving, that means information, including email, is being exchanged with the Internet.

If you see the pie wedge but no arrows, that means there's a Wi-Fi system that your tablet has found, but you haven't told the system to connect.

Depending on your settings, you may also see four other communication icons:

- ✔ **Wi-Fi Direct.** Similar to the standard Wi-Fi icon, this icon's arrows go left and right instead of up and down. This icon appears if you're using your tablet in local communication with another device that can exchange data without going on the Internet.

- ✔ **Bluetooth.** A stylized angular B tells you that the tablet's Bluetooth radio is active; you need to *pair* your tablet with another device and exchange security codes.

- ✔ **Connected to Computer.** A pitchfork-like symbol indicates that your Tab S2 NOOK is connected to a desktop or laptop computer. Confusingly, this icon can appear either in the notification panel (on the left) or the status bar (on the right), depending on the devices you're using.

✔ **Nearby Device.** If you've allowed nearby devices to come within the cone of connectivity of your Tab S2 NOOK via Wi-Fi, Wi-Fi Direct, or a mobile hotspot, you'll know it when you see this icon — a little tablet that seems to be doing the twist.

Other status or notification icons

Here are a few more icons you may see from time to time:

✔ **Mute Enabled.** A little speaker with a slash through its cone tells you audio has been silenced. (Wouldn't it be nice if you could aim that at the kids who want to loudly chat all through a red-eye flight to Istanbul?) You can mute your tablet by merely pressing and holding the – side of the Volume button until it's all the way off.

✔ **Alarm Activated.** Not a burglar alarm — a wake-up alarm. You can set an alarm, with a musical salute, from the Alarm Clock app. When it's on, a reminder appears on the notification panel.

✔ **Airplane Mode Activated.** If you turn on Airplane Mode (the quickest way is a two-finger pull from the top of the screen and then touching the icon) the tablet turns *off* Wi-Fi and Bluetooth radios but otherwise works. This way you can read books and use certain other apps, but block communication. A little jet airplane appears in the status bar to remind you that the radios are off. Retrace your finger-steps and turn *off* Airplane Mode to turn radios back *on.*

✔ **Blocking Mode.** Turn on this feature to block notifications, alarms, or both. Tap the Settings (gear) icon, choose the Device tab, and then tap Blocking Mode. Do this if you're in a place where noises are inappropriate, or if your tablet is on public display and you don't want other people to see your alarms or notifications. This icon, a slashed circle somewhat like a "Do not enter" sign, appears in the notification panel.

✔ **Error.** Houston, we have a problem. If you see a triangle with an exclamation point in it, do not panic. Yet. I've never seen one of these warnings on a Tab S2 NOOK, but if I did, here's what I'd do: Shut off the tablet, go for a brief walk around my office, and then turn it back on. Shutting off the device might clear memory of corrupted data. If the problem comes back, see the troubleshooting tips in Chapter 16 of this book; when all else fails, call Barnes & Noble or Samsung.

Googling for Mr. Search Bar

The official search engine of the Samsung Galaxy Tab S2 NOOK is Google, but you can use a different search engine if you prefer.

Google Search only works if your tablet has an active Wi-Fi connection.

The main Home screen has a Google search bar near the top. It's pointed out in Figure 2-1. You'll recognize it because it says Google on the left, has space in the middle for a search term, and has a microphone icon on the right. See Figure 2-4.

Figure 2-4: The Google Search app accepts typing or dictation.

Dictation is a very convenient way to conduct a search, and it works pretty well. You need an active Wi-Fi connection and to speak as clearly as possible. You'll still have times where the computer can't tell whether you meant "toe" or "tow," or "all" or "awl," but the quality continues to improve.

1. **Tap in the blank space on the Google bar.**

2. **Speaking clearly and directly at your tablet, say,** "Okay Google."

   If you do it right, you'll hear a beep and see the microphone symbol turn red.

3. **Speak your search command.**

   Depending on whether you ask a question or state some search terms, and also depending on the speech recognition engine, you may get a spoken answer or a screen full of search results.

Grabbing a Quick Menu of Notifications

You can pull down commands from the top of the screen with a one-finger salute: Swipe down to show the notification panel.

You can get to more on-off switches through here:

✔ Slide the panel of switches to the left.

✔ Touch the icon (three boxes and arrows) to the right of the Settings (gear) icon in the notification panel.

✔ From most screens, use a one-finger pull from the top. See Figures 2-5 and 2-6.

Figure 2-5: The quick panel offers controls for many functions. You can slide them left or right to show more options.

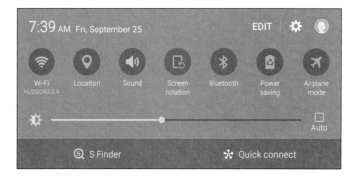

Figure 2-6: Here are additional quick panel options. Tap any to turn them on or off.

Flying the Tab S2 Wayback Machine

Mr. Peabody was the brainy beagle who took his owner, Mr. Sherman, on great adventures in the classic work of literature, "The Rocky and Bullwinkle Show." (Yes, I know it was a cartoon show in the late 1950s and early 1960s; it's not just age that makes a classic, by the way.) He used a device he called the WABAC machine (the "wayback" machine) for time travel. That was surely the most advanced machine ever invented by a beagle. It hasn't yet arrived on the Galaxy Tab S2 NOOK. What we do have is the Recent key.

Touch the Recent key to see the last five (or so) apps you've used; you can even scroll left to see a few more. Tap any app to return to it. To get rid of the list (see Figure 2-7), press the Back key or the Home key.

Multi-window icon

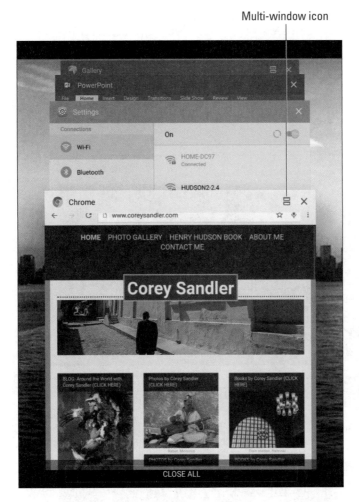

Figure 2-7: The Recent key is at the bottom of the screen; press it to see apps you've used of late.

Multitasking Lots of Windows

Some of us have a great deal of difficulty doing more than one thing at a time. Others can walk and chew gum. And just a few can write a letter, consult a map, and whistle a happy tune simultaneously.

The trick is to use a feature called *multi windows,* not to be confused with the Microsoft Windows operating system. You can, for example, ask the tablet to open an Internet window for a Google search while you're in the middle of composing an email, or look up an address while consulting a map. See Figure 2-8.

Not all apps are capable of this form of electronic magic. You'll need to look for a special icon for the multi-tasking wizards. It's pointed out in Figure 2-7.

Figure 2-8: Of asparagus and the island of Malta, in a two-screen multi window.

Here's how to use multi windows:

1. **From any screen, touch and hold the Recent button at the bottom of the front panel.**

2. **If the app you're using supports multi windows, tap another app to open it in split screen view.**

 Look for apps that have a stacked set of rectangles — like a multiple window — in their icon.

You can also launch recently used apps directly into multi window view. Here's how:

1. **Tap the Recent button on the front of the tablet.**

2. **Tap the multi window icon (two stacked rectangles above an app).**

The app starts in multi window view. Other recently used apps that support multi windows appear below the app you launched first.

Tap a second app to add it to the second window.

When multi windows are active, you can display a control panel that sits between the two windows. Here's what you can use it for:

 ✔ **Switch Windows.** Touch the icon that shows a pair of curved arrows chasing each other around a circle to swap the positions of the two open apps.

✔ **Drag and Drop Content.** Touch and hold on certain items and then drag from one window to the other. For example, you could copy an image or a calendar entry. Not all apps support this feature.

✔ **Minimize Window.** Tap here to *minimize* (make small and out of the way) the selected window. It appears onscreen as a small circular icon that can be moved about on the screen; tap it again to open it as a multi window.

✔ **Maximize Window.** Choose this command to open the selected window in full screen view, which automatically minimizes the other window.

✔ **Close App.** Tap this command to close the currently selected application. If two windows are open, the selected one closes and the other stays open and available.

3
Typing by Tapping and Talking

In This Chapter

▶ Moving, changing, and generally messing around with the keyboard

▶ Practicing penmanship

▶ Dictating instead of typing

The first time most people lay hands on a tablet, they're impressed with the screen and the ability to tap an app and read the web or consult email. But then comes the inevitable question: How do you get your thoughts and wishes from your brain to your fingers and into the tablet?

Here are the words you need to know: virtual, handwritable, voice-recognizable, plus a bit of intelligent prediction. Oh, and swipeable.

✔ *Virtual,* as in an onscreen keyboard that appears when you need it; usually at the bottom of the screen where you need to enter text, but in most situations you can also float and move it.

✔ *Handwritable,* as in a touchpad that changes your writing — block letters or even most forms of cursive — into words.

✔ *Voice-recognizable,* as in the tablet listening to your voice and putting your words onscreen.

✔ *Predictive,* as in the ability of the tablet to make an educated guess about what you've started typing.

✔ *Swipeable,* which is somewhere between handwriting your characters and tapping them. For reasons known best to Samsung, the ability to swipe is included in the software for the tablet but when you take the tablet out of the box and turn it on, *swiping* isn't turned on. I tell you in this chapter how to turn it on and how to add other versions.

Finding the Keyboard to the Kingdom

Figure 3-1 shows the standard Samsung keyboard, which is based on a traditional, typewriter-like keyboard.

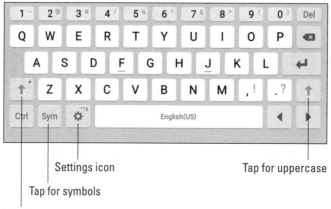

Settings icon   Tap for uppercase

Tap for symbols

Tap for uppercase

Figure 3-1: The basic keyboard with uppercase characters, which are standard for the start of a sentence.

Keep these tips in mind:

- ✔ How do you **hide the keyboard**? It depends. Try tapping the Enter/ Return or Done key, which closes the keyboard in most instances. Or, press the Back (arrow) key at the bottom of the screen.

- ✔ To shift into **uppercase characters**, tap the up arrow at the left or right side of the keyboard. The first letter of the next word you tap will be uppercase, and the next will be a lowercase letter.

- ✔ To type in **all caps,** press and hold the up arrow on the keyboard for a second or two and then type. Tap one or the other arrow to turn off caps lock.

- ✔ To type an **accented character,** press and hold on a letter. Slide your finger onto the special character and release it when the one you want is highlighted. See Figure 3-2 for examples of accented characters in their lowercase and uppercase versions.

Figure 3-2: These are the accented letters for e.

✔ To **insert a symbol,** tap the Sym key for a keyboard that has special characters, including mathematical operators and some of the essential symbols for Internet use, like the @ sign and /. In certain situations, the symbol keyboard offers more symbols, including square and curlicue brackets and bullets, stars, and markers.

To get to the secondary set of symbols, tap the Sym key. On the symbols keyboard, tap the key marked 1/2. To go back up a level, tap 2/2. In Figure 3-1 you can see one of the symbol keyboards.

✔ To **insert an** *emoji* (also known as an *emoticon*), press and hold the Settings (gear) icon to the left of the spacebar. Tap the happy face to display emojis like those in Figure 3-3.

Figure 3-3: There are dozens of *emojis* and special symbols available from the onscreen keyboard.

Adjusting the Keyboard Settings

As a lifelong user of typewriters and then computer keyboards, I know the advantage of a well-designed physical board with well-spaced keys and a good, solid clicky response. I can touch-type at a remarkable speed (and even hit the right keys most of the time). That said, it's truly amazing to switch over to a virtual keyboard on a tablet and experience its ability to adapt.

The quickest route to keyboard settings is from the onscreen keyboard. To the left of the spacebar is a key that can hold one of five icons. See Figure 3-4. Press and hold it to display the choices to modify the reactions of the keyboard. The choices are

✔ **Google Voice.** Tap the microphone icon to dictate.

✔ **Handwriting.** An onscreen panel opens to allow you to draw characters by hand.

✔ **Emojis.** A quick route to the emojis and a wide range of other symbols.

✔ **Keyboard.** You can choose amongst normal, floating, and split keyboard designs. You can move the floating keyboard around on the screen; this is helpful when the standard placement might block something onscreen. The split keyboard does exactly what it sounds like: splitting the keyboard into two smaller pieces, one of which is also a floater.

✔ **Settings.** A direct route to the panel of the settings that directly affect the behavior of the keyboard.

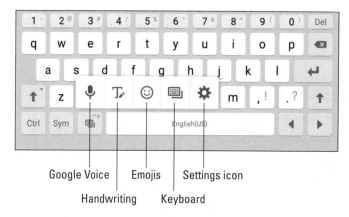

Google Voice   Emojis   Settings icon

Handwriting   Keyboard

Figure 3-4: Press and hold the key to the left of the spacebar to choose how you want to enter text, or to jump directly to the keyboard's settings.

Input languages

Your Samsung Galaxy Tab 2 NOOK will most likely arrive with U.S. English as its default language.

✔ To **add other keyboards,** tap the Settings (gear) icon on the keyboard and then tap the green + mark.

✔ When you add a language, you're asked if you want to **update the list of available character sets.** Go ahead and do so; you might find some very interesting choices, including some languages you might never have heard of.

✔ **Choose a new keyboard** by touching and holding (a long press) the spacebar; then slide left or right.

✔ To **turn on or off a foreign language keyboard** that you've downloaded, tap the Settings (gear) icon on the keyboard; tap the + Select Input Languages command. Then add or remove a checkmark beside a language. In Figure 3-5, you see one at work.

Figure 3-5: One of the beauties of a digital device is its almost infinite adaptability. Here I enabled the Cyrillic characters for a Russian keyboard.

You must have at least one language selected. Then you can switch from one to another by sliding left or right along the spacebar. Be careful on the Setup screen; you could accidentally remove the checkmark from English if you have another language enabled. If you do that and find yourself unable to communicate, you'll have to retrace your steps to this screen to re-enable English.

Smart typing

Think you're so smart? So's your onscreen keyboard. It can do things like this if you turn on those features:

- **Predictive text.** The tablet will try to guess what word you're typing as you type. It does this several ways: by consulting its own list of commonly used phrases, by making electronic note of unusual words or names you may have entered and, where appropriate, by consulting your Contacts list for names. Keep an eye on the black panel in the middle of the screen. If you see the word you want, tap the word.

From time to time, you're certain to let a misspelled or just plain odd word slip through. Your tablet will think that's exactly what you meant to say. If you see a suggestion for a word that's wrong — one that you don't want to have to deal with again — press and hold your finger on that word. When the tablet offers to remove it, tap OK.

- **Auto replacement.** You type *Thank* and the tablet guesses you next want to say *you*. If so, tap that word and proceed.
- **Auto check spelling.** Or, as most people would say it, auto spell check.
- **Auto capitalization.** Put a check in the box to automatically capitalize the first letter of any sentence.
- **Auto spacing.** This option is important when you use dictation or swiping (which you read about in this chapter). The tablet adds a space between each word without you having to press the spacebar.

✔ **Auto punctuate.** The tablet inserts a period (also known as a *full stop*) anytime you tap the spacebar twice.

Key-tap feedback

Strictly a matter of personal preference, but you might want to hear a little click each time you press a key. Or perhaps you prefer a vibration.

Another option is Character Preview. When you tap a character, the letter or symbol is shown in a cartoon-like bubble.

Moving the Keyboard

You can't shrink a keyboard with a pinch of your fingers, but you can make it *float,* which gives you a smaller, movable version.

To produce a floater, do this:

1. **Display the regular keyboard.**

2. **Press and hold the Settings (gear) icon on the keyboard (left of the spacebar).**

   A menu appears.

3. **Tap the icon that shows a stack of keyboards.**

   That icon is ordinarily all the way to the right.

4. **Tap Floating.**

When the floating keyboard is onscreen, you can move it by pressing and holding the little tab at its top. To return to the regular keyboard, press and hold the Settings icon on the floating keyboard and then tap the icon with the *tiny* stack of keyboards once again.

Improving Your Penmanship

Now for something completely beyond the ability of the computer keyboard I'm using to write these words. Your tablet's operating system can read words that you write.

Use your finger; never use a pen or a hard-pointed stylus!

Some models of Samsung devices, including the Samsung Galaxy Note smartphone series, do offer a soft-pointed stylus with some additional special features in the pen. That's not the case with the Galaxy Tab S2 NOOK.

Handwriting, for some users, is a really cool feature, and it usually works. Here's how:

1. **Display the regular keyboard.**

2. **Press and hold the Settings (gear) icon on the keyboard (left of the spacebar).**

   A menu appears.

3. **Tap the icon that shows the letter T beside a tiny little pen.**

   The keyboard is replaced by an electronic version of a yellow legal pad.

4. **Touch your finger to the pad and start drawing characters.**

These tips can help:

- You can either print individual characters or use your best (or worst) cursive. If you print, you're going to need to practice a bit to avoid pausing too long between letters; a pause is considered to be the end of the word.

- If your chicken scratch-like entries gets misread, tap a suggested word in the panel or tap the backspace key.

- The dashed horizontal line differentiates between uppercase and lowercase letters, or to enter punctuation. To spell my name, I could either make a significant difference in size between the C and the rest of the characters, or place the *C* above the line and the *orey* below it.

- A short hooked mark above the line is interpreted as a single or double quote. That same hook placed below the line is read as a comma.

When the device has interpreted your handwriting, it displays a cleaned-up version with much better penmanship. See Figure 3-6.

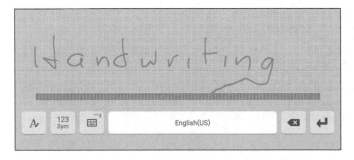

Figure 3-6: You can draw characters using your fingers, allowing the system to differentiate between capital and lowercase letters and those that go below the baseline, like q, g, and j.

Talking It Out: Google Voice

And then you can try ordering your Tab S2 NOOK around by issuing verbal orders with Google Voice. This used to be the stuff of science fiction. "Open the pod bay doors, HAL."

A microphone icon appears only in apps that accept voice input. And the feature generally requires you have an active Wi-Fi connection to the Internet. Only certain apps allow basic dictation without Internet access.

Turning it on

Here's how to dictate a sentence into a memo, an email, or most other apps that are set up to use the keyboard:

1. **Display the regular keyboard.**

2. **Press and hold the Settings (gear) icon on the keyboard (left of the spacebar).**

3. **Tap the microphone icon.**

   A larger red microphone appears, in anticipation of your words.

4. **Speak now.**

   Talk toward the microphone, which is the tiny hole just below the Volume key on the right side of the tablet.

Keep these tips in mind when you're talking to your Tab:

- **Be brief.** If you pause for a few seconds, the tablet will assume you've finished your sentence. If you speak too quickly or say too many words, the tablet may become bored and stop listening.

- **Say your punctuation.** Pause briefly after a word before you say *comma* (or exclamation mark or question mark or semicolon or . . .).

- Touch in the upper panel to **edit words.** Press the Settings icon again if you want to open the keyboard for final touches.

- If you want to **use another language** for dictation, your Tab S2 NOOK is happy to give it a try. Tap the Settings icon and then tap Select Input Languages to add a new language.

Lately, I've been using the dictation feature on the Tab S2 NOOK to practice my accent in speaking French. I figure if the device can correctly decipher what I'm saying, my pronunciation is close to the mark. *C'est merveilluse!*

To censor or not

Watch your mouth! Google Voice has a setting that allows you to block offensive words. Strictly in the interest of research, I tried it out, and the da**ed thing wouldn't include all of my words. Or you can turn off the block command and curse to your heart's content. By the way, Apple and Amazon *aren't* considered offensive words, even on a device made by Samsung and sold by Barnes & Noble.

To turn the censor on or off (sounds dirty to me), go to the Google Voice settings and add or remove the checkmark next to Block Offensive Words.

Making Google Voice settings

To customize some of the features of Google Voice, do this:

1. **From any Home screen, tap the Apps icon and then tap the Settings icon.**
2. **Tap Language and Input.**
3. **Tap Google Voice Typing.**
4. **Place checkmarks next to the options you want (or remove checkmarks from options you don't want).**

Swiping the Keyboard

As you know by now, the Galaxy Tab S2 NOOK doesn't come with a physical keyboard. Instead, a keyboard appears onscreen when needed. You can tap in the letters you need. (Many users get better results using the side of their pointer finger rather than the fleshy part.) Or you can use Google Voice to dictate, if you have an active Internet connection.

The Samsung Galaxy Tab S2 NOOK, as released in late 2015, was available only with an 8-inch screen. Samsung, though, also offered a version with a 9.7-inch screen, and that version could work with an accessory cover that adds a physical keyboard to the tablet. B&N may or may not ever offer a NOOK based on that larger screen, but you *could* purchase the 9.7-inch Galaxy Tab S2 and install the NOOK software on it and add the keyboard.

There's no easy way around this: Some people absolutely swear by Samsung's swipe keyboard, and others swear at it. Over the years, I've done both, but it's kind of growing on me. Even if it sometimes converts my pearls of wisdom into *portals of weirdness.*

There is one more way to enter characters; it's not for everyone, but some users find it to be very helpful once they have mastered the technique. It's called "swiping" and it is somewhere between typing and drawing characters. It works like this: Touch the first letter of a word you want to enter and then move your finger evenly and smoothly to the next letter you want to enter and from there to the following letter and so on.

To type *cat,* you tap the letter *c* and then proceed diagonally leftward to *a* and then diagonally rightward to *t.* Lift your finger, and if the universe is properly aligned, the word for a domesticated (or not) feline appears in whatever document you are working on. See Figure 3-7.

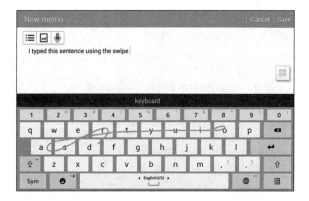

Figure 3-7: You can see my swiping path, where I was finishing up the word *keyboard.*

Practice for a while and spend time telling the system to throw away errors instead of throwing them back at you (and certainly not to get all huffy about it). I mean, who's in charge here anyway? Start slowly. Even then, you'll probably end up with more characters than you would using the old one-finger hunt-and-peck method.

Here are a few advanced tips:

- ✔ **Capital letters.** To go into uppercase, tap a letter and then drag your finger above the keyboard.

- ✔ **Double letters.** If you want to spell a word with double letters, make a little loop on the doubled character.

Here's how to turn on swipe:

1. **From any Home screen, tap the Settings icon.**

2. **Tap Language and Input.**

3. **Tap Samsung Keyboard.**

4. **On the left side of the panel, tap Smart Typing.**

5. **In the main panel, tap Keyboard Swipe.**

6. **Tap Continuous Input.**

Earlier models of Samsung tablets and smartphones came with a similar system from a third-party called Swype. And there's another version of the same sort of system, called SwiftKey Flow. You can download and install Swype or SwiftKey Flow from the Google Play Store if you want to try either.

As far as I am concerned, there's not a whole lot of difference between Swipe, which isn't turned on in the Tab S2 NOOK, and Swype or SwiftKey Flow, which you can download. I use Swipe on my tablet, mostly happily.

4

Getting Set to Go

*O*ne of the hallmarks of the human race is the fact that almost from the very start we have been determined to communicate in a lasting way, beyond mere grunts and ephemeral spoken language. I travel the world almost obsessively and have seen ancient sites decorated with the equivalent of billboards: good hunting over here, fresh water over there, the party house is the third door down on the left. Signs were chiseled into stone, painted onto walls, inscribed on papyrus, hand-illustrated in early books, and then machine-printed all the way until near the end of the 20th century when we all beheld the first portable electronic publications.

I guess what I'm getting at is that a NOOK tablet is, at its core, merely amongst the latest forms of communication. Quite advanced and quite adaptable and requiring a battery and a means of connection to the invisible but almost omnipresent Internet, but still a cousin to those ancient means of communication.

Because a digital tablet has so many advanced features, as a user your first interaction with the Samsung Galaxy Tab S2 NOOK must involve *configuring* — setting up — the device so that it looks and acts the way you want. Later on, you return to those same configuration and settings screens to fine-tune its behavior.

Being a First Timer

Everybody has a first time, sooner or later. It's exciting and terrifying and often awkward. But it has to be done, and eventually (often sometime around the second time) it all becomes familiar because you have now learned what goes where, and when.

It's that way, too, with the Samsung Galaxy Tab S2 NOOK.

In this section, I discuss the steps you need for the *very first time* you turn on your new tablet. The first time is different because it involves registering the device with at least three separate providers. You may also be tempted to add other accounts (like Facebook, Twitter, and Dropbox). I suggest that you keep it simple, sweetheart. Add optional services later, after you have your NOOK tablet up and running.

In a moment I make passing mention of the EULA, which isn't (by any definition) a musical instrument, but instead a mess of legalese to which you must agree in order to use the various systems and software of the tablet. You have two choices here: agree or return the tablet to its maker.

Setting up a Google account

The first major step involves setting up (or adding an existing) Google account for your machine. Why does this come first? Because the underlying operating system of the Samsung Galaxy Tab S2 NOOK is a version of Android, which is developed by and maintained by Google.

With a Google account, your tablet is set up to automatically receive updates to the operating system (or notifications that updates are available), and also gain access to other Google services, Gmail. And you use the same account to go to Google's Play Store, where you can download apps to expand the capabilities of your device.

When you turn on your device for the first time, you automatically go to a screen where you can enter the username and password for a Google account you may already have, or create a new Google account from the tablet.

You can sign up for a new Google account from your Samsung Galaxy Tab S2 NOOK, but it might be easier to preregister from a regular desktop or laptop computer. Regardless, for most users, it's a good idea to have the same username and password on both devices. If you also have a smartphone, use the same account. This allows you to synchronize calendars, Gmail, and apps you install on your tablet or phone (or both).

Here's how to sign up for a Google account from a desktop or laptop computer that's connected to the Internet:

1. **Open a web browser and go to** www.google.com.
2. **Click the Sign In link.**

3. **Click the Create New Account link.**

4. **Choose a login name and password.**

    Now you can use that same account when you register your NOOK tablet.

The fact that you have so much information and perhaps one or more credit cards included in your Google account should tell you one important thing: Use a complex password and change it from time to time.

Signing on for the first time

Your tablet has been fully charged, right? If not, get thee to Chapter 1.

1. **Press and hold the Power/Lock key to turn on the tablet.**

    The key is on the right side of the tablet.

    Brace yourself: It's going to take a while before the tablet comes to life for the very first time. Four, five, maybe even six or eight whole seconds. Think of it as a cute little puppy waking up from a dreamy sleep; it's going to take just a little bit of extra time while it figures out who it is, where it is, who you are, and if it feels all warm and fuzzy. When that's all done, it's going to roll over on its back and let you rub its tummy. The puppy, that is. Your Tab S2 NOOK is going to just sit there, but it will eventually be ready to welcome the strokes and taps of your fingers.

2. **Give your device a name, like I've done in Figure 4-1.**

    Why bother? This is how you'll recognize your tablet when you attach it by USB cable to a PC or laptop, or when you use Bluetooth or Wi-Fi Direct or other wireless technologies. I explain more about these technologies in Part II of this book.

    You can call your tablet anything you want. But remember, someday someone else may use your NOOK or connect to it or just see its name appear on a list of nearby wireless devices. Device names are generally visible to anyone within radio range. Can I suggest you consider for a moment how you want the world to think of you, or at least of your device?

    The other thing: Don't give your device a name that in any way would hint at its password.

3. **Touch the screen about two-thirds of the way down from the top and swipe from left to right.**

    You can use any finger on either hand.

Later in this chapter, I show you how to require a more demanding key to unlock your tablet. You *lock* your tablet to protect against unauthorized use: You don't want just anybody to read your email or notes, riffle through the books you've purchased or, perhaps most frighteningly, to use your accounts to buy books or airline tickets or entire airliners.

Figure 4-1: Please allow me to introduce myself: This is your tablet's ID in Wi-Fi, Bluetooth, and wired communication with other devices.

The very first set of options — Accessibility — is mostly aimed at users who might have difficulty reading small print, certain colors, or performing particular actions. I put accessibility options at the end of this chapter, and you can go there for guidance any time you need to.

Firing Up the Wi-Fi

Owning a tablet without regular or at least occasional access to the Internet is kind of like owning a broken pencil: pretty pointless.

Without Wi-Fi, you can't register your device with Samsung for updates and apps and offers, sign in to B&N for NOOK Shop access, or contact Google and get stuff from them. You also can't go to the Internet or get email without establishing a Wi-Fi link.

Four links in the Wi-Fi chain

When you first turn on your Tab S2 NOOK, you're guided right into the Wi-Fi setup.

Very important point here, please: You need certain elements to successfully connect your Tab S2 NOOK to the Internet through a Wi-Fi system. You have to set them up correctly. Work on that now. Here's what you need:

- **Turn on your tablet's Wi-Fi radio system.**

- **Be near a router.** You must be within range of a functioning Wi-Fi *router* (a signal transmitter/receiver), also called a *WAP* (Wireless Access Point). The Wi-Fi router itself has to communicate with the Internet. Your tablet may connect to a router but get no further than the box on the wall. If you can establish a link with a Wi-Fi system but get no further, check with the owner or operator of the router, or find another one to use.

- **Choose a signal.** You must connect to an available signal. Some Wi-Fi signals may be open to any user. Others (most, these days) require a password and sometimes a username or other details.

The Samsung Galaxy Tab S2 NOOK is a Wi-Fi device; it doesn't have a cellular radio. (Parts of the Galaxy Tab S2 can work with cellular systems; this book covers only the Wi-Fi features. You'll also have to add the NOOK app to your tablet, which is easily done by visiting either the NOOK.com website or Google's Play Store.)

I discuss Wi-Fi and two device-to-device close-proximity systems, Wi-Fi Direct and Bluetooth, in detail in Chapter 5 of this book. If you have a non-standard setup in your home, office, or elsewhere, you might want to go there now and return to this page later.

For 98.2 percent of users (I just made that number up, but by 98.2 I mean "nearly everyone"), connecting to a Wi-Fi system is quite simple. You probably already have one in your home or office. You'll also find them in most public libraries and many stores and restaurants. Barnes & Noble, as part of its intense desire to get you to buy a NOOK tablet and visit their stores, offers free Wi-Fi access. You can even read free samples or certain books in their entirety while you're in the store.

Hunting for Wi-Fi

The steps you go through are very similar to what you have to do any time you use your tablet somewhere new. And so, I explain the process of finding and signing on to Wi-Fi. When you turn on your Galaxy Tab S2 NOOK, it hunts around for any available Wi-Fi networks.

You will likely find three types of Wi-Fi network:

- ✔ **Open networks** aren't protected by any password or login requirements. Just choose the network, and you're on the Internet. It's *probably* safe, but be very careful about the sites you might visit; I would advise *not* doing your banking or making a purchase involving a credit card on an open network. If you have no choice, go ahead. Then plan on changing passwords and monitoring your credit card and bank statements regularly, which is something you should be doing anyhow.

- ✔ **Open networks with login** don't need a password, but the browser asks you to log in. You may have to provide your name, address, email address, and other information. In some cases, you may be asked to prove you are who you say you are by providing a smartphone number and then verifying that information by responding to a text message sent to the phone. Use your judgment about how much information you want to provide, and *don't assume this sort of system is protected from hackers, either.*

- ✔ **Locked networks** require a password and sometimes other information, such as a login name and security settings. If the locked network is in your own home or office, it's probably safe for things like banking and shopping.

But still: Change your passwords and regularly monitor your credit card and banking statements.

Enabling Wi-Fi on the tablet

When you first sign on to your tablet, turn on the Wi-Fi.

Why does the Tab S2 NOOK have an on/off setting for this essential function? Because when you're reading a book or watching a video or listening to music stored on your tablet, Wi-Fi is unnecessary and you can save some battery power by turning it off. And there are certain places — like an airplane in flight — where using transmitting radios isn't permitted, and for that reason there's also a switch to enable Airplane Mode, which turns off Wi-Fi and Bluetooth radios.

Here's how to set up your tablet to communicate with Wi-Fi:

1. **From any Home screen, tap the Apps icon and then tap the Settings icon.**

2. **Tap Wi-Fi and then tap On/Off.**

   When you turn on the radio, the tablet automatically scans for available networks within range and then displays them. See Figure 4-2.

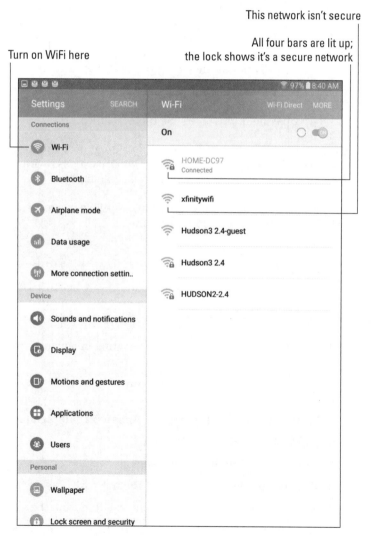

Figure 4-2: You'll see system names and signal strength. Networks that require a login name, password, or both are indicated with a lock icon.

3. **Tap the name of the network to which you want to connect.**

   The strongest signal is first; the icon shows the signal strength. A small lock icon means the network is locked; you'll see the word Secured below the network name. You can tap the name to read details.

   - *If it's an open network,* the connection happens automatically, which takes a few seconds of back-and-forth communication between the devices. If you do it right, the name of the network changes from black to a color, and you'll see Connected below its name.

   - *If the network is locked,* a screen asks for your username and password. In most secured cases, all you need is the password. Some devices require additional settings. Tap Advanced to show more options, including proxy and IP settings.

   - Some systems show a registration screen that requires information such as your name and address. And certain systems require payment for you to use their facilities.

Be cautious with systems that demand a great deal of information from you unless you know and trust the owner. And use a password that's different from ones you use for sensitive sites like banking.

If you return to a place where you have previously successfully connected via Wi-Fi, your tablet will try to reconnect.

Manually connecting to a Wi-Fi network

Some systems are set up in a non-standard way because of security or unusual equipment or sometimes just *because.* You can manually add a Wi-Fi network to your system.

Before you start, get the network information in advance from the owner of the system.

Here's how to set up manually:

1. **From any Home screen, tap the Apps icon and then tap the Settings icon.**

2. **Tap Wi-Fi and then tap On/Off.**

3. **Tap More and then Add Network.**

4. **Type in the information about the network.**

   Hopefully, you already got this information from the system owner.

5. **Tap Enter Network Name to type in the name of the system.**

   In technobabble that's *Network SSID.*

Wi-Fi status indicators

When the Wi-Fi system is on, look at the status bar at the top of the Home screen for icons that tell you about the status of the connection. When your system is connected, active, and communicating with a wireless access point or route, you'll see the indicator of a curved stack of arcs with up and down arrows below it.

If a Wi-Fi access point is available but your NOOK isn't connected to it, or if there's some sort of communication issue that must be addressed, you'll see the arcs with a question mark below.

6. **Tap Security, choose the right protocol, and enter your password.**

7. **Tap Show Advanced Options to enter additional options such as IP settings and proxy settings.**

8. **Tap Connect to store the new information and begin communication.**

Switching Wi-Fi systems

When you're using a particular system, the tablet stays with it as long as it has a usable signal. If you notice the speed dropping, or if you get an onscreen message about a weak or unstable signal, go back to the Wi-Fi connections page and see if there's a stronger signal listed.

Signing Up for Accounts and Other Preliminaries

After you connect successfully to a Wi-Fi system that's on the Internet, your tablet (or, actually, your tablet's owner, which is probably you) needs to agree to all sorts of legal fine print from hardware and software providers; sorry to have to tell you, but these agreements serve almost exclusively to protect *them* from claims by *us* for failure to satisfy. It's their game, and they make the rules.

In addition to this, you need to set the internal clock and calendar and a few other housekeeping details.

Click here; read the fine print later

There's no way to avoid it: The lawyers will make you agree to their terms in the euphoniously named *EULA* (end-user license agreement). It's either that or put the tablet back in its box and return the device to the place you bought it.

There's nothing out of the ordinary in the terms of the EULA, other than promising to turn over the keys to your house and the technical specs for the gravity-free hovercraft you've just designed. It's all in there, except for the part about the house and the hovercraft.

You'll have to accept a take-it-or-leave it deal from Samsung and Google to use the device, and from Barnes & Noble for the NOOK Shop. Tap Confirm to agree. Tap Confirm even if you don't want to.

Use a credit card with premium insurance or buyer's assistance programs. For example, certain American Express, Visa, or MasterCards let you return purchases for a full refund, even if the store says otherwise. And some cards extend (usually by a year) the standard warranty of many products. Here's an instance where it does pay to read the fine print in an agreement, or call your card's customer service to discuss these sorts of protections.

It's a Google world after all

If you already have a Google account, it generally makes sense to use that login and password across most (or all) of your digital devices. You can set up an account on the Tab S2 NOOK or register from a PC or laptop and then enter the name and password on your tablet.

When you first sign in to your tablet, you're get to create or sign in to an existing Google account. It's worthwhile, with two caveats:

- ✔ Think twice about revealing too much personal information to the public.

- ✔ Protect what you unveil with a strong password.

With a Google account you'll also be able to back up your data, including apps, app settings, system settings, and Wi-Fi passwords.

Another part of the Google registration asks if you want to allow apps to better determine your location.

- ✔ This is a good thing when you want to use an online map.

- ✔ The less-than-good thing is that Google or advertisers might want to place ads on pages that are frighteningly specific to your location. (In theory, the advertisers don't know your name or physical address, but it's still a bit somewhere between curious and unsettling to some.)

The Google universe, in addition to the Android operating system for your NOOK, also includes the Chrome Internet browser, Gmail, YouTube, and Google Earth, and more. You don't need to register to use the base search engine and many other services, but you need to agree to terms of service (a EULA) for apps that live on your device, like Google Chrome. See Figure 4-3.

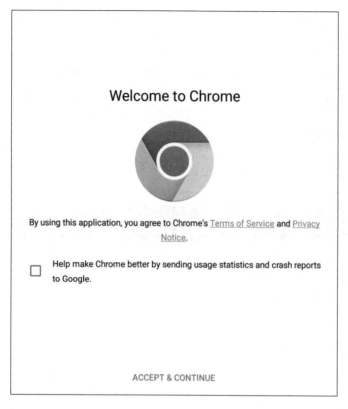

Welcome to Chrome

By using this application, you agree to Chrome's Terms of Service and Privacy Notice.

☐ Help make Chrome better by sending usage statistics and crash reports to Google.

ACCEPT & CONTINUE

Figure 4-3: To use the Chrome search engine and other apps on your tablet, you'll need to agree to terms of service that protect them from claims by you.

Signing up for a NOOK account

You did buy this particular model, the Samsung Galaxy Tab S2 NOOK, because of its integration of the NOOK Shop, right? You're going to want to create a Barnes & Noble account.

If you already have an account, your tablet can retrieve any eBooks and periodicals already in your account from other NOOK devices or from PCs, laptops, or other tablets running a NOOK app.

You can create a B&N account from your personal computer ahead of time. Then all you need is your username and password when you set up your tablet. You can create a B&N account from www.bn.com, www.barnesandnoble. com, or www.nook.com. They all go to the same place.

1. **If you don't have a NOOK account, tap No, I Need to Create an Account.**

2. **Tap Create an Account.**

3. **Fill in the form with your name, email, password, and other information.**

   You can have only one credit card linked to your NOOK.

4. **Check the time that's displayed while you're setting up.**

   Use the up or down arrows to adjust the time; pay attention to the AM or PM settings and tap that indicator if you need to change it.

5. **Tap Submit.**

   To see an example of a NOOK Account registration on your tablet, see Figure 4-4.

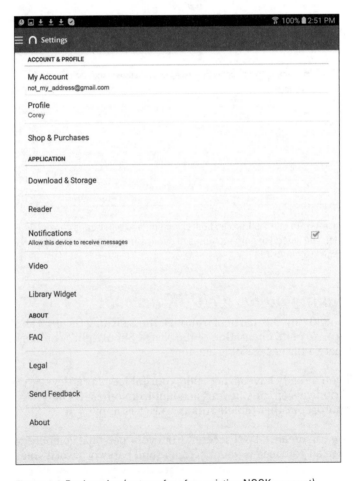

Figure 4-4: Registration (or transfer of an existing NOOK account) leads to the Account & Profile page. Adjust shop and purchase permissions, add or remove profiles, and change the associated credit card.

In addition to the NOOK reading and shopping tools on the Samsung Galaxy Tab S2 NOOK (and previous NOOK models), Barnes & Noble offers free software that lets you read (and buy) publications on devices including desktop and laptop PCs, Macintoshes, iPads, iPhones, and various Android devices. It's easy to start reading on one device and finish on another; what you can't do is have the same book or publication open and connected to the NOOK Internet system on two devices at the same time.

Going into Private Mode

Making someone enter a pattern, PIN, or password before they can use your tablet is like locking the front door. But if you *really* want to secure your tablet's contents, consider encrypting the device, or the external microSDHC card, or both.

Why would you want to do this? If you're merely storing eBooks and a few photographs, videos, and music files, this might be a bit of overkill. But if you plan to store personal or business files that would be damaging or embarrassing if seen without your permission, you can encrypt them. Now, it must be said that the level of encryption within an Android device isn't government spy-agency level. (And, as you know, even Top Secret government files can leak like a sieve.)

An encrypted Tab S2 NOOK is difficult (if not impossible) for an amateur to read. Your strongest defense is a complex, unobvious password.

You can set up private folders for certain applications, including:

- ✓ Gallery
- ✓ Music
- ✓ My Files
- ✓ Video
- ✓ Voice Recorder

Certain other third-party apps may also use the same system or add their own form of encryption.

Setting up Private Mode

Here's how to set up and use Private Mode:

1. **From any Home screen, tap the Apps icon, and then tap the Settings icon.**

2. **Tap Private Mode.**

3. **Select an access type from amongst those offered: Pattern, PIN, Fingerprint, or Password.**

4. **Follow the prompts to record your access code or other information.**

It doesn't make sense to use a password like *password* or *private,* or to write the password on a sticky note and attach it to your tablet. Oh, and don't forget your password or PIN or pattern, either. You won't be able to gain access to the material without it, and the only way to reset this form of security is to do a complete (hard) reset, which deletes all your personal material and some of the system settings and is in just about every respect a true pain in the ear.

To help protect your privacy, tap Auto Off. This automatically turns off Private Mode anytime the screen turns off. Otherwise, the Private folder you unlocked is accessible to anyone who uses the tablet until the next time it's completely shut down and restarted. See Figure 4-5.

Don't forget the code, though, or whatever is held in the folder (and I truly don't want to know) will be irretrievable by you and me, although I'm sure some government agency somewhere in the world might be able to get in to read your recipe file (which is what I assume you have locked away; I really don't want to know).

Moving an item into a Private folder

To move an item into a private folder, follow along:

1. **Find and select the folder in the Gallery (or in another folder).**

   It has to be eligible to use this procedure.

2. **Tap More.**

3. **Tap Move to Private.**

4. **Enter your PIN or password or pattern or allow scanning of your fingerprint to complete the transfer.**

Viewing items from a Private folder

When you've closed a private folder, you can't see the items in it within MyFiles or Gallery or other applications until you return to Settings and turn on Private Mode, and enter the password, pattern, or fingerprint protection you required.

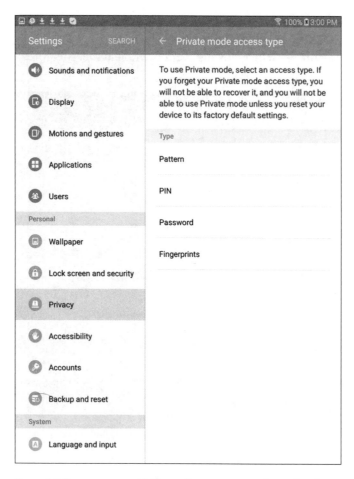

Figure 4-5: You can encrypt folders of images, text, and certain other types of files behind a password, pattern, or fingerprint.

Doing First Things Last: Accessibility Options

If you have impaired vision or need specific accommodations when using the touchscreen and other Tab S2 NOOK features, you have options. You'll have a chance to make these settings the very first time you turn on your Samsung Galaxy Tab S2 NOOK, but you can make those changes later.

Here's how to get to the accessibility settings:

1. **From any Home screen, tap the Apps icon and then tap the Settings icon.**

2. **Tap Accessibility.**

3. **Choose from and enable options under Vision, Hearing, Dexterity and Interaction, or More sections.**

   See Figure 4-6. The following sections explain these features.

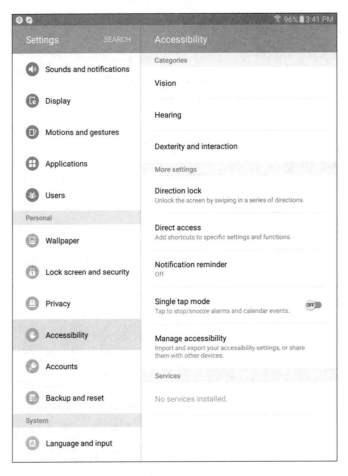

Figure 4-6: The NOOK can adapt to make it easier to use. You may also be able to include more adaptations from third parties as apps.

Accessibility

The first screen deals with some very basic settings:

 ✔ **Auto Rotate Screen.** This option is available in other places, too. Tap a checkmark to rotate the view onscreen if you change the way you hold the tablet. If you don't want it to rotate, leave this option off.

✔ **Screen Timeout.** Select the period of time before the screen shuts off. I recommend at least two minutes. It depends on how often you let your mind wander; I regularly drift off into very important but soon forgotten daydreams of several minutes in length.

Vision

These options can enlarge text, reverse the colors to increase contrast, and let you adjust for color blindness. Here are some of the many options:

✔ **Font Size.** The default setting is Small, but you can go up four stages to Huge or down two increments to Tiny.

✔ **Magnification Gestures.** Touch and slide the switch at the top of the panel to enable this feature. It lets you zoom in and out on an image by triple-tapping the screen; while zoomed in you can pan from side to side by dragging two or more fingers across the screen, and you can temporarily magnify something on the screen by triple-tapping and holding.

Triple-tap doesn't enlarge the keyboard. Also, magnification gestures may slow down some apps.

✔ **Negative Colors.** Touch this option to change black to white or to change colors to versions that are easier to see. You can also change some colors in the next option.

✔ **Color Adjustment.** Tap to display a description of the available adjustments, and then move the slider switch to On if you want to proceed. You'll see color samples. It's recommended that people using this tool make adjustments in an environment with normal indoor lighting.

   • **Grayscale** changes all colors to shades of gray.

   • **Magnifier Window** enlarges everything shown on the screen.

✔ **Speak Passwords.** If you put a checkmark in the box, the tablet will read out any entry you make in a password box. (Obviously, you want to do your best to maintain privacy when the system is announcing passwords in this manner.)

✔ **Text-to-Speech Options.** You can choose between the Samsung or Google text-to-speech engine. They both are quite capable; touch Listen to hear an example to select the one that's clearer to you. You can also adjust the speech rate, the speed at which the computer voice jabbers.

✔ **Accessibility Shortcut.** This option adds accessibility options to the Power/Lock key. If you *do* turn on advanced features like Explore by Touch, I recommend adding this shortcut to allow for a quick exit from that feature.

Hearing

These customization features include adjustments for stereo and balance and the ability to turn on subtitles (for apps that offer them). See Figure 4-7. Here are the choices:

- ✔ **Sound Balance.** If you've got a set of earphones attached or are using an external set of speakers to play back music or the audio of a movie or television, you can adjust the sound balance to adjust the amount of sound going to the left or right earpiece; touch and hold the indicator and slide it left or right as desired. Touch Set to accept a change. Tap Cancel to back out and shut off the racket.

- ✔ **Mono Audio.** If you're listening to your tablet using a headset with only one earphone, you can merge the stereo channels into a single mono signal.

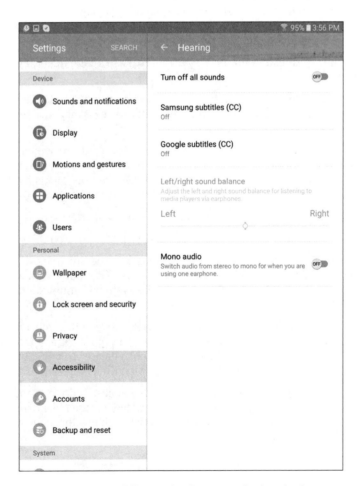

Figure 4-7: The Accessibility panels allow customization of color profiles, sound styles, and interaction.

✔ **Turn Off All Sounds.** It does what it says; someone who is deaf or who otherwise doesn't want unnecessary noise can choose this option to mute the tablet.

✔ **Google Subtitles/Samsung Subtitles.** Touch and move the slide switch to enable one or the other or both schemes to display onscreen subtitles for certain apps. The Google system lets you change text size and the color and background of the subtitle; Samsung goes a few steps further by letting you choose a font and other effects.

Dexterity and Interaction

Some of the settings here are quite helpful for users with physical challenges that may limit the use of one hand or make it difficult to use the physical keys on the side or top of the tablet. The choices here include

✔ **Assistant Menu.** You can add a small Quick menu on most screens with larger, easier-to-use icons for many features, including volume control, power off, settings, and zoom. You can choose a dominant hand. It comes preset for righties.

✔ **Press and Hold Delay.** The tablet is set up to respond to a press-and-hold for certain functions; you can define just how long that hold has to be.

✔ **Interaction Control.** Here you can fine-tune some of the ways you use your hands on the tablet, including blocking areas of the screen so that they don't respond to touch; this is useful if you hold the tablet with one or more fingers on the screen at all times.

You can also control auto-rotation of images and other functions.

More Settings

These options are included here:

✔ **Notification Reminder.** Here you can instruct the tablet to beep — at an interval you select — to remind you of any unread notifications.

✔ **Single Tap Mode.** This option lets a single tap stop or *snooze* (temporarily delay) an alarm or calendar reminder.

✔ **Manage Accessibility.** You can save all the changes you've made to vision, touch, and sound options and update the file as needed; you can also share your setup with another device if this file is created.

Additional accessibility apps and utilities can be downloaded from the Google Play Store.

Part II
Communicating Across the Galaxy

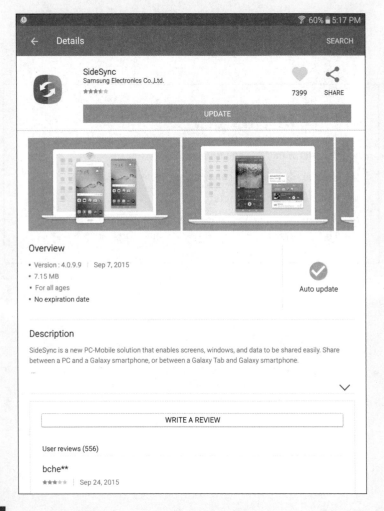

Handle email server connection trouble with Samsung recommendations at www. dummies.com/cheatsheet/samsunggalaxytabS2nook.

SideSync
Samsung Electronics Co.,Ltd.
★★★★☆

7399   SHARE

UPDATE

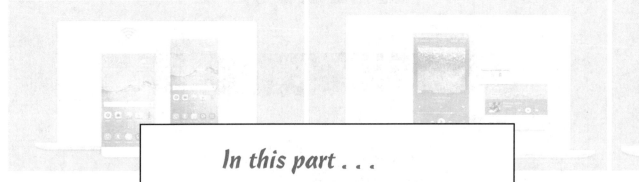

Overview

- Version : 4.0.9.9
- 7.15 MB
- For all ages
- No expiration date

Auto update

In this part . . .

- ✔ Connect with Wi-Fi and Bluetooth.
- ✔ Use the USB cable to connect your tablet to a computer.
- ✔ Add and change contacts.
- ✔ Browse the web and choose between mobile and standard sites.

Description

SideSync is a new PC-Mobile solution that enables screens, windows, and data to be shared easily. Share between a PC and a Galaxy smartphone, or between a Galaxy Tab and Galaxy smartphone.

ᐯ

WRITE A REVIEW

User reviews (556)

bche**

★★★☆☆   Sep 24, 2015

5

Making Further Connections

In This Chapter
- ▶ Working wirelessly
- ▶ Reading about Wi-Fi
- ▶ Biting into Bluetooth
- ▶ Using USB and memory cards

*I*n addition to Wi-Fi from your Tab S2 NOOK to the Internet, your handheld wonder can use Wi-Fi Direct to communicate with many other devices in the immediate vicinity. The same handheld wonder can use a different kind of short-range radio system — Bluetooth — to talk to and otherwise enjoy relations with more electronic thingies.

But as a reminder: The Samsung Galaxy Tab S2 NOOK *doesn't* have a cellular radio. Your smartphone does, and certain other more expensive tablets do, but not this NOOK. (You can add Skype or other *voice-over-Internet-protocol* [VOIP] apps to make phone calls if you have a strong Wi-Fi connection.)

This chapter expands your use of wireless non-cellular communication and then gets you *wired*.

Working without a Wire

Chapter 4 explains how to reach the Internet through a Wi-Fi wireless connection. I put that information there because everything else that follows is dependent upon at least that initial wireless setup.

Here, I discuss Wi-Fi generalities and then look at other options to connect your Tab S2 NOOK.

You can also usually find a Wi-Fi signal at public libraries, some government buildings and public spaces, and at many cafés. And Barnes & Noble, the seller of your Tab S2 NOOK, offers a free Wi-Fi signal in nearly all its stores.

If you need help creating a Wi-Fi network, call your Internet provider or call or visit Barnes & Noble, which promises to provide at least basic levels of support to all buyers of their NOOK devices.

Bottom line: Use the signal that works best with your Tab S2 NOOK. The Wi-Fi utility seeks out the strongest connection it can find, and usually switches to an alternate all by itself if conditions change.

Advanced Wi-Fi settings

The Wi-Fi system should work well as delivered, but you can adjust performance to meet your needs with advanced settings. See Figure 5-1.

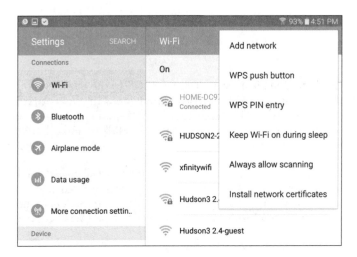

Figure 5-1: The Advanced settings for Wi-Fi allow you to keep your radio active, put it on a timer, and control scanning and connection options.

To reach the somewhat hidden screen, do this:

1. **From any Home screen, tap the Apps icon, and then tap the Settings icon.**

2. **Tap Wi-Fi, and then tap On/Off.**

3. **Tap More to see the advanced Options screen.**

4. **Choose your options:**

   • **Add Network.** This is a way to manually add a Wi-Fi network, including advanced configurations.

- **WPS Push Button.** Many routers or WAP devices let you transmit all their configuration information to a nearby device like your tablet. Enable this option, bring the devices within a few feet of each other, and press the button on the router to automate the process of connecting to a router.

- **WPS PIN Entry.** View the PIN used by your device to set up a connection to a WAP or router that requires this level of security.

- **Keep Wi-Fi on During Sleep.** Choose among Always (you get email and notifications while the tablet's asleep, which is a good thing except that it uses battery power), Only When Plugged In (which deals with the battery issue, assuming an AC outlet is handy), or Never (which shuts off the radio and saves battery power).

- **Always Allow Scanning.** If you put a checkmark in this box, your tablet lets Google Location Services and other applications scan for Wi-Fi networks even when other radio features are off. This may allow certain mapping programs to keep track of where you are even without a Wi-Fi signal, although full maps features aren't available without an Internet connection.

- **Install Network Certificates.** Some websites have their own certificate of authenticity, and certain browsers or browser settings don't allow you to connect — or will advise against connection — without seeing such a certificate. This option allows you to install certificates on your tablet as needed.

Wi-Fi Direct

Across the relatively short history of personal computers, smartphones, and tablets it has long been common for the latest, greatest new hardware to be way out front of the software needed to use its features. Or to put it another way, we had many many solutions that were in search of a problem. Samsung Galaxy Tab devices have been offering a technology called Wi-Fi Direct for several years, but only now is it becoming possible to use.

Wi-Fi Direct lets your tablet connect directly to another device *without going through a WAP or router.* Only one of the Wi-Fi devices has to be specifically designed for Wi-Fi Direct; the other needs plain old Wi-Fi capability.

For example, your tablet could connect to your smartphone and use its facilities. Or your smartphone could pick up files from your tablet. And perhaps most intriguingly, you could send a file across the room to a Wi-Fi–enabled printer to produce a hard copy.

Here's how to turn on Wi-Fi Direct:

1. **From any Home screen, tap the Apps icon, and then tap the Settings icon.**

2. **Tap Wi-Fi and then tap On/Off.**

3. **Tap Wi-Fi Direct.**

   Your NOOK automatically scans for nearby Wi-Fi Direct devices.

4. **Select a device and then follow prompts to complete the connection.**

   You'll see a special version of the Wi-Fi icon in the status bar: a set of arcs or dishes and below that a pair of arrows pointing toward each other.

   To disconnect from Wi-Fi Direct, tap End Connection or return to the Wi-Fi configuration panel and turn off Wi-Fi Direct.

Special Networks from Samsung

Samsung also offers two special types of networking: SideSync and QuickConnect. They each fall in the category of "If you've got exactly the right combination of hardware in exactly the right situation, this is the greatest thing since the invention of the electric plug." If all is not exact, they are temptingly out of reach.

SideSync from tablet to phone

SideSync allows your Tab S2 NOOK tablet to work as an extension of your smartphone: You can control the phone from the tablet, make or receive calls, send and receive text messages, and even drag and drop files between the two devices.

Provided, of course, that the smartphone in question is a current model Samsung device. SideSync doesn't work with Apple phones, nor with Android phones from other makers. You may have to install a SideSync app on your Samsung smartphone, depending on how current it is. I needed to do that for my Samsung Galaxy Note 4; it was available at no cost from Google Play. On the Tab S2 NOOK side, I needed to update the SideSync app. See Figure 5-2.

There are no details on using SideSync in the Samsung manual either, but you can learn more about the feature by exploring the Samsung website or by calling the Samsung support desk or the support professionals at your cellphone provider . . . providing your cellphone is supported by this feature.

Figure 5-2: Samsung offers apps from the Google Play Store. You may need to update the SideSync app on your Tab S2 NOOK.

When you have the component installed on a smartphone or other device and enabled it there, you launch SideSync on your Tab S2 NOOK. Then you're able to share resources. See Figure 5-3.

QuickConnect from tablet to TV

Here's another nifty new idea — a way to use both Bluetooth and Wi-Fi wireless system to stream content from your tablet to a large-screen TV or from a TV to your tablet. You can tune into a show and view it on the tablet, or project videos or pictures from the Tab S2 NOOK to the TV.

Sounds (and looks) good, if not great, depending on the resolution of the image and on the proper combination of hardware. QuickConnect works with the latest Samsung TV sets (and a handful of other TVs that have licensed the technology). And there's the prospect of QuickConnect apps or utilities that can be added to PCs or Macs.

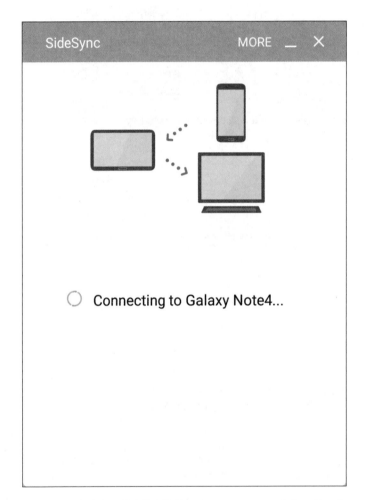

SideSync   MORE   _   X

○ **Connecting to Galaxy Note4...**

Figure 5-3: My Galaxy Tab S2 NOOK is connecting to my Galaxy Note4 smartphone. The link works at short distances.

Clearly, SideSync is still being developed. I can see a not-too-distant future in which your Tab S2 NOOK will serve as a relatively large-screen extension of a compatible smartphone leveraging the best features of each device: cellular and data connection from the phone, the NOOK's higher-quality camera and screen. See Figure 5-4.

Figure 5-4: I'm viewing the Gallery of photos stored on my smartphone on the larger screen of the Galaxy Tab S2 NOOK. The screen of the phone overlays a portion of the tablet.

Virtual Private Networks

Some institutions, businesses, and advanced individual users may insist on setting up a *Virtual Private Network* (VPN) to exchange sensitive information over the Internet. The nuts-and-bolts of setting up such a system is beyond the scope of this book, but your Galaxy Tab S2 NOOK is perfectly capable of working with one.

One extra step, although I recommend that all NOOK users do this anyhow — in order to use a VPN you must set up a screen lock, PIN, or password and unlock your tablet before use.

Here's how to set up your Tab S2 NOOK to use a VPN:

1. **From any Home screen, tap the Apps icon and then the Settings icon.**
2. **Tap More Connection Settings.**
3. **Tap VPN.**
4. **Tap Add VPN.**
5. **Follow the onscreen instructions.**

After you configure your tablet to work with a VPN, here's how to connect to it:

1. **From any Home screen, tap the Apps icon and then tap the Settings icon.**
2. **Tap More Connection Settings.**
3. **Tap VPN.**
4. **Tap the VPN you want to use to select it, and then enter your login information.**
5. **Tap Connect.**

To edit or delete a VPN, do this:

1. **From any Home screen, tap the Apps icon and then tap the Settings icon.**
2. **Tap More Connection Settings.**
3. **Touch and hold the VPN you want to edit or delete.**
4. **Follow the onscreen instructions.**

King Bluetooth Lives

Another technology for direct wireless connection of devices is Bluetooth. It connects devices at a maximum distance of about 30 feet for simple tasks, a process called *pairing*. On the Tab S2 NOOK, you can use the Bluetooth radio to share photos, contacts, music, and other files and to connect to devices like wireless earphones and speakers, and to wireless physical keyboards. See Figure 5-5.

The technology is, of course, named after Harald Bluetooth, the tenth-century king who united ragtag Danish tribes into a single kingdom, apparently with the aid of a wireless tablet of some sort. True — at least the name part.

To protect your tablet from receiving unwanted pairing requests, don't let it be found by other devices until you agree to let it be discovered.

Figure 5-5: The Tab S2 NOOK found the Bluetooth signal from the desktop computer on which I'm writing these words; I can make a screen capture on the tablet and move it wirelessly to a folder on the PC for editing.

Understanding Bluetooth

Here's how to establish a Bluetooth pairing. These steps deal with turning on the Bluetooth radio in the Tab S2 NOOK; make sure the equivalent radio is turned on and made *discoverable* on the other device.

Take these steps:

1. **From any Home page, tap the Apps icon, and then tap the Settings icon.**

2. **Tap the Bluetooth icon (an angular B) and tap On/Off to enable it if necessary.**

   When the Bluetooth radio is on, you'll see the angular B icon in the status bar.

3. **Tap Scan to manually perform a new scan.**

Pairing Bluetooth devices

Both sides of the Bluetooth equation need to agree to communicate, although the process only has to be done once. When two devices are paired, they should automatically recognize each other and connect any time they're both on and within range.

Here's how to pair the devices:

1. **From any Home screen, tap the Apps icon, and then tap the Settings icon.**

2. **Tap Bluetooth, and then tap On/Off.**

   The device you want to connect with must be *discoverable,* which is the opposite of saying that it mustn't be set to hidden. Consult the instruction manual for the other device for the steps to make it discoverable.

Your Galaxy Tab S2 NOOK should already be set up to be visible, which is another way to say discoverable. If not, place a checkmark next to the option that offers to make it Visible to Other Devices.

3. **Tap Scan.**

4. **When you see the name of the device with which you want to communicate, tap it.**

Your tablet should connect to the other device. In certain combinations, the target device may require you to enter a passcode or PIN; get that information from the owner of the target device or from its instruction manual. In some situations, each device will transmit a code to the other, and you need to verify the connection by entering the code you see on the screen.

Bluetooth is a very helpful technology — when it works — but in my experience there are still too many variants of the pairing process to provide a single set of instructions here. Don't hesitate to seek get help from the maker of the Bluetooth device or to contact Barnes & Noble or Samsung.

Unpairing Bluetooth devices

To remove the automatic connection or pairing function between two Bluetooth devices, do this:

1. **Make sure your Bluetooth radio is turned on.**

2. **From the Bluetooth settings page, tap the Settings icon next to the paired device.**

3. **Tap Unpair.**

Bluetooth radios use a lot of battery power. Turn off that function when you aren't using it.

Bluetooth limitations

Once again, the hardware capabilities of your Samsung Galaxy Tab S2 NOOK may not be equaled by the software or operating system on your tablet or on a computer or other device to which you connect.

Some but not all computers, smartphones, or other devices let you transfer files in either direction with a tablet. Check the settings of Windows, Android, Apple's OS X on its computers, or Apple's iOS on mobile devices to see what's allowed.

I could write a sentence here that says transferring files using Bluetooth is easy-peasy anywhere, anytime, and in any combination of devices. But that would be wrong. In fact, I recommend using Bluetooth only for simple tasks like beaming music to an external speaker or headset.

You can usually find a way to perform certain other tasks like syncing contact, calendar, and task information from one device to another, but in truth I think Wi-Fi or direct USB cable connection is easier for transferring files.

Getting Physical: USB and Memory Cards

This section steps away from wireless communication and details actual physical contact for data transfer. I'm calling it _part one if by wire, and two if by microSDHC card._

To me, the simplest way to transfer a bunch of files from a desktop or computer to your tablet, and the simplest way to manage files on your tablet, is to use a USB cable between the two devices.

You can use the same USB cable that connects your tablet to its AC adapter for recharging to move data.

Making the USB connection

USB _(Universal Serial Bus)_ is, simply said, a wiring scheme that carries data and electrical power. About the only thing you need to know is which end is up, and which end is micro.

The USB cable that came with your tablet is standard. If you need a replacement, you can get one from a computer store or an online seller.

1. **Plug the micro end of the USB cable into your tablet.**

   The _micro_ end of the cable is the small connector. It fits in only in one way. Don't force it.

2. **Remove the larger end of the cable from the AC adapter.**

3. **Put the small adapter somewhere where you'll be able to find it again.**

4. **Attach the larger end of the USB cable to a port on your current desktop or laptop computer.**

   It, too, only goes in a particular way. At the computer end, you need to match the open side of the connector to the block side on the port. Open to block; block to open and you're in like Flynn.

   If you're one of the lucky ones, that's all that needs be done. If not, you should see a message on your computer (not on the tablet) telling you that it needs to install a driver to recognize this new piece of hardware now attached. The desktop or laptop computer should be able to do this all by itself if it has an active Internet connection. If you run into trouble, call Samsung or Barnes & Noble for help.

TIP

When you make the USB connection, you should see a message on your tablet. For a closer look, swipe down from the top to display the notification panel.

5. **Tap the Media Device option.**

See Figure 5-6. This option is best for moving files to or from your Tab 4 NOOK. Mac users may need to install a small, free utility on their computer.

Figure 5-6: Use the Media Device (MTP) option for easy file transfer to or from your NOOK.

6. **Find your tablet in the File Explorer (on the PC) or the Finder (on a Mac).**

7. **On the computer, click to open the tablet.**

You'll find one top level for the tablet and one for the card you may have (should have) installed in the expansion slot.

On a Windows machine, you can right-click a folder or virtual drive to read more about its properties and how much data is stored within.

You might see the tablet referred to by its model number; the first edition of the Samsung Galaxy Tab S2 NOOK is the SM-T710.

If you're going to add files *from* the PC to the tablet, in most cases you'll want to install them on the card; it has more space. You can create any folder you want; I suggest leaving the folder names of the device alone. Create new ones on the external memory card instead.

The Android operating system organizes itself based on file type:

- Any PNG or JPG file goes in the Gallery.

- Photos you take with your tablet's built-in camera are stored in the DCIM folder. Other folder names are more obvious: Music, Movies, Documents. See Figure 5-7.

- NOOK eBooks are stored in the NOOK folder.

- Files you've downloaded to the tablet are in Downloads.

- Files created using some apps are in Documents.

- Some apps create their own folders, including Overdrive for library eBooks and Kindle for reading material from Amazon's store.

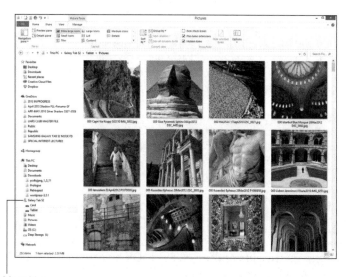

My tablet

Figure 5-7: I used the USB cable to transfer photos. I stored them in a new folder that I placed within the Pictures folder on the tablet's memory card.

Use the same basic file operations of the computer to copy or move files from one device to the other, in either direction. You can:

- ✔ Open a folder on the tablet or its card and rename or delete files.
- ✔ Drag and drop files from the PC to the tablet, or the other direction.
- ✔ Copy files on a PC or Mac, move the cursor to a folder on the tablet, and paste them there.
- ✔ Drag and drop entire folders in one direction or the other.

If you're connecting your Tab S2 NOOK to a Macintosh computer, you must eject the tablet's Disk icon before you can turn off USB storage on the Tab and remove the cable. Windows users can simply unplug the cable without any extra steps.

Using USB to Go

Another fairly recent new product line is called USB to Go, and it has devices that can connect to any other device with a form of USB port.

The Samsung Galaxy Tab S2 NOOK has a microUSB port — the same one used to charge the battery and to connect by cable to a desktop or laptop computer.

If you buy a USB to Go device, you can use the same cable that goes to the tablet's battery charger; connect the large end to the new device. Without any further need for pairing or security codes, you should be able to attach flash memory sticks and external low-power hard disk drives.

It's a wonderful prospect but still in its infancy as this new NOOK comes to market. Check with the manufacturer of USB to Go devices to see if they certify compatibility with the Samsung Galaxy Tab S2 NOOK.

It's In the Cards

Another way to transfer data to and from your tablet is to treat the microSDHC card as if it were a floppy disk. You can remove the tiny sliver of memory from its slot on the side of the Tab S2 NOOK and bring it to a desktop or laptop computer and install it there.

After installing the card, use the same drag-and-drop or copy-and-paste technique you'd use if your tablet were connected to a computer by the USB cable.

You can attach a microSDHC card to a computer two ways:

- ✏ **Insert it into the slot in your laptop/computer that accepts the card.** Be sure to match the type and size of card to the proper slot. See Figure 5-8.

   If your computer has a slot for the larger (matchbook-sized) SD card, you can use a microSDHC-to-SD converter; you may have received one with your microSDHC card when you bought it. Slide the micro version into the larger converter and then plug the converter into your computer.

- ✏ **Buy an external memory card reader that accepts various card sizes.** Make sure it works with your microSDHC either directly or indirectly. You may need to use a converter, as discussed in the previous method. Card readers plug into a standard USB port on your laptop or desktop.

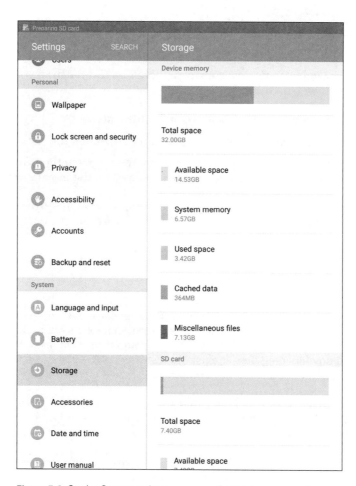

Figure 5-8: On the Storage tab you can see the total space you have left on the tablet as well as on the SDHC card. I added an 8GB card, and after formatting by the system, it has 7.40 GB of room.

Be careful handling the somewhat fragile microSDHC memory card. Don't touch the gold contacts. Also, properly eject or unmount the microSDHC card from the computer before physically removing it. If you don't know the procedure on your particular computer, shut down the entire computer in the normal way and then remove the microSDHC card.

Sending Air Mail

Email and the cloud are two last means of transferring files to and from your tablet. They both require an active Wi-Fi connection.

Sending yourself email

You can send or receive emails with attachments and then download the files for storage.

For example, to move a copy of a photo or a text file from your desktop to your tablet, do this:

1. **Send yourself an email with the files attached.**

2. **Open the email on your tablet and download the files.**

3. **Later, use a file manager to move the file from the Downloads folder to another folder within the device or on the memory card.**

The same process works the other direction. Send files from your tablet to yourself, and open the email on your desktop or laptop computer. That's how I transferred most of the screenshots you see in this book: Grab a shot, go to the Gallery, and share the image by email.

Using the cloud

Another solution, especially good for large files, is the cloud. What do I mean by the *cloud?* It's a storage system that exists out on the Internet — anywhere — that you can get to with your tablet. You use it for uploading and downloading files. It exists as a storage place of its own, not directly attached to your tablet or computer.

One of the beauties of the cloud sort of system is that it's (to use an old computer word) *asynchronous.* Both sides of the equation don't need to be online or connected at the same time.

Dropbox is one example. Another is Microsoft's OneDrive, which offers free storage and services. You may be able to get by with the basic amount of storage, or you can buy more. To use these services, you either

✔ Get them using an app on your tablet.

✔ Use the web browser to reach their site from a tablet or a computer.

After logging in with a password, you upload files to the site or download ones already stored there.

I use this sort of service to store a full set of my most important files when I travel. In that way, if my tablet or smartphone or laptop fails or goes missing, I can sign in from another device. Be sure to use a secure password to protect any sensitive material you store in the cloud.

Printing from the Tablet

The idea of a tablet, of course, is to have the world in your hand: digital versions of books, magazines, newspapers, documents, and the Internet. But sometimes you need — or at least want — something in print. How can you get a document or file from your Samsung Galaxy Tab S2 NOOK to a printer?

You can accomplish this three ways:

✔ Send a copy of a file as an attachment to an email. Open that attachment on a desktop or laptop computer that's connected to a printer.

✔ Send a file to a service bureau, like those offered at a number of office supply stores, and have them do the printing for you. (I'm hesitant to do this with any document containing sensitive personal or financial information.)

✔ Use apps and *plug-in* adaptations to the operating system that allow the Tab S2 NOOK to transmit a file over Wi-Fi, Wi-Fi Direct, or Bluetooth. This technology is still developing; check with Samsung about its own printers, some of which have this capability. Check with other printer manufacturers that have wireless capabilities for information on availability and configuration of plug-ins.

Here's how to adapt your Tab S2 NOOK for this purpose:

1. **From any Home screen, tap the Apps icon and then tap the Settings icon.**

2. **Tap More Connection Settings.**

3. **Tap Printing.**

4. **Tap a print service and follow the onscreen instructions.**

5. **Tap Download Plug-In (if necessary).**

From within the Settings page, you can go to a page of apps that you can download to your Tab S2 NOOK for wireless connection. See Figure 5-9.

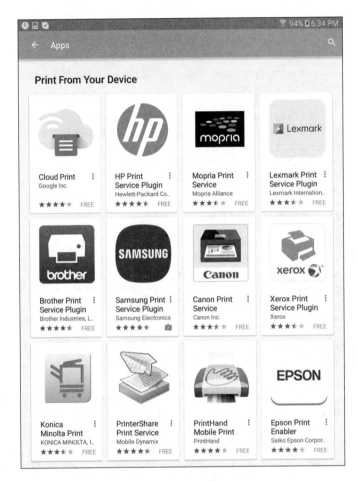

Figure 5-9: Many major printer companies are offering plug-ins that adapt the Tab S2 NOOK to broadcast files to printers with built-in Wi-Fi or other wireless systems.

6

Putting Things in Contacts

*I*n 1968, a year before Apollo 11 landed the first humans on the moon (with a spacecraft that had a computer less powerful than a pocket calculator), the French actress Brigitte Bardot had a hit song called "Contact," a triumph of what we used to call bubble-gum music, this one with a loopy outer space theme. "Une météorite m'a transpercé le cœur. Vous, sur la terre, vous avez des docteurs. Contact!" she sang. "A meteorite pierced my heart. You, on the earth, you have doctors. Contact!" (It's a truly awful song, very much worth checking out on YouTube.)

Today, all she would have needed to do is tap the Contacts icon on her Samsung Galaxy Tab S2 NOOK and she would have the landline, cellphone, email, Skype number, Facebook account, Twitter feed, and intergalactic spatial coordinates.

One of the greatest unsung accomplishments of the computer era is the concept of synchronization. And the Galaxy Tab S2 NOOK is among the devices that's finally bringing it all together. *Synchronization* is the sharing of all those scraps of information: names, titles, addresses, email addresses, phone numbers, Twitter handles, websites, past present and future calendar items, photos, videos, pages from the Internet.

The various apps that come with your Tab S2 NOOK (and most add-on apps available from other sources) talk to each other in the background so that when you make an entry in your calendar, the details of people you'll meet or communicate with by phone or over the web are at hand. You can send or receive the details of a calendar appointment by email, and you can reach into your Gallery to send an image while in the middle of a text chat.

And one step more: This synchronization isn't limited to the information on your tablet; if you set up your accounts right, your tablet will merge information from desktop and laptop computers, smartphones, web-based email and calendar programs, and other tablets. To do so, each device has to connected to an active Wi-Fi or cable Internet connection.

Just about everything can become connected. Take a picture with your tablet's camera and tag a buddy; that image goes to your list of contacts. Get an email or message from that person, and his or her picture appears along with the text. It works the other direction as well: Use the information in your contacts to send someone a book excerpt or a recommendation.

The particular model of Samsung Galaxy Tab S2 NOOK produced for Barnes & Noble doesn't have a cellular radio capable of connection to voice and data systems maintained by cellular phone companies. However, it does have a Wi-Fi radio, and with it you can make phone calls using apps like Skype, which use *Voice Over Internet Protocol* (VOIP) technology. The Skype app is available for free through the Google Play Store and other sources.

Roaming Friends and Countrymen

If you've set up and used a Google account, you likely have a list of friends and acquaintances. When you link your new Tab S2 NOOK to that same Google account, those contacts come right over to your tablet.

Your contacts can include your social networking app friends and, with a little bit of fancy electronic footwork, you can *import* (bring to your tablet) information from other sources, like Microsoft Outlook and Apple Contacts and iCloud.

If you want to import contacts from a source other than apps from Google, Samsung, or Barnes & Noble, check the Play Store on the Tab S2 NOOK to see if there's an app to do this for you. For example, Microsoft's Outlook app lets you import contacts and calendar items from that service to the Android equivalents on your tablet, and keep each side in sync with the other; a change to the details of a contact in one is reflected in the other.

Take a look at the contact in Figure 6-1.

If you haven't yet set up a Google or Samsung account, go to the app on your tablet to do so. You can also set up an Outlook account by using the web browser and searching for that Microsoft site. Or set up accounts using the full keyboard on a desktop or laptop computer and then inform the Tab S2 NOOK of the existing account you want to use on the tablet.

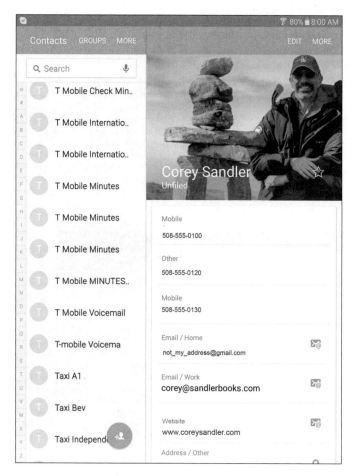

Figure 6-1: That's me, posing with an Inukshuk in the high Canadian Arctic, where accessing my phones, email, and website is difficult. But almost anywhere else in the world, contact! (By the way, those *aren't* my real phone numbers.)

Everything but the Kitchen Sync

Your tablet can *synchronize* with many different accounts, so if you change an email address on your tablet, that change is reflected on other devices, too.

Be careful about what sorts of information you share; assume that anything — and I mean anything — can and will be used against you in a court of marketing or worse. Don't share your Social Security Number or your banking information, and try to avoid giving hints that a clever evildoer might use to guess the password for other accounts.

Figure 6-2 shows some other accounts that can merge information into your tablet, or that can get information from your Tab S2 NOOK:

- ✔ **Samsung account.** You may not even know you have one, but if you signed up for a Samsung account when you were setting up your tablet, or if you did so for another Samsung device like a smartphone, you're in.

- ✔ **Google account.** They may not yet own the world, but they're on their way. Do you have an account for Gmail or YouTube? They're part of the Google-sphere, and that counts.

- ✔ **Skype.** The VOIP communication service (owned by Microsoft) that can be used to make phone calls or send text messages over Wi-Fi connections.

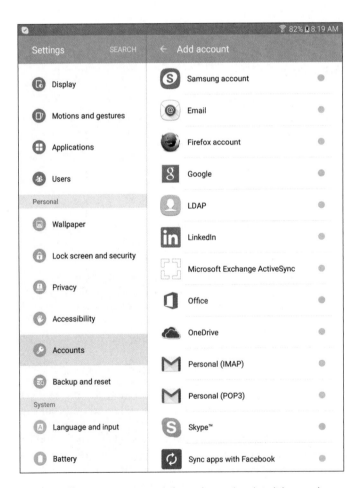

Figure 6-2: You can get contact information and update it by syncing various accounts from different services and on various devices.

✔ **Microsoft Exchange ActiveSync.** Businesses, organizations, and some Internet providers use this to synchronize email, contacts, calendar listings, and other live data.

✔ **LDAP (Lightweight Directory Access Protocol).** Some businesses and web services use this service to organize directories.

✔ **Facebook and Twitter.** If you've got an account with these folks, your information — including your friends and their contact information — can be shared with your tablet.

If you already use Gmail and other Google apps, your contacts there automatically sync with your new Galaxy Tab S2 NOOK, provided that you use the same username. Just associate your NOOK with the Google account and you're good to go.

Creating a contact by hand

About that stack of business cards I collected on my most recent trip: I just might want to add some of them as contacts. I'm sure that was the intent of the person who gave it to me.

Here's how to digitally (using your own digits) create a contact:

1. **From any Home screen, tap the Apps icon and then tap Contacts.**

   You can open the Apps menu and look for the orange outline of a head labeled Contacts and tap that. Or you may have set a Contacts shortcut on one of the Home screens.

   There's a My Profile listing at the top. The first thing I do is make an entry there, and then rename it as *Me*. I do this as a way to slightly increase the chances that someone finding my tablet will contact me to return. Yes, I know that's a long shot, but it's better than no shot at all.

2. **Tap the Add icon, which sits in an orange ball near the bottom of the screen.**

   The Add Contacts screen appears. See Figure 6-3.

3. **Choose where to save the contact:**

   • **Device.** That's your tablet. If you choose this option, the contact is saved only on your Tab S2 NOOK and not automatically available for sharing with other listings.

   • **Google.** The contact is synced with your online Google account. Not only does this create a backup copy of your contact, but it lets other Android devices (such as a smartphone or another tablet) have access to the contact.

   • **Samsung Account.** The contact is synced with the listing maintained by that company and available on other devices from Samsung, including a smartphone or another tablet.

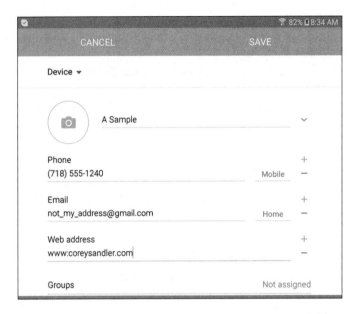

Figure 6-3: I'm creating a contact here. You can add or remove fields. You might want to use the floating keyboard to make the screen easier to see; see Chapter 3 for those steps.

- **Add a New Account.** You can add a Microsoft Exchange ActiveSync account. The problem is, if you import from this sort of account and then merge the results into your Android contacts list, the information's not protected by the cocoon of security at its original location.

In a perfect world, I'd recommend the Google account. Think twice about what information you share, use a tough password to protect your accounts, and change that password often. Oh, and best of luck.

After you select a place to store your new contact, the Create Contact form opens.

4. **Tap in as many of the contact fields as you'd like: name, phone number, cell phone number, email address, mailing address, website.**

   To the left of each field you'll see a label like Work or Home. Tap the down arrow to reveal all the options you can use for the first or subsequent fields. And tap Custom to display the onscreen keyboard to create your own label within the field. See Figure 6-3. Where offered, tap the down arrow to see more fields.

5. **Tap+to add new types of entries.**

   Depending on the original source of the contact entry, you may be able to include other essential information like birthday, anniversary, or favorite brand of beer. And with a little bit of ingenuity you can repurpose other listings by choosing the Custom option and entering a new title for the field.

If you want to tidy up the contact to remove empty text fields, tap the red – (minus) button to delete a field.

You can

- Assign a contact to an existing group, like Family or Friends.
- Create your own group, like a Human Chess Players Federation group.
- Tap Add Another Field for more options.
- Add notes or a field for a person's nickname.

To add a photo to the listing, follow these steps:

1. **Tap Contact Photo or the blank picture space at the top of the contact.**

   It has a plus symbol on it.

2. **Tap to select a photo from your tablet's Gallery.**

   If the person whose contact you're creating is right in front of you, tap Take Picture to use the tablet's built-in camera.

3. **Crop the picture with the provided tool, if it's available.**

   The box is square, while nearly all images are rectangular. Something has to give.

Importing contacts from a computer

You can also *migrate* (to use a geekish term) your collection of names, addresses, and email addresses from your desktop or laptop PC or Mac *to* the Tab S2 NOOK.

The trick is this: *Export* your contacts list from the computer in a compatible format that can be *imported* into the Tab S2 NOOK. Not just any format will work.

1. **Open your email or contacts program on your computer and look for a command to export records.**

   It may be under the File menu. If you can, go ahead and export your contacts as vCards to a location on your computer.

   If you're lucky, you'll find an option to export the files as *vCard* files, in the VCF file format. This option is available on the Mac and on certain mail programs on Windows machines, including Windows Mail and Windows Live Mail. It is *not* available in the widely used Outlook program on Windows machines. You may be able to find a utility to install on your desktop computer, or an app for your tablet, that will convert files from one format to another.

2. **Connect the Samsung Galaxy Tab S2 NOOK to the computer using the USB cable.**

3. **Transfer contacts to the tablet.**

4. **With the files on the Galaxy Tab, open the Contacts app on your tablet.**

5. **Choose the Import/Export command.**

6. **Choose Import from SD Card.**

7. **In the Save Contact To option, tap Phone or Tablet.**

   You know the Tab S2 NOOK is a tablet, not a phone, but the Android operating system was developed for smartphones first and the menus aren't always consistent.

   You may end up with some duplicate contacts. You can handle that later by joining multiple contacts; I deal with that later in this chapter.

Importing contacts through Gmail

Another way to get contacts from a computer onto your tablet is to use an intermediate web-based service, like Google's Gmail. This is one way to deal with computer programs like Outlook that don't produce vCards.

The process here is to export files as a CSV file (known to propeller-heads as a comma-separated values file), which is basically a set of details in a particular order separated by commas. Something like: Corey, Sandler, 508-555-0199,corey@notmyrealaddress.com. Sorry, spammers who want to contact me to deliver a $5 million award from a contest I never entered, provided I hand over the title to my house: That isn't my real phone number. It's a certified phony number in the 555-01xx range maintained by telephone companies for use in movies, songs, and books. "We're sorry. Your call cannot be completed as dialed."

Exporting a name card

Another way to share information between devices is to share a name card by sending it to another device as a vCard file. (On a computer, it appears as a file with a .vcf extension.)

You can share a card by

- Attaching it to an email or other message
- Transferring it across a USB cable to a computer
- Sending it via Bluetooth or Wi-Fi Direct to a nearby tablet or other device with which you have established a trusted communication

Here's how:

1. **From any Home screen, tap the Apps icon and then tap Contacts.**
2. **Tap a contact to display it.**
3. **Tap More and then tap Share Name Card.**
4. **Select a method of sharing from the options displayed. Then follow the onscreen instructions.**

Grouping and Degrouping Contacts

If you've only got a handful of contacts, you can just leave them in a single short list. And then meet some new people.

When your collection grows to many dozens, you can make some contacts members of a group, or make some of them favorites. Here's how to categorize:

1. **Open the Contacts app.**
2. **Tap the Groups tab.**
3. **Create your own group and assign contacts to it.**

   Or choose from pre-labeled groups such as Family, Friends, and Co-workers. The Not Assigned group is actually a group, as opposed to contacts that haven't been assigned to a group, if you get my meaning.

4. **Tap Save.**

   To add a single contact to a group, simply edit the Group field for that contact.

Cooking up multiple group contacts

You can add group members by the dozen, or the baker's dozen, if you like. Here's how:

1. **Tap Contacts, then tap Groups.**
2. **Tap the group you want to use.**
3. **Tap Menu, then choose Add Member.**

   Contacts that are available for categorization are displayed.

4. **Tap the name of each contact to add, or tap Select All.**
5. **Tap Done to add the contacts to the group.**

Sending email to a group

Here's one of the best reasons to create a group of contacts: You can send a single email message to all the members of the group in one fell swoop. Here's how:

1. **From any Home screen, tap Apps, then tap Contacts.**
2. **Tap Groups, and then tap the group you want to email.**
3. **Tap More and then Tap Send Email.**
4. **Tap individual contacts to select them or tap the checkbox at the top of the screen to select all.**

   You'll only see those members of group for which you've entered an email address.

5. **Tap More, and then Tap Send Email.**

The fifth Beatle: Removing group members

Sometimes it's time to thin the herd. Here's how to remove some or all members of a group:

1. **Tap Contacts and then tap Groups.**
2. **Tap the group from which you want to remove members.**
3. **Tap Menu. Then tap Remove Member.**
4. **Tap the name of each contact to be removed, or tap Select All.**
5. **Tap Done to remove the contact(s).**

Renaming a group

And when time comes to change the name of a group, you can do that, too:

1. **Tap Contacts, and then tap Groups.**
2. **Tap the group you want to rename.**
3. **Tap Menu, then tap Edit Group.**
4. **Tap the group Name field and type a new name.**
5. **Tap Save to seal the deal.**

Deleting a group

The end comes for all, including some groups on a Tab S2 NOOK. Here's how to be rid of one or more:

1. **Tap Contacts, then Groups, then Menu. Then tap Delete Groups.**

2. **Tap the names of groups you want to delete or tap Select All.**

3. **Tap Done to complete your order.**

4. **Tap Group Only to delete the group name.**

    Or tap Group and Group Members to send both the group and all its members to the digital dumpster.

Playing Favorites with Contacts

We all play favorites, whether we admit it or not. You can keep this to yourself if you want, but you can apply a designation of favorite to one or more of your contacts.

How does a favorite differ from assigning a contact to a group? Favorites can extend across multiple groups and can be made up of only some of the members of a group, or include people who aren't in a group of any kind. But when it comes time to send out a "Party time!" email, or any other sort of major announcement to a select group, you can blast it out to your chosen favorites. See Figure 6-4.

Marking a contact as a favorite

Shush. It's our little secret, okay? It's so easy you don't even need to edit the listing. Here's how you give a contact a golden star as a favorite:

1. **Tap Contacts.**

2. **Tap the contact you want to honor with the favorite distinction.**

3. **Tap the grayed-out star and turn it gold with pride.**

Viewing contacts marked as favorites

To see your secret list of favorites, do this:

1. **Tap Contacts.**

2. **Tap the Favorites tab.**

    You'll see only those contacts with the golden star.

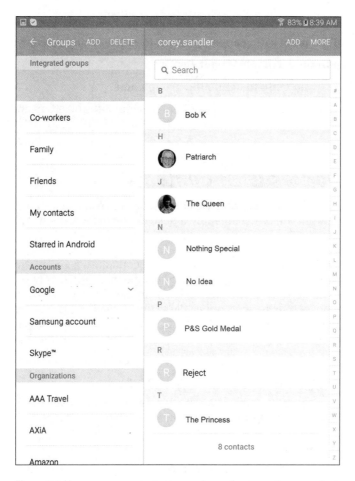

Figure 6-4: You can see contacts as members of groups, those marked as favorites, or those you've recently or frequently contacted.

Removing a favorite from a contact

Sometimes things just don't work out. Was it something I said? Were you politically incorrect? Maybe it was the shoes. Here's how to take away a single gold star or a whole galaxy of them:

1. **Tap Contacts and then tap Favorites.**

2. **Tap Menu and then tap Remove from Favorites.**

3. **Tap an individual contact or tap Select All.**

4. **Tap Done to complete the process.**

Managing Your Contacts

Much of the time, your contacts sit quietly in the background, providing information when you need to fill out an email address line, send a photo, or communicate about books from the eReader.

But to go directly to your contacts to examine, add, delete, or edit listings, do this:

1. **From the Home screen, tap the Apps icon.**

2. **Tap the Contacts icon (a little orange head).**

   You can place a shortcut to Contacts on one of the Home screen panels.

You can easily end up with a huge number of contacts, and good for you. My theory is: When in doubt, add a contact. You can always delete, edit, or merge *(link)* later.

Not every contact has a picture, and the picture can come from any of the sources of information you're tapping to construct the list. For example, if you have a photo assigned within your Gmail account, that photo will come along with the address, email, and phone number to your tablet.

Searching for a contact

There are many ways to find a particular contact, starting with the most obvious:

1. **From any Home screen, tap the Apps icon and then tap Contacts.**

2. **Tap the Search field and use the onscreen keyboard to type a few characters of their name.**

3. **When you see the contact you're looking for, tap it.**

Another way to find a particular contact is to tap a letter in the vertical alphabet list along the side of the Contacts screen. A letter of advice: Depending on the source of the contact, you may need to jump based on the last name or first name of the person you seek.

Contacts are sorted alphabetically by last name. Within that section, they're sorted with first name first. So, under L you'll find Abraham Lincoln ahead of Robert Todd Lincoln with Mary Todd Lincoln in between. Scroll through by swiping your finger, or jump to someone by tapping a letter.

Changing the order

If you're the sort of person who likes to keep track of your contacts based on their first names, your Tab S2 NOOK can do that, too. Here's how to change the sorting order:

1. **Start the Contacts app.**
2. **Tap the Menu icon (the three lines) in the upper right.**
3. **Choose Settings.**
4. **Tap List By.**
5. **Tap First Name or Last Name.**
6. **Press the Back key to exit.**

Editing or deleting a contact

Things change. This is something I've learned from a relatively long (thus far) and sometimes confusing life. And so you may need to edit or even delete an existing contact. Here's how:

1. **Open the Contacts app.**
2. **Tap the contact in need of rectification.**
3. **Tap the Edit (pencil) icon.**
4. **Tap the text field you want to change.**

    Use the onscreen keyboard to make changes.

Or do this:

1. **Tap the Trash icon.**

2. **Tap OK to confirm you really want to make the contact go away.**

    If this contact is synced to Google or other online accounts, deleting it on your tablet also deletes it from anywhere else it resides.

Sending Email from Your Contacts

Since the Samsung Galaxy Tab S2 NOOK is a Wi-Fi device without a cellular phone connection, it lacks standard phone facilities. The main means of communication from the tablet is email, although you can add apps like Skype to make phone calls and send text messages over the Internet.

You can start an email from your contacts list:

1. **From the Contacts app, tap a contact.**

   You see a contact name.

2. **Tap an email address.**

   If a contact has more than one email address, select the one you want to use.

3. **Tap an email option.**

   The Tab S2 NOOK is set up to send email through Gmail, although you don't have to stay with that choice. When I added the Outlook.com app to my tablet, that choice began appearing as a mail option. See Figure 6-5.

4. **Type your message.**

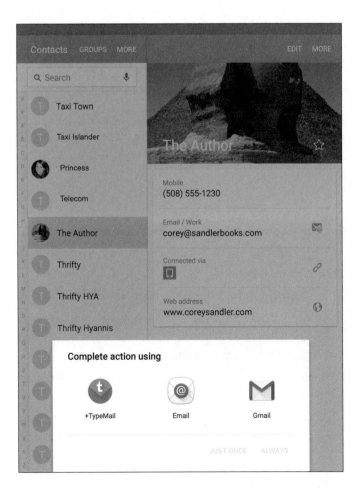

Figure 6-5: If you tap an email listing, you can send a message using one of the email accounts.

A different way to send an email is to choose the contact and tap the Menu icon in the upper right. Then tap Send Email.

And, as you see in Chapter 7 about email, you don't have to start the process in Contacts. You can open a page to send an email and type in a name; the tablet will hunt in Contacts for the address.

Handling Repeat Contacts

It's quite easy to end up with two, four, six, or more duplicate entries in your Contacts. You might have made an entry for your friend Jack Smith under "Smith, Jack" and "Jack Smith" and "John Smith," for example. Or you might have identical name entries but differing email or phone information in each.

Nixing duplicates

Because the Galaxy Tab S2 NOOK can grab contacts from Google and Samsung and Facebook and Twitter and more, dupes are quite common. See Figure 6-6.

Your first option is to go to Contacts and edit or delete duplicates or out-dated entries. Or you can *link* entries so all the information is brought together in one place.

Here's how to link:

1. **Open the Contacts list.**

2. **Open a contact that has duplicate entries.**

   The Connection section tells you the source of that entry.

3. **In the Connection section, tap the Link (chain) icon.**

4. **Tap Link Another Contact (at the bottom).**

   The tablet sees if it can determine a likely duplicate and lists it under Suggestions.

5. **Tap a duplicate entry to link it to the original.**

6. **If necessary, tap Link Another Contact again, and make further links.**

   You can link as many as ten entries.

7. **Press the Back key when you think you're done linking.**

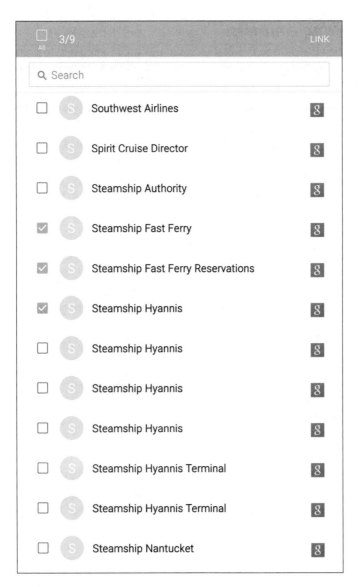

Figure 6-6: I found about a dozen entries for one ferry service, built up over the years on different accounts.

Unlinking contacts

Sometimes it's time to break the chain, perhaps because two contacts are no longer related or because you want to maintain different versions of a contact card. Here's how to unlink contacts:

1. **From any Home screen, tap the Apps icon, and then tap Contacts.**

2. **Tap a contact to display it.**

3. **Tap Link.**

4. **Tap Remove.**

7

We've All Got Email

*B*ecause you know that the Samsung Galaxy Tab S2 NOOK is a whole lot more than merely a bright and sprightly eReader for books, it isn't surprising that it can also send and receive messages to and from anyone with an email address. In today's age, that includes just about everyone you know. And in the truly good news, for the majority of users, email setup is automatic.

Hey Mister Postman

The Galaxy Tab S2 NOOK comes to you with two email apps: Email (part of the Android operating system) and Gmail (a web-based service that also comes from Google.) You can also add others, like Outlook.com, Yahoo Mail, and third-party email apps developed for tablets and smartphones like Typemail.

In this chapter, I concentrate on the Email app, which is quite full featured. It allows you to set up an account specific to the Tab S2 NOOK, or use the app as a way to bring to your tablet email from just about any other source, including accounts maintained by your cable television provider, a business or educational institution, and even from private domains.

What's a *private domain?* Say you run a business and have your own website; you might just accept email through that address. Something like corey@ this_is_not_my_address.com, which as you might imagine, is not my address but an example of a domain.

Writing Home about the Email App

You may have already set up your email particulars when you first configured your tablet. In that case, you might want to skip a bit of this chapter and explore the process of reading and sending mail and customization options. The rest of you might want to start by setting up a new email account.

The Email app is right there on your Home screen. You can also find it if you open the Apps panel. Look for the icon with an envelope sealed with a red @ sign. Tap the icon to see the inbox. My inbox is shown in Figure 7-1.

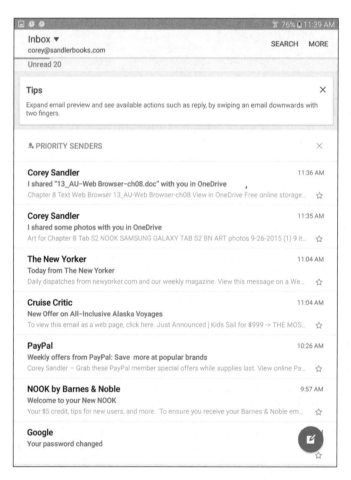

Figure 7-1: The basic email client supplied with the Tab S2 NOOK is polished and capable, offering no surprises but making no unexpected demands, either.

The Email app exists on your tablet. Using a tablet-based app allows you to read, write, and manage email even if you don't have a Wi-Fi signal. However, you can only *receive* or *send* email when your tablet is connected to an active Wi-Fi system connected to the Internet.

Setting up an email account, automatic style

If you already have an email account with one of the major providers — Gmail, Yahoo, Outlook, AOL, many Internet providers like Comcast or Verizon — you'll probably be able to add that account to your tablet with just a few bits of information. The Email app already knows the standard settings for them.

1. **From any Home screen, tap the Apps icon, and then tap Email.**

   Or tap the Email icon that may already be in place on your Home screen to open the app.

2. **Follow the onscreen instructions to set up an email account.**

   To configure additional accounts, tap More and then Settings, and then tap Add Account. You're asked to enter the username for your existing email account and password. See Figure 7-2.

   The Email app churns away, making contact with the mother ship at Google and then attempting to communicate with the email provider you use.

```
                                                    76% 11:38 AM

   Email accounts

   Select an existing account or add a new one in a few simple steps.
   Select existing account ▾
   Enter sign-in details

   Email address
   _____

   Password
   ........................................

   ☐  Show password




   MANUAL SETUP                                    NEXT  >
```

Figure 7-2: Both automatic and manual setup for email accounts begin with entering the address and password.

Setting up an email account, manual style

On the other hand, if you have your own domain or use a less-popular email provider, you may have to go through the manual setup process. Don't worry: It's nowhere as complicated as building your own rocket ship from a box of spare parts.

You have two relatively painless ways to manually set up an email account:

- ✓ With the Email app open to the Manual Setup screen, call the support department at your Internet provider. Ask them to help fill in the missing blanks for the names of the incoming and outgoing servers, plus any security scheme they use. Server names are usually something like imap.yourprovidername.com or smtp.yourprovidername.com.

  And if they aren't helpful, ask the billing department at your provider why you're paying them a monthly fee for this service which if you multiply by 12 and then by the number of years you've been a subscriber can yield a number that might make you ever-so-slightly demanding, and good for you.

- ✓ Open the email program on the computer or smartphone that already gets email from this provider. All the information you need is on the Setup screen for the existing account.

In general, don't expect much help here from NOOK or Samsung. But you might find a kindly technician who will help you get the information you need from your computer or a smartphone that already uses the account. However, the good folk at Barnes & Noble promise a high level of assistance through the NOOK desks at their stores or by telephone, and I have had good experience in that department.

Here's how to proceed *after* you get the information:

1. **Select Account Type.**

   The tablet's email app works with POP3, IMAP, or Microsoft Exchange; that's more than enough for nearly all ordinary users (and by that I mean everyone except for government spies and unemployed kids hacking away in their parents' basement). See Figure 7-3.

2. **Tap an option:**

   - **POP3.** This email scheme delivers messages from the email server onto your local computer, which may not be the best option for mobile devices. And if you lose your tablet, you could lose all unarchived email.

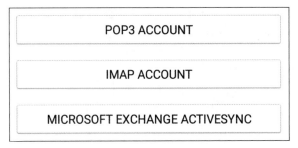

Figure 7-3: The Email app works with three common email acronyms and the protocols behind them: POP3, IMAP, and EAS.

- **IMAP.** This form of email works well with folders and mobile devices. It leaves the original messages on the email server, downloading a copy to your tablet.

- **Microsoft Exchange ActiveSync.** If you use this option, sometimes referred to as an EAS account, contact the systems manager at your place of work or other institution for details.

Use the standard keyboard to enter passwords. Don't use voice features to dictate unless you must, and do so in a private space.

3. **Type server settings for the incoming server (the system that delivers mail to you).**

   Re-enter the username and password, and then enter the name of the IMAP or POP3 server, usually in the form imap.*servername*.com or pop3.*servername*.com. Get this information from the email provider or from your desktop or laptop computer already configured to use this account.

   The Incoming Server Settings dialog box opens, as shown in Figure 7-4.

4. **Choose a Security Type from the menu.**

   Follow the same specifications that your email provider gave you. Some use none, others may demand SSL or TLS.

   Most email services use standard ports on your tablet (think of them as entrance and exit ramps from a superhighway). Check to see if your provider wants you to use a port other than the suggested one.

   The Outgoing Settings dialog box opens.

5. **Enter the address for the outgoing mail server.**

   It's usually in the form smtp.*servername*.com or similar. This server distributes your outgoing mail to the Internet.

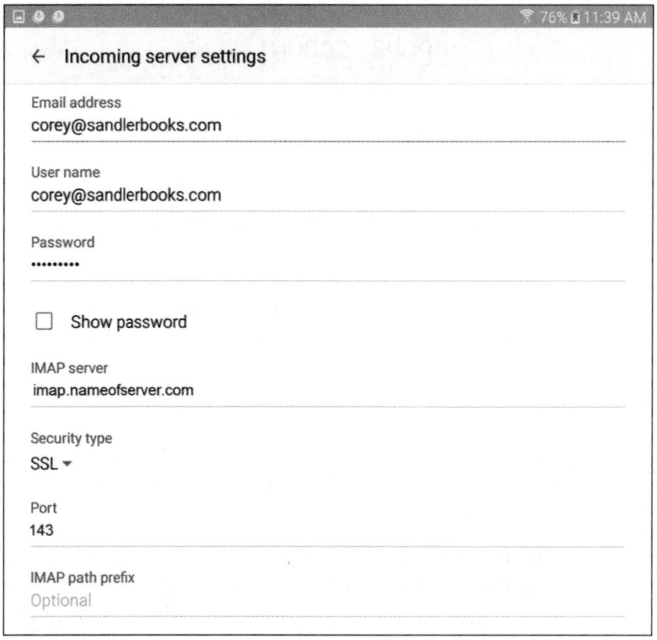

Figure 7-4: Part of the configuration panel for incoming settings of an IMAP account.

6. **Enter a security type, if required, and check that the proper port is chosen.**

7. **Tap Done.**

   If all goes well, you're taken to the incoming email panel and can see the account you added. If there's a problem, check all the settings against the ones you use on your computer or smartphone, or call the provider for assistance.

Deleting an email account

To remove an email account from your tablet, do this:

1. **From any Home screen, tap the Apps icon, and then tap Email.**

2. **Tap More and then tap Settings.**

3. **Tap the name of the account you want to remove.**

4. **Tap Remove and then confirm your decision.**

Deleting an account will delete all the email messages associated with that particular account from your tablet. IMAP and web-based email systems may keep your messages, allowing you to access them from other devices or after you reinstall an account on your tablet.

Customizing Your General Email Settings

You have a dizzying number of ways to customize your email account. Some are more important for all users; a few are important only to a few. But they're all there.

The following sections describe what you find in General Settings. You can get there from the Email app: Tap the Menu (three lines) icon in the upper right and then tap Settings.

Display options

These settings relate to how the Email app works for all accounts:

- **Auto Fit Content.** You can shrink email content to fit the screen; you can still zoom in on the details. I don't much like this option on the relatively small screen of the Tab S2 NOOK, but you can try it and see if you prefer it.

- **Notifications.** Tell the tablet whether to inform you each time a new piece of mail comes in.

- **Priority Senders.** All friends and family are created equal, but some are more equal than others. You can designate certain senders as Priority; their messages go into the Priority Sender inbox.

  You can make the Priority Sender inbox the one you go to when you open the Email app.

- **Spam Addresses.** Although it's to some extent like pushing a string up a hill, you can mark certain senders as spammers and place their addresses in a special folder. Tap this option to edit the list of spammers. You can also set up rules that filter certain types of messages directly into your spam folder. The problem here is that some legitimate email will be tagged as spam, and most spammers are fiendishly clever at getting around spam filters with adumbrations and circumlocutions, otherwise known as fancy and misleading words. Here you can add addresses of those senders who are lobbing junk into your mailbox; any messages from them automatically go into the Spam folder.

For a more full-featured email app, download one of several third-party products available through the Google Play Store. I discuss my favorite, TypeMail, in Chapter 14.

The Email app can handle many email accounts. That way you can see all your mail in one place. The app's left panel has a Combined View option, which brings together all mail from all sources rather than requiring you to look at each account separately.

Customizing settings for specific accounts

There is a fair amount of customization available in the basic email app. See Figure 7-5. To get to the advanced Settings panel for Email, do this:

1. **From any Home screen, tap the Apps icon and then tap the Settings icon.**

2. **Tap Applications in the left panel.**

3. **Tap Email in the right panel.**

4. **In Email settings, tap the account you want to adjust.**

5. **Choose your options:**

   • Edit the name of the account.

   • Tell the tablet whether to always send a CC or BCC of your message to yourself anytime you send an email.

   • Add or edit a signature for all outgoing messages. For example, I add a signature of my name, email address, website, and other details.

   • Tell the tablet whether to show all images in emails or wait for you to tap them before they are downloaded and displayed. If you have a slow connection, you can save time by limiting the initial download of emails to text only.

   • Turn on or off Auto Download Attachments. Again, you may not want to automatically download attachments if your connection to the Internet is slow. And some users worry about the possibility of a virus or malware coming in by unwanted attachments, although your tablet will automatically deal with most of these threats.

Syncing the mail

If you want the email server to send you messages anytime you're on a Wi-Fi connection, turn on Sync Email. Without that checkmark, the only time you'll get emails is when you load the app.

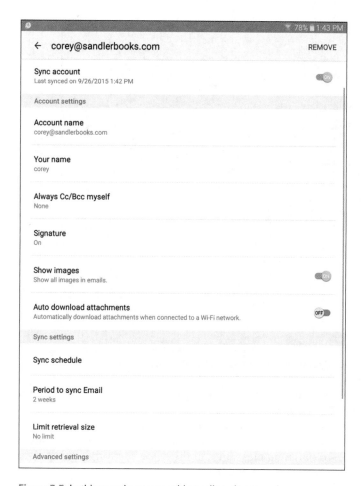

Figure 7-5: In this panel you can add or edit a signature for messages and make adjustments to the display of images and attachments.

✔ **Set Sync Schedule.** How often do you want the system to reach out to grab new messages? The shorter the interval, the more likely the tablet will slow down while you're using it for other purposes. You can also set a peak schedule for shorter intervals, and assign the days of the week and the hours that will be in effect. See Figure 7-6.

✔ **Period to Sync Email.** You can have the tablet only keep the last week or two of messages, or keep all messages back to the original date the account was set up. Setting a short sync period does *not* delete older messages; they're still available on other devices that share the same account, and you can get them if you change the sync period on your tablet.

Figure 7-6: You can set up differing schedules for syncing your mail inbox depending on the day of the week or the time of day.

Email security options

Under Advanced Settings is a section that allows you to add security to outgoing messages, encrypting them from your tablet. You can also add a digital signature to outgoing messages. In the same section, you can create private and public keys and manage them.

This level of security is generally beyond the needs of most tablet users. If you want to use encryption and keys, consult with the system manager at your business or institution about proper practices here.

I'll CC your BCC

Youngsters: *CC* stands for *carbon copy,* which used to be made by placing a piece of carbon paper under an original in a typewriter or even for handwriting. It was considered proper office etiquette to notify both the primary and secondary recipients that a carbon, or duplicate, copy of a message had been created and sent. *BCC* means *blind carbon copy,* which was a copy that the original recipient was not told had been made.

Open It Up!

After you set up the system, most of the not-quite-hard-work has been done. Tap the Email icon to see folders on the left side and mail on the right.

If you have more than one email account on your tablet, tap the menu in the upper left and choose which one to look at, or choose Combined View to bring them all to one place.

Mail that you haven't read yet has a blue first line. If a message has an attachment, you see a Paperclip icon. Tap an email to expand it for reading.

While you're in the Email app, email is organized by date; tap the Menu icon in the upper right and tap Sort By to change that.

You also see these options:

- **View As.** You can choose Conversation View, which groups all messages from a single person or address together. The problem here is that most users tend to receive most of their mail from a small number of senders, and this could easily divert your attention away from a new and important message from someone else.

- **Font Size.** You can adjust the size of the type in messages.

Now you're ready to read your mail. Tap any message to display its contents. If there's an attachment, you can see it by tapping the panel.

- **Search.** The magnifying glass icon opens a search panel where you can have the tablet hunt for emails based on sender name or a word in its subject.

- **Reply.** No need for a stamp. Just tap the leftward arrow to reply to a received message. You'll have room at the top to include a new message, like: "I found this video of a cat in a paper grocery bag and thought of you immediately."

  The Original Message option is below the message pane. Tap to remove the checkmark if you don't want to re-send the previous message but just want to reply. If there is a checkmark, you can tap the panel below to edit the original message.

- **Forward.** The right-facing arrow is the means to send a copy of a received message to someone else. You'll need to enter an email address. And you can edit the original message, which is an odd option to offer since that means you're not actually *forwarding* a message but instead sending something new.

✔ **Delete.** Get rid of, toss away, trash. The current message — or all messages from the list where you have placed a check mark in the box — will be moved to the Trash folder.

Email that you send to the trash isn't actually erased from your tablet until you go to the Trash folder and select them for final disposal. You can place check marks one by one, or tap the Menu icon in the upper right and tap Delete All.

Email that you've saved, or otherwise haven't sent, is automatically stored in the Draft folder. Tap the Draft folder and then tap any message within. You can edit it and send it from that folder, or throw it away.

Creating New Email

To write your very own email message, follow these steps:

1. **Open the Email app.**

2. **Tap the orange icon that shows a pen poised above a note.**

   This opens the email composition screen, including the keyboard.

3. **Touch in the To field and start typing the email address of the person you want to reach.**

   If the tablet finds one or more addresses amongst your contacts that include the name or first letters of the address, it will display them; you can tap one to automatically place that address in the field.

   You can add many addressees to the same field.

   Tap the down arrow at the right end of the To field to open up CC and BCC fields.

4. **Identify the nature of the message in the Subject field.**

   Not only is it good practice to give your recipients some information about the contents of the email here, but some people (myself included) tend to automatically discard any message without a subject line. It looks too much like spam.

At the top of the message writing screen you'll see a panel of icons that control the appearance and nature of the message:

✔ **Insert** Tap the little picture to insert a file: It can be an image from your Gallery, a memo, a calendar item, a Contacts listing, or a map. You can even ask the tablet to enable the built-in camera and take a picture that will automatically be added to the message. See Figure 7-7.

✔ **Font size** You can choose the size of the type used in the message. The standard size is 12 pt.

✏ **Font style.** You can choose **B** for boldface, *I* for italics, and <u>U</u> for underlining.

✏ **Type color.** Tap the <u>T</u> to select amongst 17 preset colors, or select a color of your choice by tapping in the spectrum. See Figure 7-8.

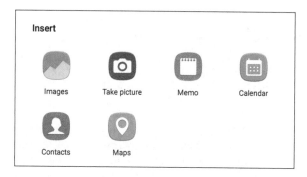

Figure 7-7: Insert a picture from your tablet's Gallery, take a photo with the camera, or attach other sorts of files to your mail.

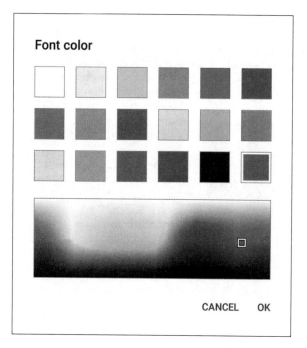

Figure 7-8: The Email app allows one of the preset colors or you can select from a palette to highlight text in color.

✔ **Background color.** Tap the reverse T (white in a black box) to choose a background color for the message; think of it as the paper color.

✔ **Other options.** You can add numbered lists or bullet lists to your messages, and add left or right indents.

Starting an Email from Other Apps

Almost every app on your tablet has a Share function. If you're looking at a photo in the Gallery and want to show it a friend, tapping the two-prong Share icon (shown to the left) opens an email message with the picture attached.

For example, the NOOK eReader also allows you to share quotes or comments, or to lend certain books. Enter an email address or start entering the name of someone you've previously communicated with, and the system will figure out who you want to send to; the Email app does the work in the background without you having to open it.

Getting Attached

You can send and receive files as attachments. For example, you can send a document to someone so she can save it to her tablet or other device. While working on this book, I sent some technical manuals and other files about Android and the Tab S2 NOOK to the tablet from my desktop computer. I got the email on my tablet — it was a PDF document that I opened using the Adobe Reader app — and then saved a copy to the Downloads folder for later. Going the other way, I sent many screen captures from the Tab S2 NOOK to my desktop computer as email attachments.

If you receive an attachment on your tablet, you'll need the proper app to read it. Tap Save to keep a copy of the attachment in the Downloads folder on your tablet's microSDHC card.

Many messages that arrive with an attachment can work with the Preview option to examine them in a small window within the Email app. The scaled-down version of Microsoft Office on the tablet opens most Microsoft Office word-processing, spreadsheet, and presentation files, for example.

8

Going Out on the World Wide Web

In This Chapter

▶ Going online with the NOOK

▶ Using Voice Search

▶ Setting your privacy levels

▶ Changing your Chrome sync settings

▶ Bookmarking websites

*T*he Internet is, in many ways, very much like the large junk drawer that most of us have in our kitchen. It's filled with important tools, odds and ends, recipes, calendars, photos, and in the end *something* you absolutely must be able to find when you need it even though it is hopelessly hidden beneath a huge stack of old newspapers.

The amazing tool we use: a *browser*. This app allows your tablet to navigate through all of the pipes and junk drawers and retail shops and libraries that make up the Internet. And browsers easily integrate with search engines such as Google or Bing and others, for better or for worse.

Your Samsung Galaxy Tab S2 NOOK comes with the Chrome web browser.

Although Chrome is the official browser for the Tab S2 NOOK, you can use any browser that works with a tablet running a current version of the Android operating system. These include Dolphin, Firefox, and Opera. You can find them at Google's Play Store, the NOOK Shop, and the Samsung store. In my experience, browsers either work or they don't work and they rarely cause problems with other apps on your device.

And there's no problem with having more than one installed and available on your Tab S2 NOOK. You can swap back and forth to test them, or even have separate Internet sessions going on at the same time on different browsers.

 A browser can take you anywhere on the web. You may find it easier and a bit quicker to use a special-purpose shortcut or app for certain sites. The Tab S2 NOOK comes with apps that go directly to Dropbox, Gmail, Google, Netflix, and YouTube — all websites. You also find apps that connect to stores for NOOK, Google, and Samsung.

Looking from the NOOK

You need an active Wi-Fi signal to use the Internet from your tablet. Without it, your browser will load but not browse.

Going onto the Internet from the Tab S2 NOOK is very much like making the same journey from a desktop or laptop computer, except that you'll be using your fingers to do the walking. See Figure 8-1.

Menu icon

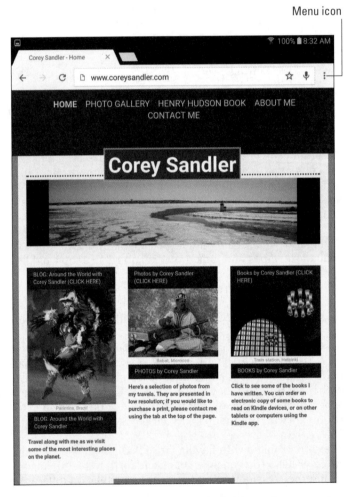

Figure 8-1: A page in the Chrome browser (which just so happens to be my home page) at www.coreysandler.com, which is one way you can get in touch with me, read my blog, or look at some of my photographs.

Basic controls within the browser

The browser window has some important command keys, including

- ✔ **Back.** Tap the < arrow or the curving arrow to return to the previous page.

- ✔ **Forward.** Tap the > arrow to go to a recent page forward.

- ✔ **Home.** Tap to have the browser display the designated Home page on the Internet.

- ✔ **Bookmarks.** Tap to visit the page or bookmarks, saved pages, and history within your browser. You can also manage those listings from this page.

- ✔ **Refresh.** Tap the circular arrow to reload the current web page.

Going to a web page

Tap in the address field and use the onscreen keyboard to enter the web address. Then tap Go on the keyboard.

You can also enter a search term into the same address field and allow the browser to take you to the results of a search engine exploration.

Using browser tabs

To open a second tab within the browser, tap the + Add Tab button.

To close a tab, tap the X Close Tab button alongside the tab to be shut.

Bookmarking a page

To bookmark the currently displayed web page, do this:

1. **Tap Bookmarks, and then tap Add.**

2. **Using the onscreen keyboard, type in a title for the bookmark.**

3. **Tap Save.**

To open a bookmarked web page, tap Bookmarks and then tap an entry.

Saving a web page

To save a web page on your tablet, tap More and then Save Web Page.

TECHNICAL STUFF

Omnibox on your tablet

One of Chrome's claims to fame was what Google called the *Omnibox,* the merging of the address bar and search bar. If you typed in some or all of a recognized website, Chrome would suggest the full address based on your prior history or its own vast records of other searches. On the other hand, if you were to enter the words or phrases of a search, Chrome assumes you want to use a search engine and it'll bring you to the most obvious of all suspects: Google.com. Most other browsers have adopted a similar scheme. See the accompanying figure.

The Chrome browser, and many others, try to keep one step ahead of you as you type in characters; if you see the word you want before you complete entering it, just tap it in the prediction bar.

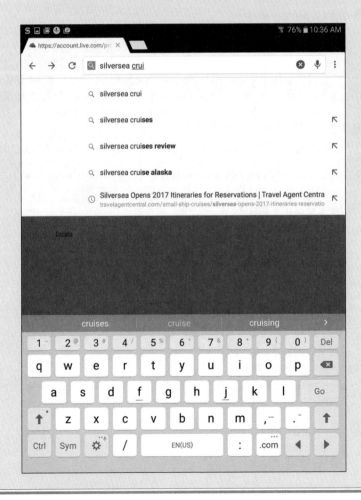

Keep these things in mind while browsing:

✔ If you know the name of the web page you want to go to, just tap the address bar near the top of the page. Then use the onscreen virtual keyboard to enter its name.

✔ You don't need to enter *http://*. Most times you don't have to enter *www.,* either.

✔ When you finish typing a web address, tap the Return key at the lower-right corner of the keyboard.

✔ If the browser correctly predicts what you want to enter, just tap the web address.

✔ If you swipe a web page up toward the top of the device, the address bar and tabs disappear. To see the address bar again, swipe down.

The Chrome browser has a few more particulars:

✔ To refresh or reload a web page, tap the curved arrow icon to the left of the address bar.

✔ To stop a web page from loading — a valuable tool if there's a hangup — tap the address bar and then tap the X symbol in the address bar. It's to the left when a page is coming up; when the page comes up, that X is replaced by the refresh icon.

✔ Anything a mouse can do on a computer, you do with a tap of your finger. "Click" a link by tapping the highlighted text (often marked in blue). Select an item or make a choice from a list by tapping an icon, picture, or word.

✔ If the web page is too small for you to easily jab at with your finger, zoom in: Place two fingers on the page and spread them apart. This works on most pages.

I'm going to make a reasonable assumption that you understand the basics of a browser. I want to point out Chrome's advanced, less obvious features.

Start by examining the browser's menu. Get there by tapping the Menu icon (pointed out in Figure 8-1) in the upper-right corner of any page in Chrome. See Figure 8-2.

Here are some of the choices:

✔ **New Tab.** You can open many tabs at once, flitting from website to website. Although after about three tabs, the real screen gets too crowded to easily use. You can also open a new tab by tapping the blank tab above the address bar.

✔ **New Incognito Tab.** This new tab section has a bit more privacy than a standard web visit. I explain more later in this chapter.

Tap here to close this tab

Tap here to open a new tab

Figure 8-2: Tap the Menu icon in the upper-right corner of the Chrome browser to display this set of powerful options.

✓ **Bookmarks.** Tap to see favorite pages you've noted.

✓ **Recent Tabs.** You can revisit web pages on tabs you recently closed. This is generally a good thing for busy users.

Chrome makes it easy to see websites you've visited. Me? I've got nothing to hide except for the obvious record of time-wasting distractions that eat away from my ordinarily highly productive writing sessions. Use the Privacy option, which I discuss later in this chapter, to clear the Recent tabs and browsing history.

✓ **History.** You can go back in time within the same session or days past. And if you have other devices using the same Google account, you can see their history. The History panel can hold dozens of entries. You can clear your browsing data by tapping the button at the bottom of the History screen, or clear away individual visits by tapping the X beside a particular entry.

✓ **Share.** Tell the world, or at least your friends, family, and coworkers, about pages you've found. I discuss sharing later in this chapter.

✓ **Print.** Tap here to print from your Tab S2 NOOK to most local printers with Wi-Fi or Bluetooth; you have to set up this communication link beforehand.

- ✔ **Find in Page.** Search for a word, name, or phrase within the current web page. As you type, results get more specific. You can't search for an image, only words.

- ✔ **Add to Home Screen.** You can create a shortcut to a web page, a very useful hyper-bookmark. I discuss this later in this chapter, in the section about bookmarks.

- ✔ **Request Desktop Site.** Websites want to show you their special, reduced *mobile* versions. Which you may not like. To ask that sites treat your tablet as if it were a desktop, tap to place a checkmark in Request Desktop Site. You might have to reload or re-request the page for this to take effect.

Settings in the Chrome browser

The last Menu option for the Chrome browser allows you to customize many of the settings for the browser. The panel is divided into basic and advanced features. The following sections explain some of the more important options you can set.

Basic settings

You can set these basic settings:

- ✔ **Search Engine.** The default search engine to look for websites or information on the web is Google's own `www.Google.com`. You can, though, ask that the browser automatically use another engine such as Yahoo!, Bing, Ask, or AOL.

  Google has become so popular that it's almost a generic term. Though Google, Inc. has a squad of lawyers prepared to do battle in defense of their trademark, you'll still hear people saying they intend to "google Teddy Roosevelt" when what they mean to say is they intend to "use the Google.com search engine to find out more about President Theodore Roosevelt."

  You don't have to change search engines if you just want to try another one from time to time. Just go to Chrome and, in the address bar, type the site: yahoo.com, bing.com, ask.com, and so on.

- ✔ **Autofill Forms.** This feature automatically fills in certain types of form information, such as your name, address, and telephone number. In a separate category, it automatically fills in a preferred credit card (including your name, card number, and expiration date). You can fill in one or the other or both fields, and there's also an on-off switch to enable or disable autofill.

  My preference is to include the name and address information only, and leave blank the credit card data; it seems to me too big of a risk to have the card poised to jump into place on a screen all by itself.

✔ **Save Passwords.** Here you can save logins and passwords for websites. This feature has an on-off switch at the top of the form, and then you can touch any individual saved entry to edit or delete it. You'll also find a listing called Never Saved, and here you see websites that asked whether you want to have login information saved, but where you told the browser not to do so.

My preference for Save Passwords is to save only those websites I don't consider a risk to my personal information or finances. For example, I do keep passwords for things like certain news sites and shopping sites where I do *not* store credit card numbers. And I maintain a whole separate set of passwords for sites that hold information I want to keep from prying eyes.

✔ **Home Page.** Here you can select a particular page as the one your browser will display each time it loads; mine is *The New York Times*. There's also an on-off switch to enable or disable this feature as needed.

Advanced settings

You can set these advanced settings:

✔ **Privacy.** Here you find a valuable collection of features that can reduce the possibility of snoops learning about places you have visited.

✔ **Navigation Error Suggestions.** Place a checkmark in the box to show suggestions anytime the web address you have entered in the browser doesn't work or a connection can't otherwise be made.

✔ **Search and URL Suggestions.** Put a checkmark to enable a prediction service that shows related queries and popular websites that sometimes — not always — guesses what you're looking for. If you don't see what you want, keep typing in the search bar until you do.

✔ **Touch to Search.** On some websites and in certain situations, when you touch a word, your tablet (when connected to Wi-Fi) uses Google Search to provide a definition, picture, or other information without leaving the current web page. You can turn this feature on or off.

✔ **Prefetch Page Resources.** Your tablet can try and be one step ahead of you as you read a website, requesting and temporarily storing links and information you just might tap next. For example, if you're looking at an online retailer and reading the description of a new camera, the browser might note that there are two big buttons nearby: Specifications and More Pictures. Chrome might *preload* one or both pages into the tablet's memory. If it guessed correctly, you might save a few seconds of your invaluable time.

Most users find both preloading and bandwidth management worthwhile. However, if your tablet slows down or certain pages don't display properly or at all, try turning off Preload Webpages or Bandwidth Management (or both) to see if that solves the problem.

✓ **Usage and Crash Reports.** Some Internet providers and hardware makers (including Samsung) are interested in knowing about usage statistics and crash reports; the information collected here is supposed to be used to improve apps and other software and your personal data is supposed to be not collected. You can choose to enable or disable this feature.

✓ **Do Not Track.** Enabling this feature means that as you visit each web page, your request to view information includes a request that your visit isn't tracked or recorded. It's a nice idea, but you have no certainty that web pages you visit will honor this request.

✓ **Clear Browsing Data.** This may be the most important option for privacy. Options on this screen allow you to remove, from your tablet's memory, any or all of the following: your browsing history, any data held in the tablet's short-term cache memory, cookies and site data placed on your phone by certain websites to track your visit, saved passwords, and autofill data. Tap to place a checkmark and turn on an option, and tap Clear to wipe them away from the tablet.

Clearing browsing data doesn't remove any records maintained by websites you have visited. In most situations, a website can determine the unique address on the Internet of your tablet or its Wi-Fi access point, and may also keep track of any information you have chosen to provide.

Going incognito in Chrome

One way to reduce your exposure to prying eyes is to open an *incognito window* within Chrome. The browser automatically declines to save a record of whatever page you've opened or downloaded within that window

Specifically, your browsing history, including pages you open and files downloaded while going incognito, isn't recorded in your browsing and download histories. Any new cookies installed in your tablet while incognito are deleted *after you close all incognito windows.*

You can switch between incognito and regular browsing, and even have both types of windows open at the same time. But the extra protection is only available in the incognito session(s).

Chrome will quite subtly mark the fact that a window is *incognito* (Latin for "unknown") by placing a tiny icon of a spy, complete with dark glasses, on the screen. See Figure 8-3.

Going incognito affects only the records that would otherwise be automatically maintained on your tablet. The websites you visit can (and probably will) still note that a tablet at your address on the web made a visit.

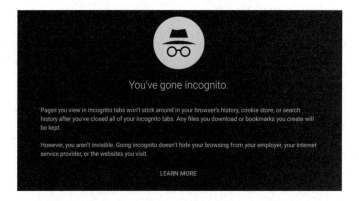

Figure 8-3: Going incognito removes most traces of web browsing from your device. Notice the little spy guy? But it doesn't scrub your visit at the *other* end of the Internet machine, the websites and all the servers in between.

You can open an incognito window two ways:

- ✔ Press and hold (or long-press) a link on a web page. A small panel opens; choose Open in Incognito Tab.

- ✔ From Chrome, tap the Menu icon and then tap New Incognito Tab.

To exit an incognito window, click the X at the corner of the tab.

Speaking Your Mind with Voice Search

You can enter requests by typing on the virtual keyboard or by handwriting entries on a character recognition panel. But hear now, here's something else: computer-assisted dictation, which you can use when your tablet is connected to an active Wi-Fi system.

1. **Tap the microphone icon (at the right side of the address bar).**

   You'll see a little box on screen with a slightly larger icon of a microphone and the instructions, "Speak now." That's your cue.

2. **Speak now, as clearly as you can, in the direction of the tiny microphone on your tablet.**

   The voice recognition is quite accurate, understanding nearly all of my search requests about 85 percent of the time.

Voice Search can help with simple questions like these:

- ✔ What time is it in Tblisi?

- ✔ Will it rain tomorrow in Casablanca?

✔ Where was Alexander Graham Bell born?

✔ How do you say "That's enough" in Latin?

The system's smart enough to make some logical leaps. I asked, "Will I need an umbrella today?" and it figured I wanted the forecast.

The d**ned thing can even understand many curse words, at least to the point of ignoring them if they're an unnecessary part of a question. See Figure 8-4.

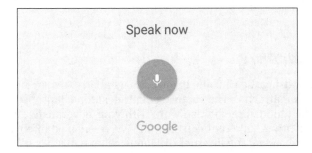

Figure 8-4: Voice Search does a pretty good job of interpreting your spoken commands, although some of its interpretations can be a bit odd.

Sharing Is Caring

With apologies to Lennon and McCartney of the Beatles: "I read the news today, oh boy, and saw a photograph that blew my mind." It was a picture of a line of about 20 people waiting at a bus stop. Each and every person was staring intently into his own tablet or a smartphone, lost in his own world. Presumably, the oncoming bus driver was paying attention.

Anyhow, my point: Though sometimes it's hard to believe it, the act of browsing the web can (and should) be a communal activity. I know that I love to find funny or interesting stories or entire pages that I can send to my wife, my kids, my friends, and total strangers.

Although you *could* copy a web page and paste it into an email, that's time-consuming (and doesn't guarantee that this pearl can be viewed properly). The better way is to send a *link* for the page you want to share. Here's how:

1. **In Chrome, open the web page you want to share.**

2. **Tap the Menu icon in the upper-right corner.**

3. **Tap Share.**

   A menu opens.

4. **Pick a way to send the page.**

   The Share Via menu offers just about every possible means of communication from your Tab S2 NOOK. You'll see the built-in Email app as well as any third-party email apps you've added, as well as Cloud storage, calendars, and many other options. The more apps you add to your tablet, the more sharing options appear here. Tap any of them to begin the process of sending a link to share.

Signing In to Chrome

An advantage of using the Chrome browser is its ability to sync between all of the devices you attach to the same account: desktops, laptops, tablets, smartphones included. It might also work with your new toaster, or garage door opener, or other state-of-the-art device: We've entered into what some technologists are calling the Internet of Things, where all sorts of devices have their own address on the Internet and can be controlled or monitored from anywhere with an Internet connection.

Here's what happens when you sign in to the Chrome browser while using an active Wi-Fi connection: All your web page bookmarks, tabs, history, and other browser preferences are saved to your Google account. At the same time, any changes you made while using another computer, tablet, or smartphone that uses the same Google account are synced to your Tab S2 NOOK. You can manage the data by going to the Google Dashboard. Signing into Chrome also opens the door to personalizations you've made to other Google services such as Gmail, YouTube, and Google Maps.

If you've set up your Tab S2 NOOK to automatically sign in to your Google account each time you turn it on, you're all set.

To turn on or off automatic sign-in, do this:

1. **From the Home screen, tap the Chrome icon.**

2. **Tap the Menu icon in the upper-right corner.**

3. **Tap Settings.**

4. **From the Basics section, tap the Google sign-in name you registered when you set up your Tab S2 NOOK.**

5. **Tap to remove or enter a checkmark in the Auto Sign-In option.**

   No, that isn't my email address.

If you borrow someone's computer or tablet, or use a public computer, don't sign in to your Google account. When you set up Chrome with your Google account, a copy of your data is stored on the computer you're using. Other users can get that information there.

To remove your data, delete the user you're signed in as. Using your Samsung Galaxy Tab S2 NOOK with Chrome is relatively safe, as long as you keep the device protected by a password and under your control.

Protecting Your Privacy

You can go back to the future or ahead to the past by tapping the ← (back) arrow or → (forward) arrow at the far left of the address bar. The back arrow is available when you've gone at least one page forward by tapping a link. The forward arrow is usable any time you've gone back at least one page in the current tab.

Being a revisionist: Clearing your history

You can also consult your history of web browsing; see Figure 8-5. You may find this a very valuable tool, allowing you to quickly return to a page you visited earlier today, or yesterday, or weeks ago; web pages that are *dynamic,* meaning that their content is constantly changing (like a newspaper front page, for example) may not work properly here because the article you were reading may have been deleted or moved.

Tap an entry in the History list to return to the page. You can clear the History list on your Tab S2 NOOK quite easily. Here's how:

1. **Tap the Menu icon within the Chrome browser.**

2. **Tap History.**

   Recent Tabs is another option. If you're signed in to Chrome, you can see web pages that you've opened on your Tab S2 NOOK as well as any desktop, laptop, smartphone, or other tablet that shares the account.

   Allow me to emphasize that point: If you sign into Chrome on various devices, places you have visited will be recorded here in sections called This Device, which means the Tab S2 NOOK, as well as on Other Devices, which could mean your desktop or laptop computer or your smartphone or someone else's computer if you signed into Chrome there.

3. **Tap Clear Browsing Data.**

Don't assume that any search, web page visit, email, message, chat, or any other action you perform on the Internet is private. Internet users can never expect to have complete and total privacy; even if you keep your own tablet clear, your requests to search engines and Internet providers are all routinely recorded or logged or otherwise noted.

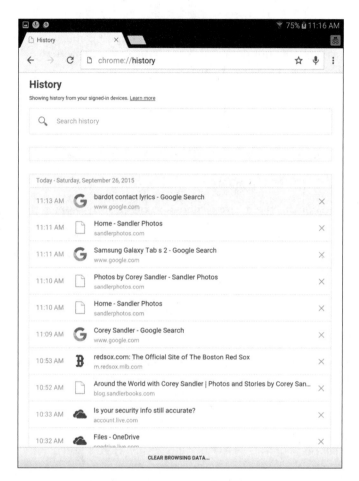

Figure 8-5: Your browser keeps track of where you've been; it even records the date and time.

To begin with, your *Internet Service Provider (ISP)* probably records all traffic that goes through its equipment. And then the web page at the end of the line will likely keep track of any user that visits — or at least their IP address, which is the electronic connection between your Wi-Fi modem or wired modem and the Internet.

If you use a different browser on your Galaxy Tab S2 NOOK, check the settings page to find a Security and Privacy panel. You can sweep away *local* evidence of your excursions on the Internet.

Adjusting site settings

Chrome allows you to adjust certain settings of websites you visit. See Figure 8-6. To get to the page where you can adjust these settings, do this:

1. **Tap the Web icon on the Home screen.**

   Or tap the Chrome icon within the Apps menu or any shortcut you may have created for Chrome.

2. **Tap the Menu icon in the upper-right corner.**

3. **Tap Settings.**

4. **In the Advanced section, tap Site Settings.**

The following sections talk about some of the options in this menu.

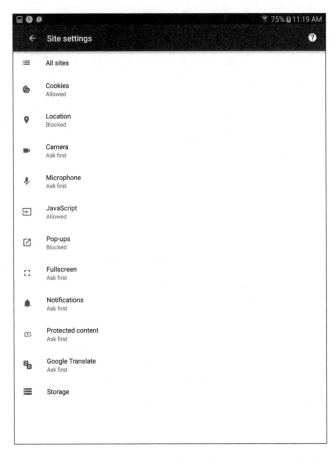

Figure 8-6: Content settings let you kill cookies on contact and make other determinations for websites you visit.

Accepting or declining cookies

I mention *cookies* a bit earlier, which some websites leave behind on your system. Some may be perfectly benign, like a reminder of the last page you visited on a complex site. Others may be not so innocent, like an attempt by an advertiser or other entity to track your movement around the web.

In theory, the cookies are anonymous. Your tablet is just a number to the cookie-dropper. However, if the cookie comes from a site that requires you to sign in, well then you're not all that anonymous after all.

You can tell Chrome (and most other browsers) that you don't want to allow cookies. The bad news is that *some* websites won't allow you to get very deep into their content without being able to leave cookies behind.

In Chrome you have two options for cookies:

- ✔ The first is an on-off switch that enables or disables the ability of sites to save and read cookie data. You can choose to turn off this feature, but some pages refuse to allow access — or at least raise an electronic ruckus if you try to visit without permitting cookies.

- ✔ The second option allows third-party websites to save and read cookie data. In theory, this means that an advertiser or a web provider could look at the cookies on your tablet. You can try disabling this feature by removing the checkmark, but you may run into the same problem as the general cookie blocker: Websites you visit may turn you away.

It's your decision. I allow cookies, but also regularly (usually daily, sometimes more frequently) clear them away. Sometimes I tell the browser not to accept cookies and wait to see which websites object; if they do, I consider whether this site has a legitimate reason to put a note within my tablet or computer.

Location settings

If you want to enjoy your tablet's ability to help find the nearest gas station or helium balloon-refilling station, you have to allow the browser to provide information to sites about where you are.

Your tablet has a GPS that can pinpoint your location to a few tens of yards in proper conditions; in addition to that, search engines are usually able to figure out your approximate location based on where your Wi-Fi router connects to the Internet.

Is this an invasion of your privacy? It probably is, but there's not much you can do to avoid it except not use a tablet or a smartphone or a telephone; I think the more important thing to concentrate on is working to limit the amount of other information you divulge to outsiders.

One other note: This is one of many features that uses battery power and data. To maximize the time between recharges of your battery, you might want to turn off location sensing and the GPS module until and unless you need them.

The other issue, the amount of data consumed, isn't usually a problem with Wi-Fi connections, but if your tablet is connected to a smartphone in certain circumstances, this could result in an unexpected data charge, especially when you're roaming away from your home region.

Camera

Some websites may seek to turn on your tablet's camera (for example, to scan a bar code). That may be a very valuable feature to you, but you should also consider the possibility — however remote — that some malicious programmer may try to spy on *you* by turning on your tablet's camera without your knowledge.

You might want to use the camera setting called Ask First, which blocks remote control of your camera without your permission.

Microphone

Just as with the camera, there are certain situations where a website might want to turn on the microphone on your tablet for things like voice recognition, dictation, or voice memos. Once again, some people worry that evildoers will try to listen in on their lives through the microphone. For that reason, consider using the setting Ask First.

Enabling or disabling JavaScript

JavaScript is a programming language that animates or customizes web pages. You can remove the checkmark from the Enable JavaScript setting if you'd like. Some websites won't run properly, or you may never notice the difference.

In the past, JavaScript has been accused of causing problems on its own, or allowing itself to be hijacked by hackers seeking to implant viruses or steal information or otherwise foul the swimming pool. That's less common today, and in any case a tablet running Android is, to some extent, less vulnerable to this sort of attack than is a desktop or laptop computer.

Block pop-ups

Among the many annoyances used by advertisers to make a buck off innocent Internet users is a *pop-up ad*. It might appear in front of a news article that you want to read or block an entertainment page.

Once again, there's a potential downside: Some websites may not run right if you block pop-ups, and some pop-ups blast right through this protection anyway. I generally leave on the pop-up blocking and hope for the best.

Some websites ask permission to be placed on a list of exceptions to pop-up blocking, which is a polite thing to do. If a site you visit regularly insists on pop-ups, and you want to grant it permission, allow it to add its address to the exceptions.

Protected content

This setting is generally benign and may not apply to you. When you allow Chrome to use the Protected Content setting, the site authenticates your device to confirm that it's allowed to display certain content (like music or videos). These providers place a special type of cookie, called a *device credential,* on your tablet or computer.

Other content settings

You can turn off Google Translate, which decodes foreign language websites for you, and also examine website settings, which are yet another form of cookies. If you see a site here that you don't expect to revisit or don't want visiting you, tap its name and then tap Clear Stored Data.

Customizing Chrome Sync settings

Although most users want to synchronize everything that uses their Google account, you can turn off specific utilities. Here's how:

1. **Tap the Web icon on the Home screen.**

   Or, tap the Chrome icon in the Apps menu or any shortcut you may have created for Chrome.

2. **Tap the Menu icon in the upper-right corner.**

3. **Tap Settings.**

4. **Tap the Basic panel on the left side, if it isn't already selected.**

5. **Tap your account name.**

6. **Under Services, tap the Sync option.**

   You see a panel of data types. If you put a checkmark under Sync Everything, then everything is synced.

   If you remove the checkmark from Sync Everything, choose from the settings: Autofill, Bookmarks, History, Passwords, and Open.

   Back out of Chrome by pressing the Back key, or return to the Home screen.

Encrypting your Google account data

Google promises that all synced data is *encrypted* (coded) when it travels between your computer and Google's servers. You can apply an extra level of encryption to the data stored on your own device. To become the encryption keeper on your tablet, do this:

1. **Tap the Web icon on the Home screen.**

   Or, tap the Chrome icon in the Apps menu or any shortcut you may have created for Chrome.

2. **Tap the Menu icon in the upper-right corner of the Chrome page.**

3. **Tap Settings.**

4. **Tap the Basic panel on the left side of the screen if it isn't already selected.**

5. **Tap your account name.**

6. **Under Services, tap the Sync option.**

   You'll see a panel of Data Types.

7. **Tap Encryption.**

   A panel opens.

8. **Your choice here is to Encrypt All with Passphrase *or* Encrypt with Google Credentials.**

   For most users, it's acceptable to leave the security work for this sort of information to Google, using credentials or passwords that are generated by the system.

   If, however, you want full control, you can enter a passphrase of a few words. Retype the passphrase when you're asked to confirm.

   If you create your own passphrase, it doesn't go to Google and you're responsible for keeping it in mind. If you forget the passphrase, you have to reset the sync process within your Google account.

Turning on Data Saver management

Chrome users can retrieve most web pages through Google's servers instead of directly from wherever they're stored. Although it ordinarily adds at least one extra hop — and a bit of time — between your request and the moment a web page appears on the screen of your tablet, Google offers the possibility of more than making up for the lost time by *compressing* the web page so that it moves faster to you. This Data Saver *bandwidth management* scheme works by converting certain types of images to smaller files; on average, about 60 percent of web pages consists of images. In addition, the Google technology also performs other tricks to reduce the overall size of web pages.

You can try bandwidth management and see if it works well for you. If it causes problems, turn it off. Here's how to turn it on:

1. **Tap the Web icon on the Home screen.**

   Or, tap the Chrome icon within the Apps menu or any shortcut you may have created for Chrome.

2. **Tap the Menu icon in the upper-right corner of the Chrome page.**

3. **Tap Settings.**

4. **Tap the Advanced panel on the left side of the screen if it isn't already selected.**

5. **Tap Data Saver Management in the panel on the right.**

6. **Turn the on/off slider to enable or disable the feature.**

You can see a report that estimates the amount of compression that has been applied in the last month. If the report says 25%, in rough terms that means that pages that've been compressed through the Google servers have been on average about 25 percent smaller by the time they arrived on your tablet, and your system has responded about 25 percent faster than it would have without this feature enabled.

Using Data Saver also enable Chrome's Safe Browsing system, which can detect many malicious web pages and protect you from certain phishing, malware, or other nasty attacks. On the downside, using Data Saver might interfere with access to premium data services provided by some Internet carriers. You can experiment with enabling or disabling this feature to see what effects you might encounter.

Leaving Bread Crumbs: Bookmarking

Sometimes you very much want to leave behind traces of places you have been on the web. You can insert *bookmarks* that record web addresses for pages you expect to want to visit again.

Among the nice things about browser bookmarks is that they don't fall out when you turn your NOOK upside down. Figure 8-7 shows a bookmark in progress. Here's how to create a bookmark for a page:

1. **From Chrome, visit the web page you want to bookmark.**

2. **Tap the Bookmark (star) icon in the upper-right corner of the address bar.**

   An unassigned web page has an empty or open star; when it's bookmarked, the star is filled in blue.

You'll next go to a page where you can edit and adjust the information about the bookmarked page.

3. **Edit or skip to Step 4:**

   • *Name.* Chrome offers a suggestion, but you can tap in the field and change the name.

   • *URL.* This is the web address for the page you are bookmarking (in geekspeak, its uniform resource locator). Leave it as is.

   • *Folder.* You can store your bookmarks in one of the predefined folders or create your own folder.

   I create folders by type: Travel, Banking, Shopping, and the like. You can scroll through the list of bookmarks with judicious finger swipes.

4. **Tap Save.**

If you don't create a bookmark while viewing a web page, you can go back in time to the Most Visited tab. Open the web page and tap the Bookmark icon.

Figure 8-7: You can add a favorite or important page.

Editing or deleting a bookmark

To change a bookmark's name or folder, or to delete a bookmark, do this:

1. **Go to the folder that has the bookmark.**

2. **Press and hold the bookmark.**

3. **Choose an option.**

   You can open the website in a new tab, open it in an incognito tab, or edit or delete the bookmark.

Adding a web page to your Home screen

The ultimate bookmark adds a shortcut to a web address on your Home screen. You can even create a folder of favorite sites and gather them there.

Here's how to add a shortcut to a web page on your Home screen:

1. **From Chrome, visit the web page you want to bookmark.**
2. **Tap the Menu icon in the upper-right corner.**
3. **Tap Add to Home Screen.**

   The system automatically adds the website name. You can edit the name if you want; the address won't change. See Figure 8-8.

4. **Tap Add.**

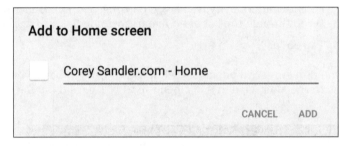

Add to Home screen

Corey Sandler.com - Home

CANCEL   ADD

Figure 8-8: Putting a shortcut on the Home screen lets you visit pages without even starting the browser.

Popping open multiple browser tabs

The long-gone but not forgotten (by some) comedy troupe *Firesign Theater* once based an entire evening's performance around the essential question, "How can you be in two places at once, when you're not anywhere at all?" On Google Chrome, while you sit wherever you may think you are, you can be in many more places at once.

You can open multiple *tabs* within one browsing session. Unused extra tabs lurk behind open screens; just tap an empty tab to visit other sites or conduct searches without closing earlier tabs. Move to another by tapping any tab title. To close a tab, tap the X in its right corner. You can touch and move tab order onscreen.

The other way to open a new tab is to press and hold (or long-press) a link you see on a web page. When you do that, you get these options:

✔ **Open in New Tab.** Select this one to do just what it offers, automatically opening a tab based on the link you chose.

✔ **Open in Incognito Tab.** This opens a new tab based on the link, but makes it incognito. Its details are in this chapter's "Going incognito in Chrome."

Part III
Reading Electronics

Visit www.dummies.com/extras/samsunggalaxytab4nook for help setting up separate accounts on the Tab S2 NOOK.

In this part . . .

- ✔ Figure out how to buy something from the NOOK Store.
- ✔ Categorize books, magazines, and newspapers in your NOOK library.
- ✔ Read on your NOOK.
- ✔ Find other sources for eBooks.

9

Buying and Reading NOOK Books

In This Chapter

▶ Shopping from your NOOK

▶ Archiving to the NOOK cloud

▶ Lending, borrowing, and reading eBooks, magazines, and newspapers

▶ Managing your library

▶ Designing your own eBook

*O*kay, so there is not time — or much of a point — in debating the relative advantages of a digital book on a tablet versus an old-fashioned book printed on paper. Lovers of electronic tablets disparagingly call printed books "dead tree" versions. Lovers of printed books wish that tablets were not so small and light and portable.

In the end, it doesn't matter what medium you use to get your information. The technology is the means of transport and display. A digital, backlit LCD screen tablet is merely another way to read the written word and absorb its content into our souls.

As I explain, Barnes & Noble has taken an off-the-shelf Samsung tablet and packaged it with a set of apps that open the door to their electronic bookstore. That's the NOOK part of the Samsung Galaxy Tab S2 NOOK, and that's what you explore in this chapter. Chapter 10 explores other sources of reading material and multimedia for your Tab S2 NOOK.

Calling All NOOK Shoppers

I'm going way out on a limb here to declare it highly likely the reason you purchased the NOOK version of the Samsung tablet is that you actually intend to do some reading: books, magazines, newspapers, and catalogs. Good news! The process is just about as easy as tapping your finger.

The Galaxy Tab S2 NOOK comes with a large block of internal memory plus a slot into which you can add a huge amount of additional memory on a card. And even that is not the end: Books and other media you purchase from Barnes & Noble are also archived back at the other end of the electronic connection and if you have removed a title from your device it can easily be restored to your NOOK anytime you have a Wi-Fi connection.

Your Samsung Galaxy Tab S2 NOOK comes with a few free books already loaded, plus samples of others. So you could, if you want, jump right in and start reading. I explain how to turn the pages and personalize the experience later in this chapter. But first, you might want to go shopping.

And you get a regular set of personalized recommendations. The more you buy, the more appropriate the suggestions become. See Figure 9-1.

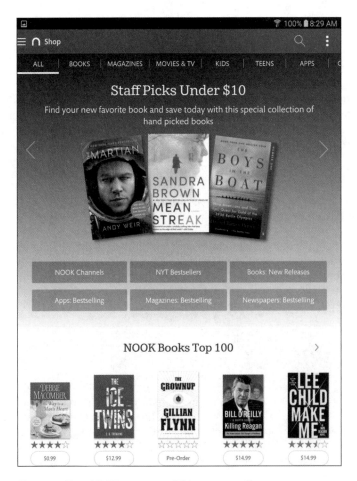

Figure 9-1: Your NOOK suggests additions to your library.

The NOOK Store on the Galaxy Tab 4 NOOK can only be portrait mode (taller than wide). You can scroll up on the page to see special offerings in each of the departments.

The full suite of NOOK apps appears along the bottom of the screen. They include:

- **Current Read** is a shortcut that takes you almost instantly from the Home page to the book or periodical you were most recently reading, depositing you on the page you last viewed.

- **NOOK Shop** is a direct connection to the online store where you can shop for books, periodicals, videos, music, and apps.

- **NOOK Search** is a specialized search tool that allows you to look for titles, authors, and even certain types of content within your own library on the tablet, or with an active Wi-Fi connection it'll search the NOOK Store and report back on what it has found.

- **NOOK Home** lets you see new recommendations and special offers from the NOOK Store, customized based on your recent purchases or other indicators of your interests.

Look at the upper-left corner of most of the NOOK apps for a Menu icon made up of three horizontal bars stacked atop each other; see it to the left here. To open the menu, either tap the icon or swipe to the right from the left edge of the screen. The options double back on the main NOOK apps of Current Read, Home, and Shop. And then the menu adds quick jumps to your personal library of content, special messages that may be sent your way from Barnes & Noble, and the Settings screen where you can customize much of the reading experience.

Making Your Own NOOK Shortcut

You can even make your own shortcut from the Home screen to any NOOK book or other content you get through the store. As an example, say you want a shortcut that allows you to quickly jump to the very book you're reading right now.

Here's how to do it, and it's not quite as difficult as it may sound:

1. **From any Home screen, pinch the screen and then tap Widgets.**

2. **Swipe your way through the available widgets, and when you locate it tap NOOK Widgets.**

3. **Touch and hold the widget called NOOK Shortcut to Book to place it on a Home screen.**

   When it's on a Home screen, you can move it about on that page or other secondary Home screens and place it there. See Figure 9-2.

Figure 9-2: Add the NOOK shortcut to your Home screen to quickly jump to the last place you were reading something (an eBook, for example) that you got from the NOOK Store.

4. Scroll through your library and find the content for which you want to create a shortcut.

Not all content is likely to fit on one screen; tap More at the bottom of your library list to see additional entries.

5. When you find the item for the shortcut, touch it.

A flexible box appears around the shortcut; you can make this box smaller or larger by touching one of the sides and pushing it in or out.

6. Tap outside the shortcut to complete the process.

You can create as many NOOK shortcuts as you can fit on your Home screen panels. And you can delete a shortcut: Press and hold a shortcut until it pulses; then drag it to the Trash icon; deleting a shortcut does *not* delete the content itself.

I discuss the shopping experience at the NOOK Store in more detail later in this chapter.

Opening and Reading an eBook

You want to start reading. Naturally enough, you begin by opening a book. And there are several ways to do just that:

✐ Go to the Home screen and tap any cover you find in the NOOK library. See Figure 9-3.

✐ Tap Current Reading to go to the place you were last perusing in a title in your NOOK library.

✐ Tap a NOOK shortcut that you created for any title in your library.

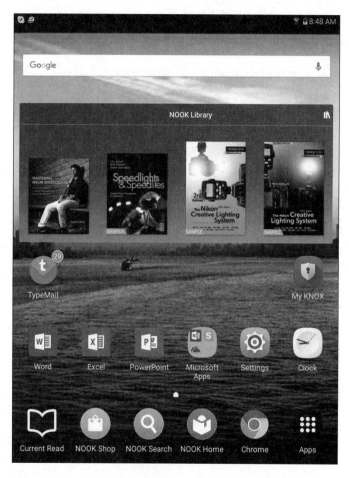

Figure 9-3: You can scroll through the current titles in your library from the shelf that is ordinarily placed on the Home screen. In this screen, I have one new book, plus samples of three others I had considered buying.

If you removed the NOOK app from the Home screen, tap the Apps icon in the lower right corner of the Home screen. Tap Apps and then tap NOOK Library. There you can tap any cover you find.

Turning the pages

Don't lick your finger and try to turn the page; that's unsanitary and will streak the glass. Instead, here's how to move within an eBook.

Going forward a page:

- ✔ **Tap anywhere along the right edge of the page.**
- ✔ **Swipe from the right side of the screen toward the left.** Think of this as flicking a page from the right side of an opened book to flip it over. Place your finger on the right side of the page and with a light amount of pressure keep it in contact as you flick it to the left.

Going back a page:

- ✔ **Tap anywhere along the left edge of the page.**
- ✔ **Swipe from the left side of the screen toward the right.**

But wait, it gets better. You can choose amongst three different animated page turn effects. One or another might be more pleasing to you, or perhaps you'd like to impress the youngsters with a bit of flash. Here's how:

1. **From any Home screen, tap the Apps icon.**
2. **Tap the NOOK Settings icon.**
3. **Tap Reader.**
4. **Tap Books.**
5. **Choose an option:**
   - *Slide.* One page slides smoothly to the other, as if there were no gravity or friction or peanut butter on the pages.
   - *Curl.* The page magically curls at one corner and rolls over to the next page. This is the one to use to impress non-believers. See Figure 9-4.
   - *None.* If you're a strictly business, no-nonsense type, choose this option and one page is almost instantly replaced by the next.

For magazines, follow Steps 1–3, and then choose Magazines & Newspapers. There you have two choices: Slide or Curl.

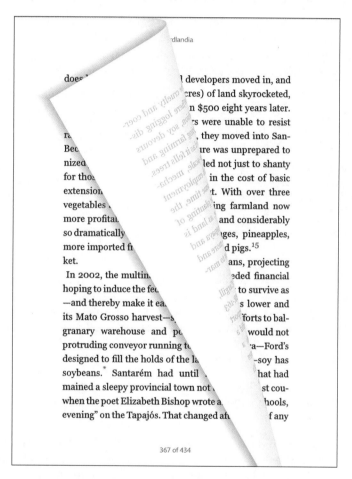

Figure 9-4: There's no way around it: the page curl effect is cool, the sort of thing to show your favorite anti-eReader Luddite.

Page turn effects are only available for books or magazines that are formatted using the EPUB specification, one of the most common means of encoding text for an eReader. If the publication uses a different formatting scheme, such as PDF, you'll just have to settle for one page flopping over onto the other, which is still pretty cool if you think about it.

Page what?

You may see a page number on the screen, which seems quite familiar and reassuring. The problem is that the page number probably won't correspond to the printed version of the book. For that matter, the page numbers are likely to vary between two Tab S2 NOOK tablets; page 47 on my screen might be page 52 on yours.

That's because you can change the size and style of type you see onscreen and also adjust margins and line spacing. That's all good, but it makes electronic book reading different from unchangeable printed versions, at least when it comes to pagination.

What if you want to compare notes about a particular passage with another person? If you're both using an eReader, you can identify a particular phrase or passage and use the Search function to find it within the book. Going between an electronic version and a printed version is a bit more complex: You have to rely on chapter numbers, which are the same in both versions.

Divining the table of contents

Maybe you don't know what page you want. Instead, you'd like to see the chapters in the table of contents. Or perhaps you'd like to search the book. Or you've decided that the typeface is too small or the page background is the wrong color. These are all fine thoughts, and with an electronic device like this one, your wishes are the NOOK's command.

To display the table of contents, open a book and then tap the center of the page. You'll see a panel with an option helpfully labelled Contents; tap it. See Figure 9-5.

The sections and chapters are here. You can scroll up or down through the listing, and best of all, the entries are active. The current chapter is highlighted by a gray bar. In most books you can jump immediately to a section by tapping the name. Scroll up or down through the contents and then tap a chapter or section to open it.

Remaking a book to your preference

And for customization of your book; there's no need for scissors, pots of glue, pencils, or erasers. You've got the tool you need at the tip of your finger.

Start with customizing the type size, font style, margins, and other page elements.

Setting your own type

To change the appearance of a page, do this:

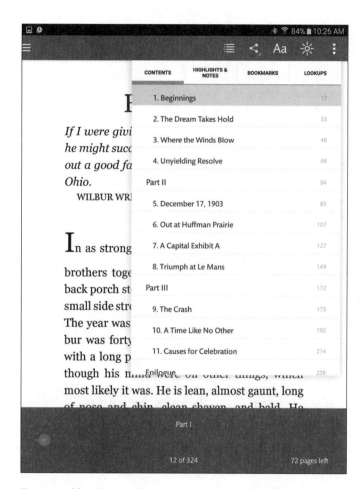

Figure 9-5: Most books offered through the NOOK Store include an interactive table of contents. You can tap any part, section, or chapter to move directly to it.

1. **Tap anywhere on the page of text.**

   The main reading tools open.

2. **Tap the Text Settings (Aa) icon.**

3. **Select type size, font, margins, line spacing, or the color theme for the page.**

For most books, you can choose from eight type sizes, six typefaces, three line spacings, three margin options, and six background colors. Feel free to experiment with the fonts to find one that's easiest to read. See Figure 9-6.

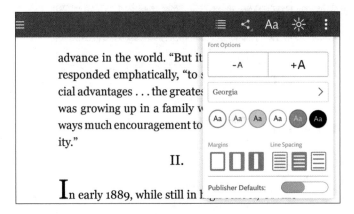

Figure 9-6: Increase or decrease the size of the text, choose a typeface, pick a color scheme for the type and background, and adjust margins and line spacing.

To be precise about it, in printing terms, *font* refers to a particular style of type at a specific size. For example, 12-point Times Roman would be a font that uses the common newspaper-style typeface Times Roman at a size where its largest letter (usually characters like M or W) is 12 points tall; in typography there are 72 points to the inch, and so this particular font would be about 1/6th of an inch high. But with digital readers, the term has been changed: In this example, Times Roman is the font and its size is 12 points.

When you're choosing a type size, start at the fifth or sixth largest for a good balance between readability and number of words that fit on the page. Feel free to experiment, though; tapping any of the As changes the size of the type that shows behind or above the menu.

Setting margins and line spacing

You can set the left and right margins that surround the text. Obviously, you want to pick the one that you find easiest on your eyes. Experiment here between narrow, medium, and wide margins for the text. The more white space there is around the text, the fewer words will fit on each line.

You can adjust the amount of line spacing in the text: single spacing, 1.5-line spacing, and double spacing. This is a relative measure; if you're using the largest type size, then the line spacing for the text will be large.

Choosing a color theme

With an advanced eReader like the Galaxy Tab S2 NOOK and its color LCD, you can choose the "paper" and the text color for most books. In some lighting situations it might be easier to have a black background with white type, or perhaps a soothing dark brown on tan background. See Figure 9-7.

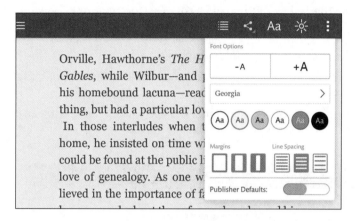

Figure 9-7: You can go with the standard or black type against a white background, or choose a more soothing combination like this one for some late-night reading.

I like to do my own book design. I generally prefer a serif font like Georgia, a medium size, and tight line spacing. And depending on how late in the day it is, I sometimes choose the Butter theme over Day.

Displaying the status bar in books

The standard setting is supposed to maximize the reading experience, and for that reason you don't see the black status bar that tells you things like the amount of remaining battery charge, whether the device is connected to a Wi-Fi system, the clock, and other notifications.

I am a natural multitasker; I become very anxious when there are fewer than four things going on at one time. I want to know the time and I want to see the subject lines of emails that come in while I'm reading a book, and more. If you want to see the status bar in eBooks, do this:

1. **From any Home screen, tap the Apps icon.**

2. **Tap the NOOK Settings icon.**

3. **Tap Reader.**

4. **Tap Always Show Status Bar to place a checkmark in the box beside that option.**

Finding a topic or passage in a book

Since every word in an electronic book exists in computer memory, it's a snap to quickly search for a particular name, phrase, or other element.

The tool is, appropriately, called Find in Book. Here's how to use it:

1. **Tap the center of the page to display the reading tools at the top.**

2. **Tap the Menu icon in the upper right. See Figure 9-8.**

   The onscreen keyboard will appear.

3. **Enter the word or phrase and then tap the Search (magnifying glass) icon.**

   The screen shows all instances of the word it finds. You can jump to any of them by tapping the listing. See Figure 9-9.

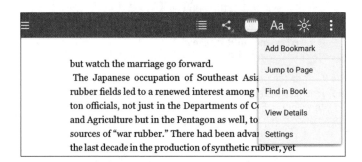

Figure 9-8: Tap Find in Book and enter a word, name, or phrase to see its presence in a publication.

If you know exactly what you want to find, enter the word, name, or phrase. Otherwise, for better results be a bit fuzzy. For example, if you want to find soy, soybean, or soybeans, then search for *soy*. A search for *soybeans* will exclude *soy* and *soybean*.

You'll see a list if the word or phrase appears in multiple places; you can jump to any particular one with the tap of your finger. The more specific you are in your search, the more likely you are to find something quickly. Searching for *eye of a needle* is going to be much more direct than searching for *eye*.

Figure 9-9: You can jump directly to any search word or phrase you see by tapping. Here you see some evidence of one of Henry Ford's other obsessions: soybeans.

To use the built-in dictionary to look up the meaning of a word, press and hold on the word. To get a more detailed definition, tap the A-Z icon when the definition pops up.

Many publishers deliver their books with a recommended design. You can make any available design changes, but if you want to quickly switch back to the way the publisher intended you to see the book, move the slider marked to Publisher Defaults On.

Placing and finding bookmarks

An electronic bookmark works just like a piece of cardboard between pages: It lets you quickly open to a particular page. You can set as many bookmarks as you like in each book.

To place a bookmark, tap the right corner of the screen. A ribbon-like icon appears, indicating you have put a bookmark there.

To see a list of bookmarks electronically inserted into a book, do this:

1. **Tap the center of the page.**

   Some options appear.

2. **Tap the Table of Contents icon.**

   I know; that doesn't seem quite right, but they didn't ask me when they designed this feature.

3. **Tap the Bookmarks option to see a list of bookmarked pages.**

4. **Tap any of the pages to quickly jump to it.**

Jumping to a page

With a printed book, you can flip through the pages, jumping from 38 to 383. With an electronic book, it's easy, but different.

- ✔ **Use the slider.** The slider, which you can see in Figure 9-10, comes up at the bottom of your eBook page if you tap. It's a blue horizontal line with a glowing dot somewhere along its path. The dot shows where you are in the book. Drag the slider right or left. If you're reading a book that someone has loaned you, a button at the right end of the slider lets you buy your own copy.

- ✔ **Enter a Jump To page number.** Follow these steps to quickly jump to a particular page in an eBook:

    1. **Tap anywhere on the text.**

       The page slider appears.

    2. **Tap the Menu icon in the upper right.**

    3. **Tap the Jump to Page option.**

       A numeric keypad appears.

    4. **Type a specific page number.**

Page numbering is relative to the typeface, type size, and other design settings you have made.

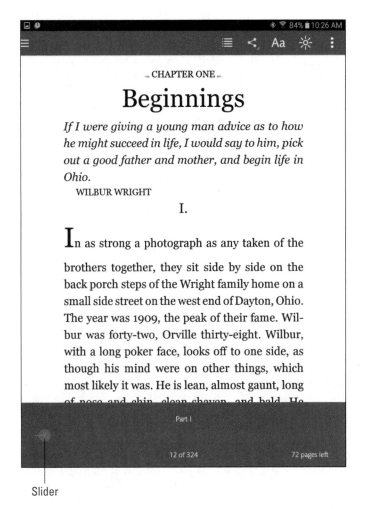

Slider

Figure 9-10: The slider appears at the bottom of a book if you tap any-where on the page.

Lending and Borrowing Books

With the Tab S2 NOOK, a lender and a borrower you can be. They're man-aged through the NOOK mother ship, at www.mynook.com.

Keep just a few catches in mind:

✔ Not every publisher will let you lend out a copy of the digital file. You can loan only books that have a LendMe badge.

✔ You can loan a book only once and only for 14 days. After then it comes back to your library.

✔ You can't read the book while it's on loan to someone else. (It's like a printed book in that way: It can't be in two places at once.)

You also can loan a book by lending the actual Tab S2 NOOK device to a trusted friend or acquaintance. If you do this, be aware that the person will have access to the Barnes & Noble store under your account name (but can't buy anything if your account requires a password to do so). And the person might make changes to other files on your tablet. And then you might have to chase after your soon-to-be former friend or acquaintance to get your NOOK back into your hands.

Here are a few more bits of legalese about electronic loans using the LendMe program:

✔ You can lend only to users who have other registered B&N devices, or apps that run on other devices such as desktop or laptop computers, smartphones, and certain other tablets.

✔ You can send LendMe offers to any email address, but to accept, the recipient must have an email address associated with a Barnes & Noble online account. That means that person is a resident of the United States or Canada.

✔ An offer expires after seven days if it hasn't been accepted.

✔ You can't loan a book that's been loaned to you.

✔ You can't save a borrowed book to a microSD card or archive it to the NOOK cloud.

Some book files are protected by a special form of encryption. The process is called *Digital Rights Management (DRM)*. If you bought a book through the NOOK Store that has DRM protection, your tablet takes care of all of the details of registration of the document at the time of purchase. (Your NOOK tablet is linked to your NOOK account.) If you get DRM-protected files from another source, you may need to provide an unlocking code or other form of identification as supplied by the seller.

Reading Newspapers and Magazines

Magazines come in all shapes, sizes, and special designs. Their electronic formats vary greatly; the way you see pages may be different from one magazine to another. Some are even interactive.

Some periodicals offer two ways to view content.

Page View

Page View is basically a snapshot of the printed page. This digital representation of the printed magazine has photographs, drawings, charts, and other elements. You'll see small images in the lower half of the screen. Page View is available in both portrait and landscape modes. See Figure 9-11.

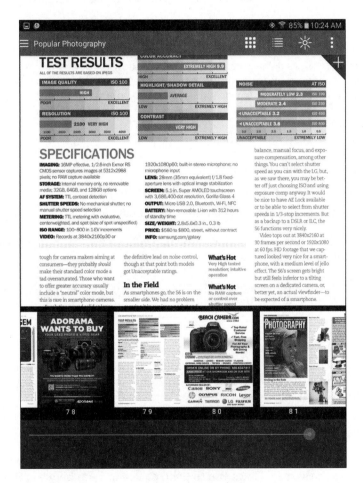

Figure 9-11: Many magazines have developed beautiful versions of their publications that include text, art, and advertisements. You're looking here at *Popular Photography.*

✐ To move through the magazine, swipe your finger along the thumbnail images.

✐ Tap a page to jump directly to it; a progress bar below the images shows where you are in the issue.

- ✔ To make the thumbnail images reappear, tap in the middle of the screen.
- ✔ As you read a page, tap the right side of the screen to move to the next page; tap the left side to go back a page.

You can move around on the page and enlarge sections if you need to, but this experience is more like looking at a photo than an interactive computer page.

ArticleView

ArticleView offers a reformatted version of a newspaper or magazine optimized for readers on the relatively small screen of a tablet. This format shows articles with few (or no) illustrations or photos. You can scroll through the text as you would in a book.

You can go directly from article to article:

1. **Tap the center of the screen.**
2. **Tap the Contents icon at the bottom of the page.**
3. **Tap the cover, table of contents, or specific article.**

You'll find the text of articles in scrollable columns; swipe right or left to move from one article to another.

In ArticleView, tap the center of the page to open the reading tools. There you can perform any of these actions:

- ✔ Tap Aa Text Settings to customize the type style, type size, and other design elements.
- ✔ Tap the grid icon to display a scrollable grid with thumbnail images of each page of the magazine or newspaper. You can jump to any page by tapping it.
- ✔ Tap Table of Contents to see a scrollable section and chapter index; tap any element to jump directly to it.

Some publications let you view content in either mode; a button at the bottom of the screen allows you to jump back and forth between Page View and ArticleView.

Other schemes

If the newspaper or magazine uses another scheme to present its information, use the left- and right swipe and pinch or zoom controls that are available to you in all publications.

Whether you've downloaded a single issue or you subscribe, newspapers are on your Daily Shelf and on the Newsstand page of your library.

✔ To open a newspaper, tap its front page. When it opens, the front page shows headlines and one or two paragraphs from the start of major articles.

✔ To read an article in more depth, tap its headline or the first paragraphs.

✔ To share parts of an article, tap in the middle of the page. From the reading tools, choose Share or Notes (if available).

✔ Bookmark a page by tapping in the upper-right corner of the page.

✔ To turn to the next page of a newspaper, do any of the following:

- Tap along the right edge of the screen.

- Swipe your finger from right to left across the screen.

- Swipe your finger from low to high on the screen.

✔ To go back a page in a newspaper, do one of these actions:

- Tap along the left edge of the screen.

- Swipe your finger from left to right across the screen.

- Swipe your finger from high to low on the screen.

Shopping an electronic catalog

When I was a youngster — a long, long time ago in a galaxy far away — there were basically only two ways to shop: going to a retail store on Main Street or buying from a catalog, which we used to call *mail order*. At one time, companies like Sears, Roebuck would produce huge catalogs of hundreds of items. It was a great entertainment to read the catalog from cover to cover, dreaming of tools and toys, shoes and sofas. You'd mail in your order with a check, and a week or two later a truck would appear with the goodies.

Almost all of the big catalogs have gone away now, replaced by the nearly infinite capacity of the Internet and its up-to-the-second inventory counts. But a few specialty catalogs have held on, and now with the NOOK they've become a hybrid life form that brings together old and new in exciting ways.

Within the NOOK Store, you can subscribe to a single issue of a catalog or agree to receive each issue as it comes; most are produced quarterly or monthly, and nearly all are free.

The catalogs are produced in great style, with colorful pictures and illustrations. Some of them also include interactive hotspots: Tap them to visit a web page that might include video or other interactive material. Now you not only can read all the details of the latest satellite-connected self-driving auto-sharpening lawnmower with built-in refrigerator and barbecue grill, but you can see it in use.

You flip through the pages of a catalog just as you do a magazine. I especially like using the page curl animation as I hunt for that perfect item I never knew I needed. See Figure 9-12.

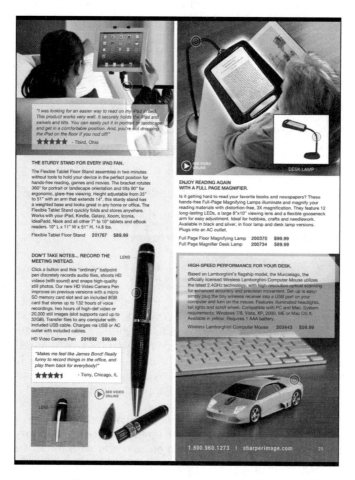

Figure 9-12: The Sharper Image presents a sharp image on the Tab S2 NOOK, with beautiful photos and videos to demonstrate all sort of products you never knew you needed.

Your tablet must have an active Wi-Fi connection to the web to view the hotspots. Some catalog companies may allow you to place an order directly from within the pages, again by venturing out on the web.

By default, all catalog hotspots are available to you. If you want to turn off the hotpots, you can do that:

1. **From any Home screen, tap the Apps icon and then tap the NOOK Settings icon.**

2. **Tap Reader.**

3. **Tap Enable HotSpots to turn them on or off.**

Getting Kids into the Act: Picture Books

The Tab S2 NOOK offers some special features for young readers (and those of you who sit by their side as they discover the joys of reading). Some picture books have a bit of animation that you set into motion by tapping the screen; others read aloud parts of the book. See Figure 9-13.

Figure 9-13: Certain picture books allow you to record your own voice, or that of your child, reading the text.

Kids' books are special

Keep these picture-book tips in mind:

- ✔ Enlarge a book by spreading with two fingers. This isn't available on all books.

- ✔ Tap the up arrow at the center bottom of the page to see *thumbnails* (small pictures) of each page in the book; scroll left or right through them and tap the page you want to visit. Or you can let a kid do it.

✔ Children's books open in landscape mode to better present the two-page spreads of most picture books.

✔ If the speaker is tough to hear, use two sets of earphones plugged into a splitter. Splitters are available at most electronics stores and shacks.

Choosing a reading style

Some children's books can narrate themselves. Others move. These special features appear only if the book includes them.

✔ **Read by Myself.** Just the words and pictures. Tap the blue button to open the book. Some special activities may be marked with a white star; tap the star to play. Better yet, let a kid tap the star.

✔ **Read to Me or Read and Play.** Read and Play books have audio tracks and interactive features marked with a white star. Tap the orange Read to Me button or the purple Read and Play buttons to hear the author or an actor read aloud.

If you're enjoying a Read and Play book, you can turn the pages only by tapping the onscreen arrows. The pages won't turn if you tap them.

✔ **Read and Record.** Daddy or Mommy (or a child!) can become the voice of a book. Here's how:

1. **Tap the cover of a kid's book that has the Read and Record feature.**

2. **On the opening screen, tap the green Read and Record button.**

3. **Tap the green Record button.**

   It changes to a Stop button. But don't stop.

4. **Start reading.**

5. **When you're done recording, tap the Stop button.**

Keep these general read-and-record tips in mind:

✔ The tiny hole on the right side of the Tab S2 NOOK, just below the Volume key, is the microphone. Don't cover it with your hand while you're recording.

✔ Hold the tablet about 15 inches away from your mouth.

✔ Try to record in a quiet place without background noise.

✔ To hear your recording right away, press the Play button. Press the Pause button when you're done listening.

✔ If you're a perfectionist (or if someone dropped a pile of plates while the microphone was on), press the Re-record button and do it again.

✔ To keep recording, swipe or tap to the next page and then tap the Record button.

✔ To stop recording, tap the Done button in the lower left. A screen asks you to choose a picture as a symbol. Type a name for the recording.

✔ To play a recording, open the book and tap the picture icon for the file you created.

✔ To re-record, change the name (or delete the audio file, tap the Edit button next to the picture icon, and then choose the option you want).

Geeking Out about NOOK Comic Books

Pow! Oomph! Wow! The Tab S2 NOOK can display specially formatted NOOK comics in portrait or landscape mode. Moving within a NOOK comic book is very similar to the steps involved in NOOK Kids titles:

✔ Tap the cover of a comic book to open it.

✔ Swipe left or right to go forward or back, or tap the right or left side of the page for the same effect.

✔ Tap in the center of the screen to bring up the reader tools, including small versions of the entire document. Tap any image to go directly to a particular page.

✔ To zoom in on text and images, double-tap or spread. Double-tap again to return the page to normal. See Figure 9-14.

✔ Bookmark a page by tapping the + icon in the upper right. After you place a marker, tap the center of the page to see reader tools, tap the Contents icon, and then tap the Bookmarks tab.

✔ Jump directly to any bookmarked page by tapping the bookmark.

Because comic books sometimes use unusual graphic designs or vary from one edition to another, the Tab S2 NOOK includes support for a special comic book reading mode: Zoom View Letterboxing. That's a pretty fancy term for a relatively simple thing: the ability to move the view from frame to frame even if they are of different sizes.

To turn on Zoom View Letterboxing, do this:

1. **From any Home screen, tape the Apps icon and then tap the NOOK Settings icon.**

2. **Tap Reader.**

3. **Tap Zoom View Letterboxing to enable or disable the feature.**

Figure 9-14: Comic books never looked this good when I was collecting my nickels and dimes to buy them each week.

Shopping at the NOOK Store

As much as I love to browse the aisles (physical or electronic) of a good bookstore, sometimes I know exactly what I want.

To search for a particular book or periodical, tap the Search (magnifying glass) icon at the top of the NOOK Store screen. Use the keyboard to type your entry.

Or press and hold the icon to the left of the spacebar of the onscreen keyboard and tap a method:

✔ Use voice recognition to say what you're looking for.

✔ Handwrite your entry on the touchpad.

My search results are in Figure 9-15. Scroll through the results by dragging your finger up or down. A blue banner shows the prices on the B&N site. If you see a gray Purchased label, you've already bought that title for the current account; once you pay, you can always download it again without paying again.

Buying a book

Sooner or later you're going to find a book you want to add to your library. On behalf of authors and publishers everywhere, we thank you for your investment in fine literature of all kind. Here's what's next:

1. **Tap the cover to see its details.**

   Sometimes you're offered a sample from the book. To drop a not-very-subtle hint to someone about the perfect birthday gift for you, tap the Share icon to send an email detailing what you've found. You can also rate and review your thoughts about the title, posting to Facebook or Twitter. See Figure 9-15.

2. **To buy an eBook, tap the blue box that shows the price.**

   Are you sure? You're asked to confirm your purchase.

3. **Confirm your purchase.**

   Some books are offered for the can't-beat-it price of free. Publishers do this to try and build an audience for a series of books. If you ask for a copy of a free book, you're still asked to confirm your decision.

   Any eBook that has a price tag is charged to your credit card and the title comes to your Tab S2 NOOK, usually within a few seconds. If an eBook's download is interrupted because of a problem with the wireless connection or other causes, the download automatically resumes the next time it gets a chance.

   The new item appears on the Active shelf on the Home screen and in your library. It wears a New badge until you open it.

Buying magazines or newspapers

You can buy individual issues of a newspaper or magazine, or subscribe to daily, weekly, or monthly delivery. Just as in the world of paper and ink, the best deals come with longer-term subscriptions. Once you buy, the first issue downloads immediately.

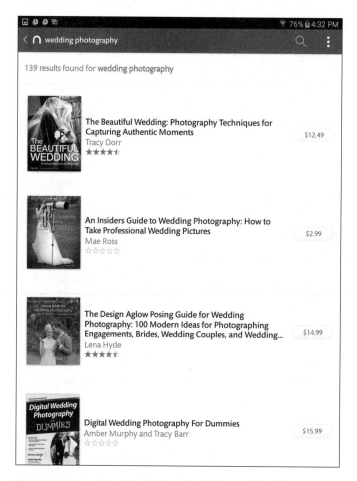

Figure 9-15: Search for eBooks by author, title, or subject. Tap one to learn more about it or to buy.

Nearly every magazine and newspaper offers free 14-day trials; you can get one free trial for each publication. If you cancel the subscription before the end of the trial, your credit card isn't charged. Otherwise, deliveries continue and your credit card is charged automatically at the monthly subscription rate. To cancel a periodical subscription, go to your account at www.nook. com, log in, and go to the Manage Subscriptions section.

To buy a single issue or to subscribe, follow these steps:

1. Tap the cover.

You'll see the price for the current issue, and elsewhere on the page you can see the price for a monthly subscription. See Figure 9-16.

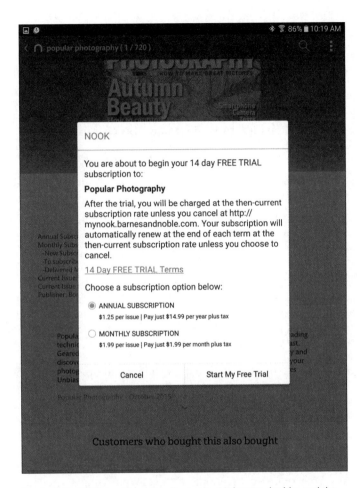

Figure 9-16: Getting a free trial allows you 14 days to decide, and the rate is usually better than buying individual issues.

2. **To buy the latest issue only, tap Buy Current Issue. To buy a subscription, tap Start My Free Trial.**

    If you subscribe, you get the first issue and have 14 days to decide whether to continue. If you cancel within those 14 days, you'll have received that first issue for free. If you *don't* cancel, you're on the hook for at least one subscription cycle (usually one month) at the subscription price — but you can cancel any time after then.

It's almost a no-brainer: Take the free trial for any magazine or newspaper you want to try. The month-to-month subscription usually represents a significant savings over buying a single issue, and you can cancel any time. Note that you can only take a free trial once for any particular publication.

3. **Tap Confirm.**

   The issue downloads.

4. **Tap the Read button.**

If you already subscribe to the print version of a newspaper or magazine, the publisher may offer a discount on digital versions. You can call or check the web page for the publication, or follow these steps:

1. **Visit the NOOK Store and go to My Account.**

2. **Go to Manage Digital Subscriptions and look for the link to verify a print subscription.**

3. **Enter your print subscription account number (usually on your magazine's mailing label).**

Subscribing to catalogs

Catalogs are free; the companies that provide them very much want you salivating over their shoes, dresses, fruitcakes, and gadgets. Some of the first offerings were from major sellers like L.L. Bean, Sharper Image, Omaha Steaks, Pottery Barn, and Ross-Simons.

When you tap the cover of a catalog, you wind up on a purchase screen very much like one for a magazine. You'll see two choices, and both are free:

- **Current Edition:** Just this once.
- **Free Subscription:** You're going to get each new edition of the catalog.

NOOK offers more than three million books, magazines, newspapers, and other types of media in its online store. What you *cannot* purchase from the NOOK Store are printed books, scented candles, lava lamps, and other physical items. To purchase them, use the NOOK's web browser to visit the www. bn.com page and place your order there.

Buying or Renting a Video

Your NOOK can also work as a handheld movie or television player, and can output most of that material to a larger television screen.

NOOK Video offers two ways to obtain video material: streaming or download.

About streaming

Think of streaming as the way you ordinarily watch television on a standard TV set; the program begins and you watch it as it arrives on the screen and then it's gone. It doesn't require any storage space on your device. You must, though, have an active Wi-Fi connection while you watch a streaming presentation. And you're likely to be rather unhappy with the experience if your Wi-Fi connection isn't fast and strong.

About downloaded video content

Think of downloaded video as if you were playing a DVD or a videotape (remember those?) of content. You'll need an active Wi-Fi connection to the NOOK Store to receive the full contents of a movie or TV show, which will be stored in the memory of your tablet. Once it's been received, you can watch the video content any time without the need for a Wi-Fi connection.

Downloading a full movie can take some time, depending on the speed and strength of your Wi-Fi signal.

There's one other distinction to be made: renting and owning. If you rent video content, it's downloaded to your NOOK and available to watch anytime within the allowed rental period. When that rental period has elapsed, your rental is over and you can't view it again without re-renting it. See Figure 9-17.

If you purchase a video, you own it and can watch it anytime you want and as many times as you want.

Downloaded videos can take up a great deal of space within your tablet. This is one reason I recommend buying and installing an additional microSDHC card for your tablet and then instruct your system to store video content on the card rather than in your device's internal memory.

Here's how to instruct the NOOK to store videos on the card:

1. **From any Home screen, tap the Apps icon and then tap the NOOK Settings icon.**
2. **Tap Video.**
3. **Tap Video Download Location and select the external SD card.**

Managing video on multiple devices

If you purchase video content from the NOOK Store, you are allowed to view that content on as many as five different devices. What does that mean? If you happen to own two NOOKs, you can watch the same video on either one. If you have a streaming video device attached to a large-screen television, or a laptop computer with a NOOK app installed, they too can stream the video you have purchased.

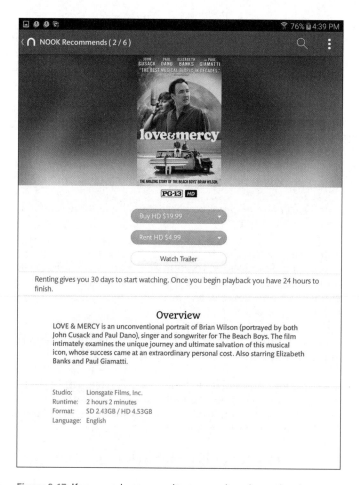

Figure 9-17: If you purchase a movie you own it and can view it as often as you want; some videos are rentals for a limited time period.

The one additional necessary step is to tell the BN mother ship which devices are authorized to access your NOOK Video collection. Here's how:

1. **From any Home screen, tap the Apps icon and then tap the NOOK Settings icon.**

2. **Tap Video and then tap Manage NOOK Video.**

   You'll see a screen that lists the NOOK devices currently associated with your account and authorized to access content.

   To remove a device from the list of authorized devices, tap its name and then confirm that you want to delete it.

TIP

The NOOK boob tube

The NOOK Store offers lots of movies, TV shows, and specialty videos. You'll find free previews of some movies and free episodes from TV series. On the Galaxy Tab S2 you can download and view both *SD* (standard definition) and *HD* (high definition) video. You aren't going to see much (or any) difference between SD and HD versions when you view a video on your tablet, but if you output the video signal from the Galaxy Tab S2 NOOK to a large-screen TV, HD will rock your socks.

You can buy videos of movies or TV shows (individual episodes in some instances or entire seasons or collections), in which case you own them and can watch them over and over again; if you have children, you'll understand that concept right away.

Some videos are available as rentals, generally for about one-third to one-half the price of buying. When you rent a video, you have 30 days after download to start watching; once you start playing a movie or show, you have 24 hours to finish. And you can watch the same show over and over and over again, but only within that 24-hour window.

The Tab S2 NOOK supports UltraViolet, which lets you stream or download a video to multiple compatible devices in a variety of formats including Blu-ray, DVD, and digital video. For releases in that format, sign up for yet another account, this one with UltraViolet. Visit www.myuv.com to link your NOOK account the UltraViolet service.

Selectable subtitles aren't supported with videos on the NOOK, at least in the first released version. *Selectable subtitles* can be added to the video at your option; if a foreign language movie is sold with subtitles embedded into the image (and not selectable from a menu) you'll be able to see them.

Closed captioning is available on some but not all video titles.

To give permission to a new device, you must sign in on that device using the same account name and password you used to purchase the video content. Add a checkmark next to the name of a device to authorize it for video viewing.

REMEMBER

Paying the bill

Unless you say otherwise, your credit card is charged when you buy something from Barnes & Noble. It's all done for you; there are no receipts to sign.

If you have a Barnes & Noble gift card, you can add its value to your account:

1. **Tap the Menu icon in the upper-right corner.**

2. **Tap Shop Settings.**

3. **Tap Credit Cards or Gift Cards and enter information there as requested.**

The NOOK Store accepts Visa, MasterCard, Amex, Discover, Diners Club, JCB, or gift cards and access codes. If you have any problems with a gift card or credit card, call customer service at the NOOK Shop or use its chat line.

You must enter your billing address, and current BN rules limit purchases to those who reside in the United States or Canada.

Adding a gift card requires entry of the card or certificate number, plus the four-digit PIN for the card.

4. **Tap Submit to complete the addition of the card to your account.**

Redeem codes and discounts

You may also receive occasional special offers from Barnes & Noble or partners that contain a special access code. To add this to your account, do this:

1. **From any Home screen, tap NOOK Shop.**

2. **Tap the Menu bar in the upper-right corner.**

3. **Tap Shop Settings.**

4. **Tap Redeem Access Code. Then enter the 13-digit number you received.**

5. **Tap Add Now.**

Archiving to the NOOK cloud

Have you ever been accused of walking around with your head in a cloud? So have I. And so, too, does your Tab S2 NOOK. Every registered user is automatically set up with unlimited storage back at the Barnes & Noble mother ship (also known as *the cloud*).

All items you get from the NOOK Store are automatically maintained in an archive at Barnes & Noble as well as on your device. You can also *remove* an item from your NOOK, which takes away its file from your tablet but keeps the link between your device and the NOOK cloud so that you can someday bring it back to the tablet.

A file that you remove from your NOOK leaves behind only an icon or picture of its cover to remind you; any time you want to get that reading material, you can *restore* it from the NOOK cloud. You must have an active Wi-Fi connection to the Internet to retrieve the file. See Figure 9-18.

Why would you remove something from your NOOK to the archive or cloud?

- ✔ You want to clear some space in the built-in memory or microSD card.

- ✔ Your Tab S2 NOOK or other NOOK device is stolen or permanently deceased; sign in to the same account to restore all the files to a new device or app.

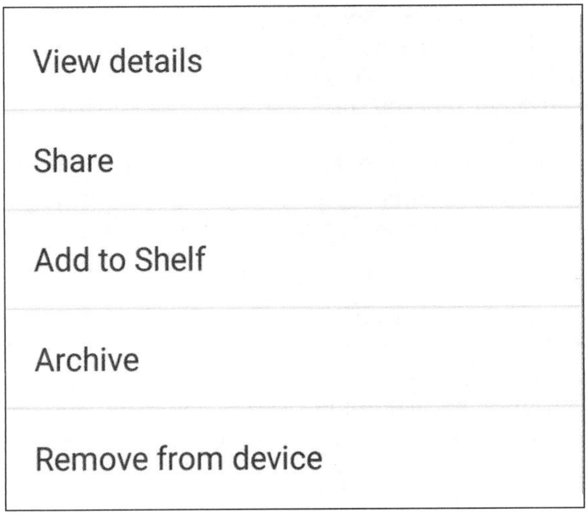

View details
Share
Add to Shelf
Archive
Remove from device

Figure 9-18: You can fill the NOOK archive with as much B&N electronic material as you want; grab it with a tap.

You can archive any of these from the NOOK cloud: books, magazines, newspapers, or catalogs. You can also reinstall apps or videos you have purchased.

The NOOK cloud is only for material that you get from the NOOK Store. You can't place personal files or media from other sources. However, you *can* connect your NOOK to a computer and make a backup folder of your personal material on that device.

Here's how to archive NOOK Store files:

1. **Go to the NOOK library.**

2. **Press and hold on the book cover.**

3. **Tap Archive.**

   The book or other publication goes away, but if you tap the Menu icon in the upper-right corner of the library, you see View Archive. From there, you can restore items. (You must have an active Wi-Fi signal to archive or restore, of course.)

There's another way, with a bit of confusing terminology:

1. **Go to the NOOK library.**

2. **Press and hold on the cover of the book.**

3. **Tap Remove from Device.**

Yes, I know this sounds like the book will be deleted and gone forever, but that's not the case. It's removed from the hardware and kept in your archive even though it doesn't say that exactly. You can get it back by going to the archive; just tap the Menu icon in your NOOK library.

There's a big difference between *archiving* and *deleting.* If you *archive* an item, you can get it back from the NOOK cloud. If you *delete* any item, you erase it from your NOOK and can't get it without going back to the original source.

After you buy a book from Barnes & Noble, you own the license to that title on up to six devices or apps registered to your account. You can leave the book file on your Tab S2 NOOK or you can archive it back to your account, which removes it from the tablet but keeps it in your available material in the NOOK cloud. The key: All devices or applications must be registered to the same account.

Performing a sync or refresh

You can also *sync* your Tab S2 NOOK to your NOOK account; doing so keeps it updated with all your currently purchased content. Syncing also lets you know about tablet updates, book loan offers, and other notices.

Items you've archived aren't synced.

Follow these steps:

1. **Go to the NOOK library.**
2. **Tap the Menu icon in the upper-right corner.**
3. **Tap Refresh.**

B&N goodies

What happens if you take your NOOK to an actual Barnes & Noble store, where there are walls and floors and ceilings? The device asks if you'd like to connect to the in-store network. (Tap Connect to agree; tap Dismiss to disagree.) If you connect, you can get:

- A free pass to read or sample certain NOOK eBooks for one hour per day. You can read as many books as you want while you're in the store, although the 60-minute limit applies for each title.

- Exclusive content and offers available only to NOOK owners using the in-store network.

Managing NOOK Profiles

As the owner of a Samsung Galaxy Tab S2 NOOK, you're the master of your digital domain. However, there are times when you may want to (or be persuaded to) share your amazing little tablet with others: spouse, friends, or even children.

So comes the question: Do you want to share any or all of the following with others:

- ✔ The content of your library of items purchased from the NOOK Store.

- ✔ Any personal material you've downloaded, uploaded, or created on the NOOK tablet.

- ✔ The right to go to the NOOK Store and buy any kind of material, without regard to appropriateness, price, or value, using your preloaded credit card.

I'll give you my answer: no way. I want more control over what my adult friends and family can do with my account, and I insist on absolute control over what children are able to view and purchase. (It's hard enough to raise a child in today's almost-anything-goes society; take any opportunity you can to set some boundaries. And good luck.)

You NOOK can support as many as six profiles, allowing different people differing types of access. Those six profiles can be any combination of three types:

- ✔ **Primary Profile.** This profile is created when first you register your NOOK. The owner of that profile, protected by a password, can make any sort of digital purchase and view any sort of content on the tablet. All purchases made on the NOOK are processed using the credit card information on file.

   The keeper of the primary profile can create and edit profiles for other users and manage their access to content.

- ✔ **Adult Profile.** You can create a profile for an authorized adult, allowing that person to purchase any type of content and to decide which of those items are visible only in this profile and which can also be viewed by a child. This secondary adult profile, though, can't control which content is visible to the primary profile holder.

- ✔ **Child Profile.** The standard settings for a child profile allow the child to only view or buy content authorized by the primary profile. The owner of a child profile can't create or edit other profiles, and can't override any parental controls.

Setting up an adult profile

To set up an adult profile, follow these steps:

1. **Sign in as the holder of the primary profile.**

2. **From any Home screen, tap the Apps icon, and then the NOOK Settings gear.**

3. **Tap Profile. See Figure 9-19.**

4. **Tap the+symbol at the upper-right corner.**

5. **Type a name for the new profile.**

6. **Follow the onscreen prompts to decide whether you want existing NOOK Store content available to the holder of the new profile.**

7. **Tap Next to complete.**

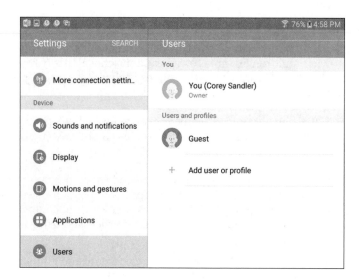

Figure 9-19: Profiles can be used to manage access to content by youngsters or by adult users other than the owner of the device.

Creating a child profile

To set up a child profile, follow these steps:

Sign in as the holder of the Primary Profile. Then do this:

1. **From any Home screen, tap the Apps icon, and then tap the NOOK Settings icon.**

2. **Tap Profile.**

3. **Tap the + symbol at the upper right.**

4. **Type in a name for the new profile.**

5. **Tap the checkbox next to Child Profile, enter the child's age, and accept the terms and conditions.**

6. **Tap Next.**

7. **Follow the onscreen prompts to select the permissions you want to give the child.**

8. **Tap Next to complete.**

Using parental controls, you can control whether a specific child (or group of children to whom you give the particular profile) can do any or all of the following:

✓ Browse the NOOK Store.

✓ Purchase from the NOOK Store only when they're given and properly use your NOOK account password.

✓ Shop only for kids' content.

✓ Access Reads for Kids, Videos for Kids, Apps for Kids, or Games for Kids.

You can also select which TV and movie ratings are offered to the child: G, PG, PG-13, TV Y, TV Y7, TV G, or TV 14.

Managing content for a profile

You can share all or some or none of the content in your library with each profile. Depending on the item, the user of the other profile may have immediate access to a book or other publication or may need to download it; if granted permission, the profile user merely taps the cover of a book that has a download icon and waits for it to arrive from the NOOK cloud.

An active Wi-Fi system with Internet access is required for any download.

Annotations to a publication, such as notes and highlights, are specific to the profile that added them. As the primary profile, if you make notes, they aren't visible to other profiles. Similarly, if someone using a different profile makes notes or highlights, they're not visible to other profiles.

And it gets even niftier: If two or more profiles have access to the same book, their reading positions in the book are tracked independently of each other. So you can stop reading on page 38 and return to that spot, while another profile holder can be at page 237.

Assigning content to other profiles

The manager of the primary profile can assign content to the various adult or child profiles. And the holder of an adult profile can limits material for child profiles (but not the primary profile).

To manage access to a particular book, magazine, or other item, do this:

1. **From the NOOK library, tap and hold on the cover of an item.**

2. **Tap Assign to Profiles.**

3. **Tap a checkbox next to a choice to allow profile holders access to them.**

4. **Tap Save.**

Switching between profiles

When you have at least two profiles set up on your NOOK, the primary profile can switch between the identities you have created on the device. Here's how:

1. **From within the NOOK Store, NOOK Library, or NOOK Home, tap the NOOK Navigation Menu (three horizontal stacked bars).**

2. **Tap the name of the current profile,**

   A list of additional profiles created for the device appears.

3. **Tap the profile name to which you want to switch.**

Deleting a profile

As the holder of the primary profile, you can delete an adult or child profile.

Deleting one of the secondary profiles does *not* delete the primary account from the device.

Here's how to remove an adult or child profile:

1. **From any Home screen, tap the Apps icon, and then tap the NOOK Settings icon.**

2. **Tap Profile.**

3. **Tap beside the profile you want to delete and then tap the Trash icon beside the name.**

4. **Tap Delete to confirm your instruction.**

Being Your Own Librarian

The library is where all documents live on your NOOK, including books, periodicals, and personal files. The *library* holds everything, but the individual *shelves* for books, magazines, catalogs, and newspapers hold only files that the system recognizes as fitting that description.

Reading covers

To some extent, you actually can tell a book by its cover on the NOOK: not so much about what's inside, but a great deal about its status or stature in your collection.

- **New.** Freshly downloaded and ready to be opened. This badge goes away after the first time you open the document.
- **Sample.** A free sample of a book or other publication.
- **Download.** A publication that's either downloading or is waiting to be downloaded from the NOOK Shop.
- **Pre-order.** A title has been announced and is for sale, but isn't available for download yet. If you buy it, the book or publication will arrive at the first opportune moment and your credit card will then be billed.
- **Recommended.** A friend or contact has suggested that you check out this title.
- **LendMe.** A book that you can loan to someone.
- **Lent.** A book you're borrowing; the badge also indicates the number of days remaining on the loan. (While a book's loaned out, the original owner can't open it.)

Building your own shelves

When your NOOK arrives, it has basic shelves of this sort: Books, Magazines, Movies & TV, Kids, Catalogs, and Newspapers. Below that, My Shelves is where you can create and fill your own collection in any way you choose. And finally, a section called My Files holds any personal files you have moved over to the Tab S2 NOOK.

Creating a shelf

You can create any shelf you want and call it anything you like. To create a shelf, do this:

1. **From any Home screen, tap the Apps icon and then tap the NOOK Library icon.**

2. **Tap More Options, then tap New Shelf.**

3. **Use the keyboard to enter a name for the shelf.**

4. **Tap Save.**

Adding items to a shelf

Now you need to move things to your shelf:

1. **Press and hold on a book or a file in the list of items in your library.**

   A menu appears.

2. **Tap the checkbox next to an item to add it to the shelf.**

3. **Tap Save.**

To add or remove content in a shelf you have previously created, do this:

1. **From any Home screen, tap the Apps icon and then tap the NOOK Library icon.**

2. **Swipe down and tap My Shelves.**

3. **Tap a particular shelf to open it.**

4. **Tap More Options.**

5. **Tap Manage Content in Shelf.**

6. **Tap to add or remove a checkmark next to an item.**

   If it has a checkmark, it'll appear on the shelf.

7. **Tap Save.**

You can

- ✓ **Rename a shelf** from the More Options section by tapping Rename Shelf and then typing a new name. Finish the process by tapping Rename.

- ✓ **Remove a shelf** by going to More Options, tapping Remove Shelf, and then confirming your intention by tapping Remove.

When you remove a shelf or remove an item from a shelf, you are *not* deleting that content from your NOOK device. The book, movie, TV show, comic, or other media remains available in the library.

Using reading tools

You have a whole other pathway to the bells and whistles. From the Reading Tools menu, you can move quickly through a book, search for something specific, share your knowledge, or change the way the page looks. I call these the *secondary reading tools,* but they're part of the same toolkit.

To see the secondary reading tools, press and hold on a word or anywhere on the page. It might take a few tries to get the hang of it: Tapping brings up the full set of tools, including the slider bar. A more determined press-and-hold brings up the secondary reading tools shown in Figure 9-20.

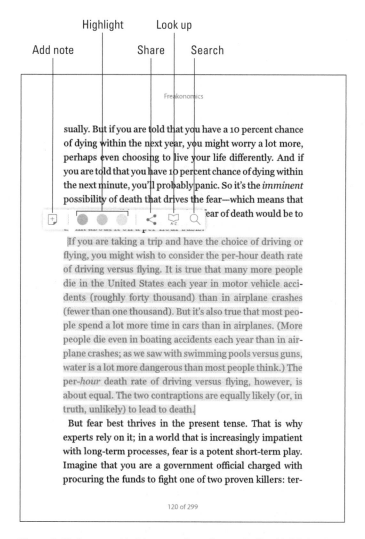

Figure 9-20: Press and hold to reveal reading tools. I've highlighted a quote from the marvelously disruptive book *Freakonomics*. It's enough to make me, a compulsive traveler, want to stay at home.

The tool highlights a word if that's what you've touched; it highlights a nearby word if you've pressed on a blank spot. Above the highlight, you see the buttons described in the following sections:

- Highlight (in blue, green, or yellow)
- Add Note
- Share
- Look Up
- Find in Book

Highlight

To select a word, press and hold on a word; then lift your finger. The word is highlighted in blue, and you'll see a darker blue vertical bar on either side of it (unless you've chosen a different color theme for the page).

To expand the highlight, tap and then drag one of the vertical bars; this tool is called the Text Selection tool. When you lift your finger or fingers (you can use your thumb and pointing finger to cover more area), the Text Selection toolbar appears.

Samsung offers free apps to work with a number of printers that can accept material beamed to them by Wi-Fi Direct. But all users can use this trick to print a passage from your Tab S2 NOOK: Select a passage and send it to yourself by email. Then use a computer and printer to make a hard copy.

Be sure you understand the proper use of citations if you're using part of a copyrighted book in an academic paper or a publication of your own.

Add Note

You can insert a comment (up to 512 characters) about the highlighted word or phrase; the date and time are included. A small icon that looks like a sticky note with a+mark will appear onscreen.

- You can search for what's in your note.
- You can view and change notes any time.
- You can make notes invisible. Why? Perhaps you want to share a selection or loan a book but keep your comments private.

To perform other actions on a note you've already made, use the primary reading tools. Here's how:

1. **Tap anywhere on the page.**

    The slider bar and system bar appear at the bottom of the page.

2. Tap the Contents icon.

The icon looks like a stack of four dotted bars. It's pointed out in Figure 9-21.

3. Tap the Highlights and Notes tab if it isn't already selected.

4. Tap one of the notes.

You're taken to the page where it's attached.

5. Tap the highlighted word on the page.

A menu appears like the one in Figure 9-21.

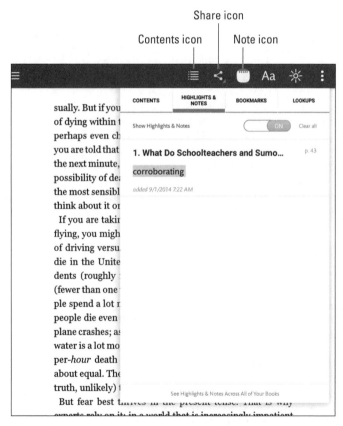

Share icon

Contents icon   Note icon

Figure 9-21: From the table of contents in a book you can add high-lights and notes and bookmarks, and also see the record of any Lookups on the Internet you have made based on the book you are reading.

6. **Tap an option:**

- **View Note.** Tap to read the comments you placed there.

- **Edit Note.** Tap to see the comments onscreen. Use the keyboard to make changes. When you're done, tap Save.

- **Remove Note.** Tap to delete the note; there's no second chance, so be sure this is what you want to do.

- **Remove Highlight.** Tap to take away the color highlighting. The color shading disappears immediately, but you can always press the word and reinstall a bit of a hue.

- **Change Color.** Tap one of three colors (aqua, lime green, or sunset yellow) to make a change.

Share

You can share a word or pick up a short passage and send it by email (or Twitter or in a Facebook post). The NOOK is ready, willing, and able to assist.

When you tap Share, you can connect to any of the communication services to which you subscribe or are installed on your device. These include Wi-Fi Direct, Quick Connect, and Bluetooth, as well as services like Email, OneDrive, Drive, Gmail, Hangouts, and Memo. If you've added apps like TypeMail or Skype or enabled Microsoft's OneNote, they appear in the list as well.

In my usage, I like to copy quotes to the Clipboard, a standard option of Share. Once the material is in Clipboard, I can paste it into an email, a Word or Memo document, or just about any other app.

Dog-earing a page

Back in ancient times, I used to tear up any old piece of paper I could find and insert it into the pages of a book I was reading. (I never could bring myself to crease the corners of a book or write in its pages. A book in my library, though read half a dozen times, still looks as pristine as the day it was bought.)

Here's how modern folk bookmark an electronic publication:

- ✔ **Bookmark the page you're reading.** Tap in the upper-right corner of the page. A small blue ribbon appears in the corner of the page. To make the bookmark go away, tap the blue ribbon in the upper-right corner of the page.

- ✔ **See all the bookmarks in a book.** Follow these steps to see everything you've bookmarked:

    1. **Tap the center of the page to open the reading tools.**

    2. **Tap the Contents icon (pointed out in Figure 9-21).**

TIP

3. **Tap the Bookmarks tab (in the Contents pane). See Figure 9-22.**

• To jump to a bookmarked page, tap a bookmark in the list.

• Tap anywhere on the page *outside* the list of bookmarks to close the list.

✔ **Clear all bookmarks in a book.** Follow along to get rid of all the bookmarks in a single book:

1. **Tap the Contents icon (pointed out in Figure 9-21).**

2. **Tap the Bookmarks tab.**

3. **Tap Clear All.**

4. **Tap OK.**

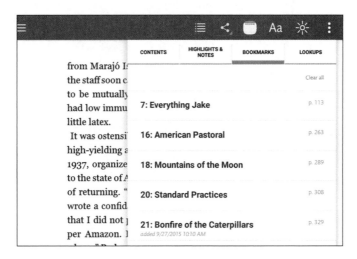

Figure 9-22: Once you bookmark a page, you can return to it quickly by displaying the list of bookmarks shown on the tab above the table of contents.

Finding Other eBook Sources

*Y*ou can buy the Galaxy Tab S2 from sources other than Barnes & Noble, and you can apply the NOOK app to tablets from a wide range of manufacturers.

We are gathered here in these digital pages to explore the particular combination of the two companies. But because this tablet also exists outside of the world of NOOK, it's important to know that you have many other sources of reading material to install upon it.

In this chapter, you look at a few major alternate sources: Google Books, Overdrive, SCRIBD, the Gutenberg Project, and even Amazon Kindle.

Snooping around Google Books

On the Samsung Galaxy Tab S2 NOOK, Google's shop is called the Play Store. On some Google-branded devices it's known as Google Play; it also had a former name, the Android Market. They're all the same: the official store for products to be used, read, watched, or listened to on a device running the Android operating system. See Figure 10-1.

The Play Store isn't playing around. It offers these categories: Books, Games, Movies & TV, Music, and Newsstand. By the time you read these words, the Play Store is likely to be approaching 1.5 million available apps, and 5 million books and other media. They claim, although I haven't counted lately, to be the largest bookstore on the planet.

You can reach the Play Store by tapping the Apps icon from any Home screen. To go directly to the bookstore that is part of Play, load Chrome or another Internet browser and go to www.books.google.com. See Figure 10-2.

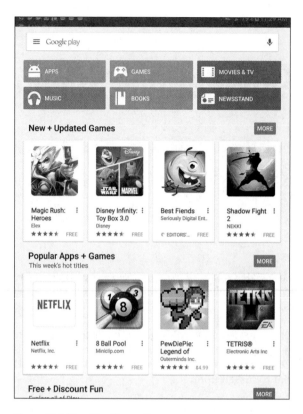

Figure 10-1: The Play Store offers apps, games, movies, TV shows, music, books, and magazines.

When you set up your Tab S2 NOOK, you got the opportunity to link the tablet to an existing Google account or to create a new one. (Using an existing account lets you sync and share apps and some other materials.)

Throughout the store you'll find items for sale as well as free products. Why free? Some developers hope to make money by delivering space on your tablet to advertisers; others hope to entice you to pay to upgrade: Get more features! Buy other products! For example, in the Play Music store, you'll find individual tracks for sale as well as discounted or free tracks or entire albums.

Similarly, you'll find books under all sorts of pricing schemes in the Play Books store. The prices for books in the Play Books store are often the same as those in the NOOK Shop or the Amazon Kindle Store, but not always. If you're concerned about saving a dollar here and there (and why not), you can compare prices from the comfort of your sofa.

Figure 10-2: The collection of free and for-purchase books curated by Google can also be reached through an Internet browser at www.books.google.com.

Some publishers allow you to read free samples, while others give away entire books in hopes of hooking you on a series. The hook-'em-with-a-free-book scheme is especially popular with romance novels, which, when successful, tends to attract loyal and voracious readers.

Play Books has an extensive collection of classic books, many of them for free or at very inexpensive prices. (The authors, most of them dead, receive no royalties.) See Figure 10-3.

Google is a huge company now, and it — along with Amazon — has among the most experienced and creative marketers in the digital industry. The pages of the Play Store are very nicely designed and the buying process well thought out.

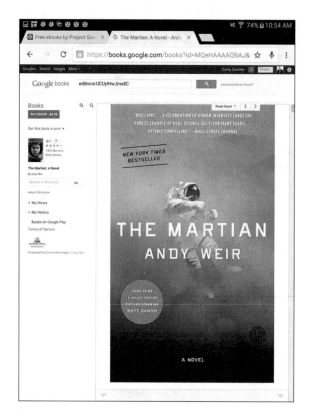

Figure 10-3: You can search for a book from the books. google.com website, or troll the shelves of the Google Play app. Here I asked to find *The Martian,* an intriguing best-seller that became a movie.

You can't loan titles you buy from Play Books to anyone; on this tablet only the NOOK library is set up to do that. However, if you trust someone enough to allow the temporary relocation of your Tab S2 NOOK tablet, you can loan the device and the books (and other media) it contains. Be sure you're clear about your desire to get it back, though.

Taking Kindle for Samsung for a Spin

Why am I talking about the Amazon Kindle in a book about a tablet marketed by Barnes & Noble to sell eBooks through its own NOOK division?

Because you can add a Kindle app to your Tab S2 NOOK; it's free, right there in the Play Store and the Samsung app selections. Amazon, like Apple, is a very tightly controlling company. The book files it provides are in the company's proprietary format. What does that mean for you? Books you buy from

Amazon have to be read using Amazon's own eReader — Kindle — which does a fine job and works like the NOOK eReader.

Out of apparent deference to its partner, Barnes & Noble, on the Tab S2 NOOK the app is called Kindle for Samsung. See Figure 10-4.

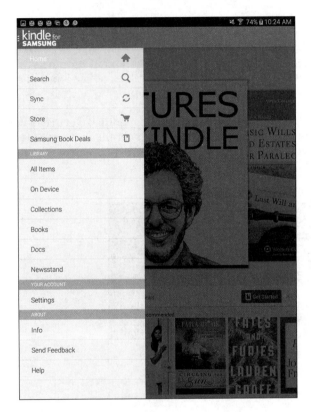

Figure 10-4: You can download and install a copy of Kindle for Samsung from the Samsung apps store or from Google Play.

Although neither Google nor Barnes & Noble can be very happy about the presence of a third bookseller on a single tablet, as a consumer you can appreciate the wide choice. You can buy current and classic books from the Kindle, as well as a growing number of titles self-published by authors or provided by other sources specifically for the Kindle. And Amazon, a ferocious competitor, also has various offers, including free books for members of its Amazon Prime service and other special promotions.

Your NOOK books won't appear in the Kindle library and your Kindle books won't be on the shelves of your NOOK library.

Going in to OverDrive at the Library

I love libraries, and as a young man I fulfilled several of my fantasies all at once by dating a children's librarian. (We both were of legal age.) But I digress. Today's libraries are quite changed from what they were just a decade or so ago. You'll find free Wi-Fi and computer terminals, plus other electronic services. And many libraries now offer online loans of eBooks; all you need is a library card and the proper app.

One of the leaders in library eBook management is OverDrive, which works with more than 27,000 libraries and schools and perhaps two million titles. You can get a copy of the OverDrive app from the Play Store. See Figure 10-5.

Figure 10-5: The free OverDrive app is available through Google Play or, in some instances, through participating public libraries and institutions.

Check with your local library to see if they participate, and see whether they're part of a network that includes other lenders in the region. Books are usually loaned over the Internet for one or two weeks, and most borrowers are limited to a set number of titles at a time. You don't have to drop off the books in a slot when you're done; the file disappears when it's due. See Figure 10-6.

Figure 10-6: My local library, the Nantucket Atheneum, dates in its present form to 1834. It's a member of the cutely named Cape Libraries Automated Materials Sharing (CLAMS); we've got a lot of clams, which we use for chowder. And we read a lot of books.

OverDrive has its own electronic reader system, and the reader is quite capable. Just as with the NOOK eReader, when you return to OverDrive after closing the app, you automatically go to the last page you were reading. See Figure 10-7.

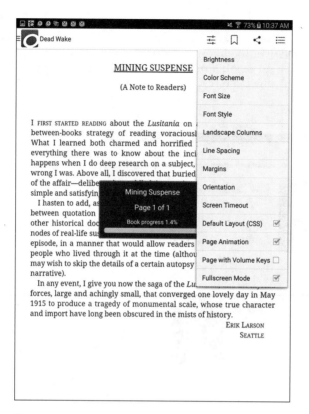

Figure 10-7: The reading tools in OverDrive are similar to those of the NOOK app, although the page turns aren't quite as snazzy.

Subscribing to Scribd

Yet another option for readers is Scribd, a platform that includes more than a million titles as well as tens of millions of other documents, available to subscribers for a monthly fee.

Like NOOK, Amazon Kindle, Google Books, and other sources, books are available on Android and other platforms. Unlike some services, Scribd is available anywhere in the world you can get a Wi-Fi signal, although some books have limitations that restrict their availability away from the United States.

You can get the app for Scribd from the Galaxy apps selection on the tablet. With the introduction of the Tab S2 NOOK, owners received an offer for three free months; the flat monthly fee was less than ten dollars for all you can read. See Figure 10-8.

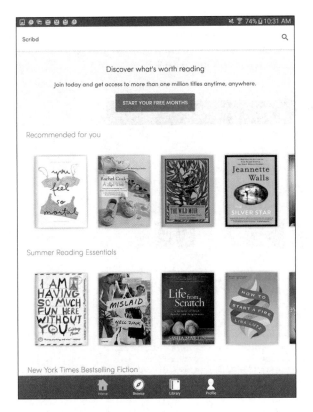

Figure 10-8: More than a thousand publishers are associated with Scribd, and payment of the monthly fee gives you access to as many books as you'd like.

Reimagining Gutenberg

I'm pretty certain that Johannes Gensfleisch zur Laden zum Gutenberg had no concept of an electronic reading tablet when he introduced, or at least popularized, the concept of mechanical moveable type in the mid-16th century. That revolutionary step allowed printers to relatively quickly create templates to print pages of text that were eventually bound together to make books. (Remember ink on paper?)

Today those characters are drawn on the screen of a digital tablet, but Gutenberg is not forgotten — especially by the volunteer members of Project Gutenberg. Most of the items in the Project Gutenberg collection are the full texts of public domain books, which are titles no longer under copyright protection.

As of late 2015, the group had about 50,000 titles in its collection. Anyone can access these titles to read them directly through a browser or download them to a tablet in one of several formats. You can explore Project Gutenberg at www.gutenberg.org. See Figure 10-9.

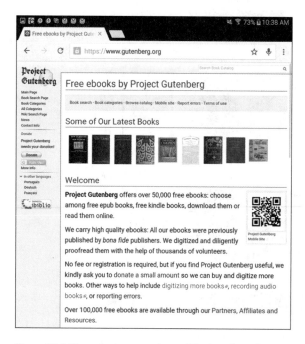

Figure 10-9: The volunteer members of Project Gutenberg have worked since 1971 to digitize tens of thousands of ancient, obscure, and otherwise hard-to-find books.

When you download a book within an app on your Tab S2 NOOK, most providers deliver the file in a format your device can use. Books from other sources might offer you a format choice; select EPUB for the best results on the Tab S2 NOOK. Second choice is PDF, which in some cases has fewer reader tools and customization options.

Part IV
Getting Creative with Camera, Video, and Music

Take a perfect panoramic picture with help from www.dummies.com/cheatsheet/samsunggalaxytabS2nook.

In this part . . .

- Use the front and rear cameras.
- Organize pictures and videos in Gallery.
- Buy music by the track or album.
- Watch a movie or TV show.

11

Snapping Pictures

*O*nce again, we converge on convergence: The Samsung Galaxy Tab S2 NOOK brings together, under one set of covers, an eReader for books, a small but powerful computer, a video and audio player, some phone functions, and a camera. Let me de-converge that just a bit: Some would argue that it makes compromises at every turn with each of its functions. That's probably true, but having almost-everything-in-one-place is a beautiful thing.

This chapter looks at the Tab S2 NOOK as a camera. Actually, it has not one, but two cameras — one on the back and the other on the front. They can take pictures or video.

Use the rear camera for pictures that you want to print or otherwise view at a size larger than that of the screen on the tablet.

I still laugh when I see people holding a tablet at arm's length and tapping at the screen to take a picture. It's a bit awkward and hard to control. But still, it's a camera and the result is still a digital photograph that can be stored on the tablet, sent to someone else's digital device, or sent out to a photo lab for a print.

Taking Pictures with a NOOK

On the plus side, the cameras in this NOOK can immediately display the pictures or videos you make (and with a screen considerably larger than the ones on plain old digital cameras or smartphones). On the downside, although the electronics of the camera in *all* tablets are quite advanced, the fact is that none of them can match the quality of the large lens on an advanced camera.

In addition to being an author, I am also a professional photographer and I travel the world with a camera that cost several thousand dollars and a zoom lens that cost a few more; my photography kit also weighs about four pounds. And when I need it, I also add in an electronic flash unit that adds a pound and costs more than a few pence.

So back to convergence. When it comes to owning a device that has so many functions and yet costs only a few hundred dollars and fit in a coat pocket and weigh just a few ounces, less just might be more in most situations. In this chapter I show you how to use the tablet's cameras in automatic mode and give some hints on how to make some advanced adjustments that bridge some of the gap between point-and-shoot and professional equipment.

The Tab S2 NOOK doesn't have a flash or LED light, so your source of light has to come from somewhere else. That isn't a big deal in most situations. Use the sun outside or a lamp indoors to light your subject. And here are a pair of tips to help with faces or details:

- Outdoors, have an assistant hold a white card or something similar to reflect sunlight onto a face.

- Indoors, turn up the lights and have someone standing outside of the image aim a light at faces or objects you want to brighten.

You can create a gallery of images on the tablet and do some basic editing, and you can share them by email, social network, or upload or transfer your files to a photo printing service and get decent prints. Think small: A 4x6-inch or 5×7-inch print should be sharp and pleasing, and photos taken in bright light should be fine at 8×10 inches. Larger than that, not so much.

Thinking about yourselfie

We are in the Age of the Selfie. For reasons that I completely fail to understand, youngsters (of all ages) seem to have adopted the practice of holding their tablet or smartphone at arm's length in front of them or even on a telescoping "selfie stick" and taking a picture — of themselves in front of a landmark, or of themselves with friends and family, or of themselves posing in front of a Happy Meal. In some situations the selfie has essentially replaced the old-fashioned concept of collecting an autograph from a celebrity. (I don't understand autograph hunting, either, so feel free to officially declare me a very computer, camera, and tablet-savvy old fogy.)

The front camera takes and stores your selfie as a photo. At its 2.1 megapixel resolution, it'll work for profile pictures and for small prints of perhaps 4×6 or 5×7 inches. Enjoy.

Taking a Camera Tour

In Figure 11-1 you can see the basic camera controls. I go through them briefly here and examine them in more detail later in the chapter.

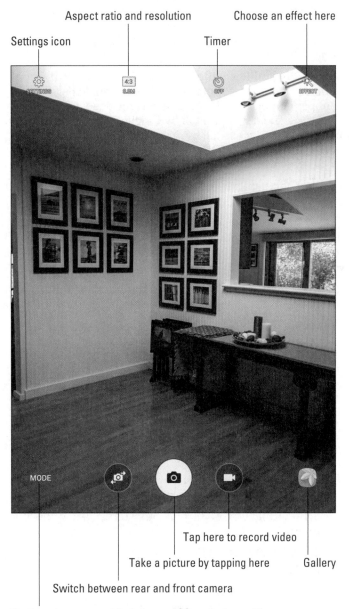

Settings icon

Aspect ratio and resolution

Timer

Choose an effect here

MODE

Tap here to record video

Take a picture by tapping here

Gallery

Switch between rear and front camera

Tap here to access white balance, ISO, and other settings

Figure 11-1: The basic camera controls for the Samsung Galaxy Tab S2 NOOK.

Camera controls for the upper screen

Start the tour in the upper-left corner and work your way across the top first:

- **Settings.** I've already noted how this NOOK tablet is nowhere near as advanced as a professional camera. However, you can make lots of manual adjustments here, including whether you want an image taken at full resolution or at a lesser resolution (which creates a smaller file). You can ask for grid lines on the screen to help compose your image. I explain more later in this chapter.

- **Aspect Ratio and Resolution.** You won't see those words on the screen, but that's what the two sets of numbers mean. In Figure 11-1 you can see the upper number of 4:3, which means the aspect ratio is the equivalent of an image about 8 inches tall by 6 inches wide in portrait mode (taller than wide), or 6 inches tall by 8 inches wide in landscape mode (wider than tall). The Tab S2 NOOK uses a more book-like ratio than other tablets, many of which use a 16:9 ratio, more like a widescreen television.

  The other number is the resolution, or number of *pixels* (picture elements or individual dots) captured by the sensor. The more pixels the sharper the picture, and also generally the larger it can be displayed or printed.

  You can't independently select resolution or aspect ratio. See Figure 11-2. Here are the combinations available for the rear camera, the one facing away from the screen:

  - **8.0 M (4:3). 3264×2448.** This is the standard setting, capturing as many pixels as possible and presenting them at a 4:3 or 3:4 ratio.

  - **6.0 M (16:9). 3264×1836.** A slight reduction in the total number of pixels collected, although that usually doesn't matter since the size is also smaller in the 16:9 or HD-like aspect ratio.

  - **6.0 M (1:1). 2448×2448.** A high-resolution square image that can be used for standard photos or for portraits for mug shots on Facebook or LinkedIn or other social or professional network pages.

  - **4.9 M (4:3). 2560×1920.** A reduced resolution version of the 4:3 aspect ratio.

  - **3.6 M (16:9). 2560×1440.** A reduced resolution version of the 16:0 aspect ratio.

  - **3.1 M (4:3). 2048×1536.** In relative terms, a low-resolution 4:3 photo.

  - **2.4 M (16:9). 2048×1152).** In relative terms, a low-resolution 16:9 photo.

Shoot at lower resolution if you have limited space for storage in the internal memory or an external SDHC card installed in the tablet. I prefer to have a large SDHC card and transfer my images to a desktop computer for editing. As far as aspect ratio, it's entirely a matter of personal choice.

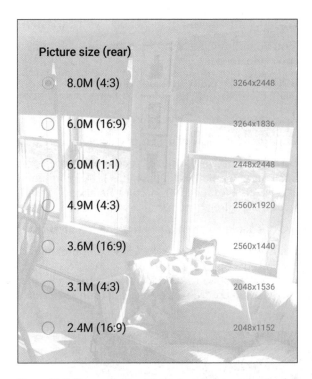

Figure 11-2: The available picture sizes and aspect ratios for the rear-facing camera.

You can shoot an image at high resolution and later send a smaller file as an email attachment. Visit the Google Play Store for free or paid apps that let you adjust the file size. Save a copy of the picture with a different name; that way you have the high-resolution image and a smaller file to share.

There's a similar set of adjustments for the front camera, although that one starts out at a much lower resolution of 2.1 megapixels:

✔ **Timer.** Tap to enable a countdown timer before the picture is taken. You can use this as a self-timer so that you can run around and get into the image or for other special requirements you might have timewise. Your options here are Off, 2-, 5-, or 10-second delay. Or you might experiment with having the tablet take a candid camera shot all by itself.

Be careful about propping your tablet and then running off to get into a photograph. You don't want the tablet to tumble.

✔ **Effect.** Tap here to add an effect to a photo. You can preview the effects on screen before selecting one. See Figure 11-3. Special graphical effects include these:

  • **Vintage.** A sort of faded or low-saturation color, like an old photo found in the bottom of a drawer somewhere.

- **Vignette.** Another old-timey effect, with darkened corners.

- **Tint.** Something like a duotone, mixing a bit of orange over top of a grayscale image.

- **Grayscale.** No color, just glorious black and white. You'll get best results with strong, contrasty lighting.

- **Faded Color.** Another version of vintage.

- **Moody.** A dark, low-contrast grayscale image.

- **Cartoon.** What's not to like? A compressed color range, low contrast, and just plain odd. In Figure 11-4, I combined the Cartoon effect with a forced shift in Color Balance. Go forth and experiment; film is free.

You have to enable an effect *before* taking the picture.

✔ **Download.** Remember, your NOOK is a computer, and that means it is almost infinitely configurable. With a connection to the Internet through Wi-Fi, tap on Download to hunt for other effects you can obtain from developers; some are free and some ask for a few dollars.

Figure 11-3: As delivered, your Tab S2 NOOK comes with seven special photographic effects; you can also download other modifications.

Figure 11-4: Playing around with the Pro settings, I selected the Incandescent white balance setting for a daylit room and then applied the Cartoon effect. This isn't the way the breakfast nook usually looks, but I like the result.

Camera controls for the bottom screen

Move now to the controls at the bottom of the screen, starting at the left corner:

- ✒ **Mode.** Jumping over to the bottom of the camera screen, tap here to select from interesting special effects or controls. You can take manual control of the sensor's sensitivity (ISO), use automatic or manual white balance, and compensate or adjust exposure by as much as two stops. (Each stop is equivalent to half or double the amount of incoming light, depending on whether you choose to under- or overexpose the image.)

Not all modes are available on both the front and rear camera.

✔ **Switch camera.** Tap here to swap between the rear camera (the one that's on the side away from the screen) or the front camera (which looks you right in the eye). The icon shows a camera with left and right arrows. In most instances you'll use the back camera for landscapes and portraits. Use the front-facing camera for video calls and selfies (self-portraits).

✔ **Take a picture.** Tap the icon on a camera to actually snap a photo, which is, of course, one of two reasons we are gathered here.

✔ **Record video.** Your other option is to tap the movie camera icon, which starts the recording of a video.

✔ **Gallery.** Tap the icon to look at the most recently taken photo or video, as well as all others stored on the device. From the Gallery, you can share your work with others by sending it over the Internet. And you can perform other actions on the files.

Tap-Clicking with a Tablet

Are you ready to use your tablet as a camera? From the Home screen, scroll through the app icons on the lower part of the screen; tap the Camera icon. Or, you can tap the Apps icon on the Home screen and find the Camera icon there.

After a brief interlude during which the tablet changes its personality, you see the main camera screen, as you saw in Figure 11-1. Tap the shutter to grab a photograph. But before then:

✔ You can hold your tablet camera wider or taller. The buttons and controls will stay where they are on the screen, but their labels will rotate as you turn the tablet.

✔ To tell which camera you're using, look at the screen. If you see whatever's in front of the tablet, you're using the rear camera. Some of you, I'm sure, are at this moment halfway down the rabbit hole with Alice in Wonderland. Remember that the _front_ camera is the one on the front, which is the side you use to see the screen; the _rear_ camera is on the back.

✔ To switch between the front and rear camera, tap the camera icon that has left and right arrows. Each time you tap it, you switch between one lens or the other. If you see your own face, tap once to use the rear camera.

✔ If the tiny lens on the back or front of the tablet gets dirty, your pictures are going to appear smudged or otherwise less-than-lovely. Gently clean the lens with a soft cloth or a tissue. If the lens has some sticky gunk on its face, you can _slightly_ moisten the cloth with just a _bit_ of water or a lens-cleaning solution like the ones used for eyeglasses. Don't press hard and don't assault the lens with a nail file or jackhammer.

✔ On the screen, tap the spot you want to focus on. In certain combinations of light and modes, you may be able to shift the point of focus slightly. For example, if you're taking a picture of a person standing in a field of sunflowers, tap that person's face so that he or she's in focus. Or, tap a distant sunflower to emphasize the beauty of nature over your friend's face.

✔ Touch the screen with two fingers and spread them apart to zoom in as much as 4 times; pinch your fingers toward each other to bring the zoom back toward 1 time. You can also touch and hold the slider that appears on the screen to manually adjust the amount of zoom.

The zooming range of the tiny camera system is limited, and it's *electronic* rather than *optical.* The Tab S2 NOOK relies on enlarging a portion of the image captured on the sensor; extreme zooms of distant objects or people will lose a little — or a lot — of quality.

✔ You'll see a short lag between the moment you tap the shutter and when the photo's recorded. This is the price we pay for all of the automated functions that are handled for you by the tablet camera: exposure calculation, white balance adjustment, and autofocus. This makes it a little more difficult to take action photos; practice a bit to learn how to anticipate motion. And don't hesitate to reshoot if someone has blinked or made a face.

Choosing camera shooting modes

If you're the sort of person who owns a microwave with a clock that constantly flashes 12:00 as the time of day, or prefers to scrunch your knees up against your chin rather than adjust the seat in your car, you just might be missing some of the finer things in life. We live in a *customizable age,* and as I'm sure you're beginning to figure out, your Samsung Galaxy Tab S2 NOOK has a button or slider or control for just about everything.

NOOK versus a Nikon

As capable as the Tab S2 NOOK is, this isn't a full-featured camera with a fine piece of optical glass for a lens. The fixed plastic lens on the tablet — like those on nearly every tablet and smartphone — is best suited to put nearly everything in focus in a well-lit setting. For experienced photographers: The aperture isn't adjustable, and therefore the depth of field doesn't vary. All photos are taken at an aperture of f1.9; to compensate for extremes of light or lack of light, the tablet can boost or reduce the electronic shutter speed and turn up or turn down the sensitivity of the sensor.

A large (or *wide*) aperture of f1.9 lets a lot of light reach the sensor, which is generally good. But photographers know that a wide aperture also makes for a short depth of field. What that means is that whatever you choose as focus should be sharp, but objects closer to you or farther behind spot will be less so. There's not a lot you can do other than pay close attention to the image you see on the screen of the tablet before you take a picture and adjust the focus point.

These sections concentrate on the camera's shooting modes. Because the rear-facing camera is better and generally serves different needs, some of its modes are different than those on the front camera.

Here's how to adjust modes: From a Home screen, tap the Apps icon and tap Camera. Then tap Mode. The following sections explain the selections you can make.

Shooting modes for both cameras

These modes work for either the front or rear camera:

- **Virtual Shot.** Create 3D-like multidirectional views of objects. This is a truly amazing feature, although I'll be the first to admit that it takes a bit of practice to get it right.

   The *Virtual Shot,* also called *Virtual Tour* in some descriptions, allows you to create a walk-through of your surroundings, like circling a 3D object. For example, you could tour your home or office, or document all the facets of a statue in a museum.

   When you enable the feature within the Camera app, do this:

   1. **Look at the screen and find the target pointer.**

   2. **Adjust the way you hold the tablet so that the pointer's in the center of the circle.**

      When the target dot is in the center of the circle, it automatically takes a picture.

   3. **Follow the onscreen prompts to move the view to the next spot in your tour.**

      Hold the tablet as steady as you can and at the same distance above the ground. Each time the target circle appears, this tells you that an image has been captured and stitched into the tour package that you are preparing.

   4. **Press the Stop button when you've completed the tour.**

      You can view the results in the Gallery on your tablet.

- **Download.** Access and install additional shooting modes from Samsung's Galaxy Apps store.

Shooting modes for the rear camera only

Tap Mode to see seven available special shooting styles, as shown in Figure 11-5:

- **Auto.** This standard point-and-shoot setting lets the camera choose the best settings. It's usually pretty good, but sometimes we humans like to believe we are just a bit smarter than a machine; occasionally we are.

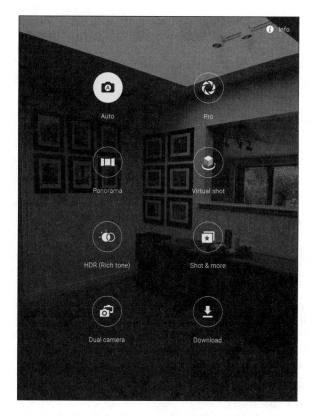

Figure 11-5: Choose your rear shooting modes from here.

✔ **Pro.** This is, in most respects, the opposite of the Auto setting, allowing you to adjust the sensitivity of the camera's sensor, as well as choose exposure values, white balance, and color tones.

✔ **ISO.** Your camera's sensor is the replacement for film, and like film it can be more or less sensitive to light. In film-based photography, this used to be called the *ISO* value. Going for a high sensitivity, or a high ISO, allows you to take pictures in low-light conditions, although the higher the ISO, the greater the possibility of *noise* (graininess) in your image.

The Galaxy Tab S2 includes manual settings between 100 and 800. In most situations you'll want to use the Auto setting, but if you're taking photos in bright sunlight of fast action (beach volleyball, perhaps?) you might want to experiment with a high ISO of 800, which will force very short shutter speeds to freeze the action, or an ISO of 100, which might produce a bit of interesting blur.

✔ **White Balance.** Light is made up of the visible spectrum, which is another way of saying that the color of light varies based on the time of day or the nature of artificial illumination. The early morning is usually cool or bluish; sunset is usually warm or toward orange.

An indoor incandescent light is much warmer (toward the red or orange) than fluorescent lights or daylight. The tablet computer is pretty good at adjusting for the prevailing light condition, but just as one example you might want to play around with this setting in unusual situations that mix light coming through the window and electrical or candlelight inside a room.

🖝 **Metering.** Your tablet makes the best possible exposure, adjusting the *shutter speed* (the amount of time the sensor records light) as well as the sensitivity of the sensor itself. But your Galaxy Tab S2 NOOK (and even professional photo gear) can become confused in a situation that has a wide range of light levels in the same scene — for example, a sunny day at the beach with deep shadows under umbrellas and extreme highlights dancing on the surf. If I weren't so hard at work writing this chapter, I'd be off to the beach right now although there's a fall-like nip in the air and the seals are still feeding and the sun is near setting, which means the Great White shark population is thinking about dinner. I think I'll stay at the keyboard.

Figure 11-6 shows your options:

- **Center-Weighted** makes exposure decisions based mostly on the lighting conditions in the middle of the scene. If you choose this option, put the most essential element of your picture in the middle of the image; that's not always the most aesthetically pleasing composition, but you can always crop the image later.

- **Matrix** has nothing whatsoever to do with Keanu Reeves and an artificial reality set up to control human minds. The Matrix setting averages out the entire scene to come up with the best exposure setting.

  Matrix metering works well when the range of light is consistent — in other words, scenes where the darkest dark and lightest light aren't all that far apart.

- **Spot** is a good one for attentive, patient photographers. The tablet sets the exposure based on wherever you tap the image. The trick is to find a place that's best for the image you want to record. Tap a face to expose best for that part of the picture, for example.

🖝 **Panorama.** Use the tablet's brain to stitch together multiple photos into one large panoramic image; this is the same idea as Virtual Shot, which I discuss earlier, except that the result is a single stitched-together image instead of a computer-created simulated video.

Brace yourself and keep the tablet as steady as you can as you slowly move it in an arc from left to right or right to left. You'll see a blue guide frame on the screen; when you move the tablet so that it fills the guide frame, it takes the next picture in the series. To stop shooting the pano, tap the Stop (square) icon. Panorama mode automatically stops if it can't recognize elements of the previous picture.

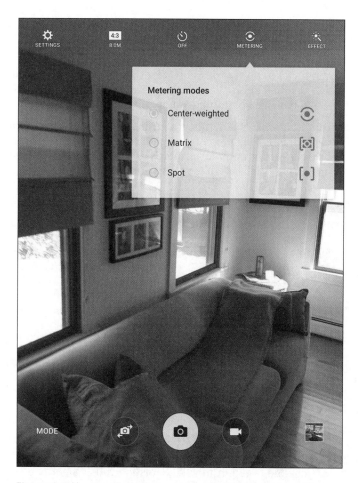

Figure 11-6: You can choose amongst three types of metering of exposure for images. Most people use either Matrix or Center-Weighted.

Panoramas work best when there are simple but recognizable backgrounds, like trees or windows. Shooting against empty skies or blank walls may confuse the camera, which may confuse the image, which will confuse you when you try to make sense of what you've got.

✔ **Virtual Shot.** A computer-stitched-together panorama movie made up of individual images.

✔ **HDR (Rich Tone).** This option gives you an image that records only *HDR* (high dynamic range) tones. Your camera takes three quick pictures at different settings and then combines them into a single image that includes exposure values you wouldn't ordinarily be able to record directly. For example, it can deal with both deep shadows and brightly lit objects.

HDR won't work well if the object is moving fast or if you're moving the tablet as you take the picture.

- **Shot & More.** When you take a *burst,* or series, of photos, this mode can allow you to apply special features such as best photo, best face, drama, and panning shots. Remember: "Film" is free, so experiment to see if the tablet can see something you might be missing.

- **Dual Camera.** Again, this is a strange feature but sometimes worth an experiment. This mode takes pictures or videos in a variety of styles using the front and rear cameras at the same time. There you are in the image, and there is what you are looking at.

Shooting modes for the front camera only

These settings only work with the front-facing camera:

- **Selfie.** Yes, here's the way to take a picture of yourself with the Taj Mahal over your shoulder, or a photo of you posing with the President of the United States or your bridesmaids or some random dude. You'll see the image on the screen of the tablet before you take the picture. You can apply effects to make yourself look less like yourself, if you want.

- **Interval Shot.** You can have the camera shoot a series of shots at a set interval — every few seconds or every few minutes — and then choose the best images from the group. (Are you thinking this might be a way to discover who is stealing the candies from the jar on your desk? It just might be enough to send the felon away to the big house.)

Making camera settings

If you're into making minor adjustments, check out the following sections, which I grouped together in what Samsung calls Camera Settings. The options vary depending on which camera you're using, and sometimes on the mode you're in.

Tap the Settings (gear) icon and choose Camera to apply the settings you want.

Camera settings for both cameras

Tap Settings from the Camera screen to customize more details of the camera. See Figure 11-7.

- **Grid Lines.** This tells the camera to display a set of grid lines on the screen as you prepare to take a picture. This is helpful in making sure the horizon is level or that buildings are upright and not tilting (with the possible exception of the Leaning Tower of Pisa). The grid lines are visible only when you're taking the picture; they aren't recorded in the file.

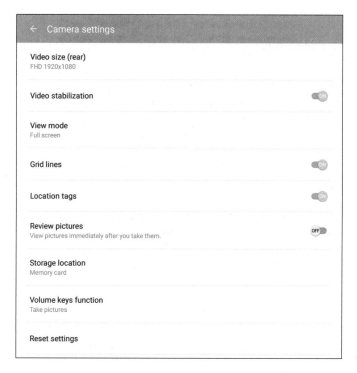

Figure 11-7: Here you can turn on grid lines, add location information to image files, set the storage location for photos and other housekeeping details.

Grid lines are, for me, are essential when holding a thin, flat, rectangular tablet camera at arm's length. It's considerably more difficult to hold a tablet camera steady than a standard camera held at your eye level and braced against your face.

✓ **Location Tags.** Your Galaxy Tab S2 NOOK has a built-in GPS receiver, which can tell the device where in the world you are. This function records that information (as latitude and longitude) in the data for the file; you can later use an app on your tablet or a program on a desktop or laptop computer to look up the location of those geographic coordinates and tell you where the picture was taken: Pisa, Italy at 43°43'N, 10°24'E.

The strength and accuracy of GPS signals can vary from place to place. Sometimes they're weak inside buildings or in areas between buildings where the view of the horizon is blocked. Weather conditions can also affect GPS signals. If you leave Location Tag turned on, the tablet applies the last good signal it had to your photos, updating your position any time it can. See Figure 11-8.

Location tags

This function will attach, embed, and store geographical location data within each picture that you take or video that you record. Use caution when you send, share, distribute, transmit, or copy these pictures and videos since they contain information about where the picture or video was taken or recorded.

The location information of a photo or video is provided based on GPS data generated by your device's location service at the time you take a photo or video.

OK

Figure 11-8: What a world! You can use your tablet's GPS system to add location information to your photos, and then you can worry about someone spying on you because you did.

In a perfect world, most of us would say, "Yes, of course. What a nifty special feature." But some people worry about privacy. What if that picture ended up in the hands of someone else — someone you don't want to know where you were when you took the picture? If you send your pictures to someone else by email, or especially if you upload them to the Internet, you lose control over whatever information is embedded in the file.

✔ **Review Pictures.** You can turn on or off the brief display of pictures after you've taken them. I generally leave this on, so that I can review the photos to make sure that there's not a fern growing out of cousin Arthur's head.

✔ **Storage Location.** If you install a microSD card in your Samsung Galaxy Tab S2 NOOK (which I recommend), here's where you can tell the tablet where you want your photos and videos stored.

In general, you should store your photos, videos, music, text files, and the like on the memory card and leave the built-in memory for apps.

✔ **Volume Key Function.** Your options are

- **Zoom Key.** Pressing the + or – side of the Volume key zooms you in or out; your Volume key is set up this way already.

- **CamKey.** You can make the Volume key into a shutter release key for photos.

- **Rec Key.** If you make the Volume key work as a Record key, pressing it in the Camera app starts or stops recording a video.

✔ **Reset Camera Settings.** If you've adjusted your camera — and I hope you will — you can quickly return all settings to the original — like when first you unboxed your Samsung Galaxy Tab S2 NOOK. This is an all-or-nothing reset, and it only affects camera settings.

Camera settings for rear camera only

✔ **Video Stabilization.** This little bit of technical magic slightly reduces the effects of shakes or bounces while the video camera is recording. I say *slightly*.

Camera settings for front camera only

✔ **Beauty.** When the camera detects a face, it sets exposure so that skin tones are well lit and skin is smoothed, a makeover without makeup or surgery. It works better in close-up portraits than in distant images, and some results are better than others.

✔ **Gesture Control.** More magic: Hold the palm of your hand out, facing the camera, and look for a yellow box on the screen surrounding your hand. Now take your hand away and the camera will take a picture a few seconds later.

Making Movies

The standard setting for the rear camera is high (or normal) resolution. The Samsung Galaxy Tab S2 NOOK uses the MP4 file format for videos. Note, too, that video files can be quite large; a 10-second clip at full resolution occupies about 21 MB of space.

Tablet, camera, action!

Eye see

The human brain is an amazingly sophisticated computer, more capable in many ways than the most advanced digital device. But the reason we're able to enjoy movies or videos is related to several optical illusions caused by the reaction speed of our brains. First is *persistence of vision,* which causes an afterimage to remain on the eye's retina (the equivalent of a digital camera's sensor) for approximately 1/25 of a second. If another image appears within that time period or less, the human brain doesn't notice a gap. The other optical illusion is called the *phi phenomenon,* which causes us to perceive continuous motion when objects move rapidly from frame to frame.

The further you get into digital photography, the harder it is to remember that a video (or to use that old-fashioned word, a *movie*) is made up of hundreds or thousands or millions of individual still pictures. In the time of film, the movie would move through a projector, and each still frame would have its moment on the screen. (Most *motion pictures,* to use another term, projected still frames at a rate of 24 per second.)

Video doesn't use film, of course, but the same principle applies. When you watch a video on TV, a tablet, or in a state-of-the-art movie theater, you're seeing individual still frames that are retrieved by the microprocessor from memory and then replaced by the next one in a series. On the Samsung Galaxy Tab S2 NOOK, the video frame rate is 30 digital frames per second.

Recording video

You can only use the rear camera, the one facing away from the screen, to record videos.

To make your own video, do this:

1. **Open the Camera app.**

2. **From the main screen, tap the video camera icon on the right side of the screen.**

   If you most recently used your camera for video, the icon should already display that icon.

3. **To start making a video, tap the Record (red dot) icon.**

   You can momentarily halt recording by tapping Pause.

4. **Tap the Stop (square) icon when you're done.**

Keep these things in mind when you're recording:

- Hold the camera tablet as steady as you can. Bring your elbows in to your chest.
- If you plan on *panning* (moving left or right, or vertically), do so slowly and smoothly.
- Record in a well-lit setting: outdoors in daylight or using lamps indoors.

Zooming in or out

While you're using the video camera, zoom in or out to make distant people or objects appear closer or return to the normal view. Touch two fingers on an image and then spread them apart to zoom in. Bring the two fingers toward each other (pinch) to zoom out.

Extreme zooms are pretty poor quality. Judge for yourself whether a video (or camera) zoom is acceptable.

After you record a video, you can

- Review it by tapping the Gallery window within the camera screen.
- Close the Camera app and tap the Gallery icon from the Home screen. There you'll see a collection of both still and video files. Tap any thumbnail (small picture) to view.

I discuss the Gallery app in detail in Chapter 12.

You can buy apps that allow you to edit the videos you make on your Galaxy Tab S2 NOOK. Some very basic ones allow simple cuts and edits, while advanced apps let you fade from one scene to another or apply other sophisticated transitions. You can also email or load your video file from the tablet to a desktop or laptop computer and use a full-featured video editor to make your own movie. That includes reordering scenes and merging videos taken at different times or different locations into one movie.

12

Getting into the Gallery

In This Chapter

▶ Putting pictures into albums

▶ Tagging people in pictures

▶ Editing videos

*Y*ou youngsters out there have grown up with the concept of digital photos, which are held in digital files that are automatically organized by date and time and can easily labelled with a title that can be searched for. Add to that the ability to embed a photo's latitude and longitude as measured by the built-in GPS unit in your tablet, and you can also find a photo by searching for the place where it was taken.

It sure beats a box stuffed with hundreds of precious, irreplaceable family photographs of events long forgotten in places that have faded from memory and sometimes of people no longer recognizable.

Your Samsung Galaxy Tab S2 NOOK has features that help you organize, label, and share your photos and videos. It all comes together in a place called the Gallery.

Visiting Your Picture Gallery

Like the smart little computer it is, your Samsung Galaxy Tab S2 NOOK is available anytime you need help, never takes a coffee break, and doesn't care if you stomp your feet and whistle as you browse the collection. And you can (and should) make as many copies as possible of digital photos and videos to protect against loss or failure of the hardware.

The Gallery app not only stores photos or videos you've taken using the NOOK cameras, but also any images you download from the Internet or email or transfer from a computer. The folder also holds any *screen captures* (pictures of what's onscreen) you've made; see Chapter 16 for those instructions.

Visit the Gallery from the Home screen. Tap the Apps panel and tap Gallery. Or even quicker, tap the Gallery app icon in the lower part of the Home screen. If you've taken photos using one of the built-in cameras, a direct link to Gallery shows the most recent image.

Going to the Gallery in this fashion brings up a screen showing all your image folders, including pictures you took on the tablet, screen captures), and pictures or videos you've downloaded to the tablet from other sources such as from a desktop, laptop, or smartphone. See Figure 12-1.

Figure 12-1: A full, unsorted display of some of the photos in my Gallery.

If you're using one of the built-in cameras of your Tab S2 NOOK, you can jump to the Gallery by tapping the preview box that appears in one of the corners of the camera screen. The images shown in the preview are *only* those you photographed using your NOOK; you get to other images in the Gallery.

Your Tab S2 NOOK can only create and display certain file types. For still images taken with the camera, files use the JPG (pronounced by techies as *jay-peg*) format, a technology that squashes the size of the file with little or no loss of quality. Camera images are stored in the DCIM/Camera folder. Screenshots use a file format called PNG (pronounced *ping*) which also squashes files without losing quality; they're stored in a folder cleverly named Screenshots.

You can transfer files from another device that are in a different format, but you get an error message when you try to see them (or they may appear damaged). Here's a way around: Convert incompatible file formats using a photo- or video-editing program on your PC or Mac before transferring them to your Tab S2 NOOK.

I sometimes use a tablet as a storage place for extra copies of important files I take with me when I travel. In that instance, it doesn't matter whether the tablet can display the incompatible format (including TIFF or RAW camera files); all I need to do in an emergency is get to a PC or laptop and upload the files to a computer that can handle them.

Viewing images

You want to see what pictures you have? Images are displayed in order of when you took them.

- ✔ Tap a folder to open it and check its contents.
- ✔ Tap an image to view it full screen.
- ✔ Scroll left or right with your finger to view the previous or next image.

Zooming in or out

You can enlarge most images onscreen to take a closer look. You can zoom two ways:

- ✔ Double-tap anywhere on the screen to zoom in. Double-tap again to zoom out to normal view.
- ✔ Touch two fingers on an image and then spread them apart to zoom in. Bring the two fingers toward each other *(pinch)* to zoom out or reduce the size to normal.

Editing images

Your Samsung Galaxy Tab S2 NOOK comes with a built-in basic image editor. Here's how to use it:

1. **While viewing an image, tap the screen once.**

   The image options appear.

2. **Tap Edit to view editing tools.**

   See Figure 12-2.

3. **Tap a tool to use it, following the onscreen instructions.**

Figure 12-2: Tap for tools, including Auto Adjust, Rotate, and Crop.

You can rotate an image from horizontal to vertical or the other way around, adjust brightness, saturation (the intensity of colors), and crop images. The Auto Adjust button may fix certain problems.

There are more than a few more capable photo-editing apps available through the Google Play store and elsewhere. Some work with full-scale editors on desktop or laptop computers.

You can always send your pictures by email or transfer them by Wi-Fi Direct or over a USB cable to a desktop or laptop computer and open them in a photo editor there. At the professional end of the scale, programs like Adobe Photoshop or Adobe Lightroom or Apple's Aperture work with files created on your NOOK tablet. So too will basic programs that are part of the Windows or Apple operating systems.

Deleting images

Film is all but gone, and taking pictures is all but free. But you don't need (or want) to hold on to every last image you record.

To delete an image from within the Gallery, follow along:

1. **Tap a folder or category to open it.**
2. **Tap More, then tap Edit.**
3. **Tap one or more items to select them.**
4. **Tap the Trash icon.**

   Or, while you're viewing an individual image, tap the Trash icon.

Putting All Your Pictures in One Basket

If you're the sort who likes to neatly separate all your pictures or videos into folders that you name, that's fine. But you can also tell the Tab S2 NOOK tablet to do a bit of sorting: The most basic way is to show folders by date or by alphabetic order.

The tablet comes with some preset albums. Think of them as folders. And certain others are automatically created by programs looking for a place to store material. For example, if you download an image using email or from the Internet, a folder called Downloads is created and automatically used. Similarly, the first time you capture a screenshot of something displayed on the screen, a Screenshots folder is created and used for storage.

But you can easily

- Create your own album while you're in the Gallery on the tablet. See Figure 12-3.
- Add a folder (which is treated as an album) while using a PC or laptop computer to work in the files on your tablet.

I explain how to create folders and transfer files using a computer connected by the USB cable in Chapter 5.

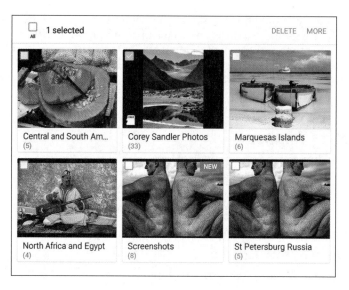

Figure 12-3: You can assign images to one or more albums, which makes it easier to organize photos for slideshows or send to a printer or photo service.

Sorting your pictures

You can examine photos, videos, and other images in ways that Marian the Librarian could never have imagined. Sort to your heart's content:

1. **From the main Gallery screen, tap Albums.**

   A submenu opens.

2. **Choose how you want your pictures sorted:**

   - **All.** You got this, right?

   - **Albums.** Show the names and the first image in each album.

   - **Time.** The oldest are at the top and most recent are at the bottom. You can scroll through all the pictures by touching and sliding anywhere on the screen. Tap a single picture to see it full screen. Tap the Back icon to return to the display of images by time.

   - **Locations.** If you turn on your tablet's Location feature, every photo and video you shoot will use the built-in GPS to figure out where it was taken. (I discuss this in more detail in Chapter 11.) And then, using certain apps, you can tell the tablet: "Show me only the pictures taken on Nantucket Island." See Figure 12-4.

   - **Favorites.** If you declare an image to be a favorite (tap the Menu icon in the upper right and then tap Favorite), selecting this method means only your favorites will show up.

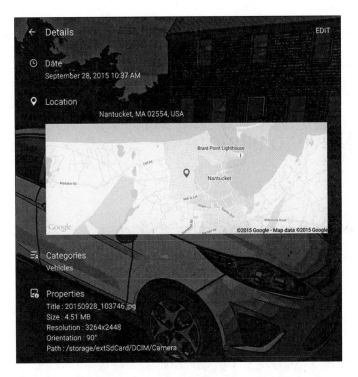

Figure 12-4: I took a photo of my car (adding the Cartoon Effect for kicks) with the Location sensor turned on. When I checked the details, the tablet presented a map showing where the car was parked.

Moving pictures into albums

To move a photo to an album from the Gallery app, do this:

1. **From any Home screen, tap the Apps icon and then Gallery.**

2. **Choose Album View.**

3. **Tap a folder with images.**

4. **Press and hold an image to select it.**

   A checkmark appears in the upper-left corner of the thumbnail.

5. **Tap the checkmark on any other image you want to move to an album.**

   See Figure 12-5.

6. **Tap More, and then tap Copy to Album or Move to Album.**

   • Choose Copy to place a *copy* of the picture in the new location and leave the original where it is.

   • Choose Move to relocate the picture to an album.

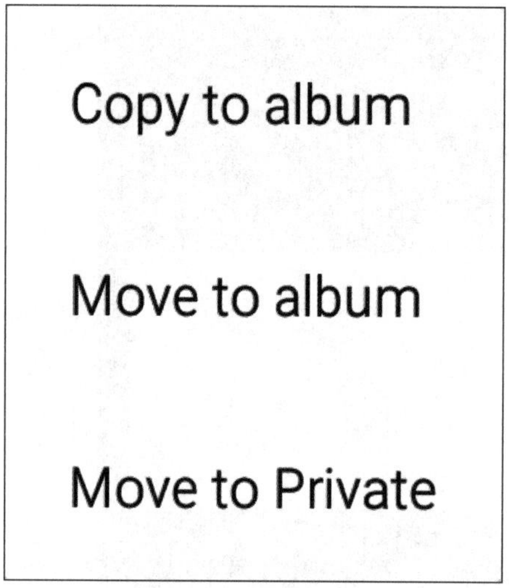

Copy to album

Move to album

Move to Private

Figure 12-5: Select one or more images by placing a checkmark in the box for its thumbnail and then tapping Copy or Move.

Putting Your Images to Work

Your images can be shared, emailed, put in a slideshow, electronically framed, renamed, printed, or used as the portrait on a new $100 bill. Just kidding about that last option, unless you happen to have your own tropical island nation and a printing press. And if so, why haven't you invited me to visit?

From the Gallery app, tap an image and then tap the Menu icon (shown here). Now choose an option:

  ✓ **Slideshow:** Start an automated presentation that goes through every photo in the current folder. You can make the show even more dramatic if you add transition effects and music. You can say for how long you want each picture on the screen.

  ✓ **Details:** You get the nitty gritty: filename and its format, the date and time the photo was taken, and which folder it's stored in. If GPS was on, you can see the location, resolution, file size, and whether the camera was held upright or on its side. In certain situations, the tablet can even determine that the subject of the image falls under a particular category, like people, vehicles, or nature.

  ✓ **Favorite:** You can tag an image as one of your faves. It won't rename or move the file, but any time you tap the Favorites folder, you'll see only those images upon which you have bestowed this particular honor.

✔ **Set As:** You can use a picture as the *wallpaper,* or background, on your tablet's Home or Lock screen, or both. You can put a picture of a person with that person's contact information, too. In Figure 12-6, I've selected an image of sea fog hanging over a glacier in Prins Christian Sound in Greenland as the wallpaper to sit behind my Home screen.

Figure 12-6: You can choose any image in your Gallery to serve as wallpaper behind the Home screen, the Lock screen, or both.

Searching for an Image

The Tab S2 NOOK lets you look for an image based on any part of its file-name, the date it was taken, its category, and other attributes. In Figure 12-7 I'm asking the NOOK to find an image that includes the word *sinai.*

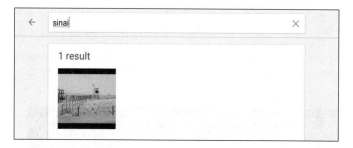

Figure 12-7: I entered the word *sinai* in the search bar and located this photo I'd taken of a forlorn Egyptian army post in the Sinai Desert. Your results may differ.

Sharing Your Images

No NOOK tablet is an island, which is a good thing if you want to quickly share your photos with your friends and the world at large. You can send photos several ways, including posting them on social networks and by sending them as email attachments.

In Chapter 5, I explain how to move your photos from your tablet to a desktop or laptop computer; from there you can use fully capable photo-editing software and share them other ways.

From the Gallery you can share by email, Gmail, Bluetooth, or Wi-Fi Direct. To share an image directly from the Gallery, follow the steps. You must, of course, have an active Wi-Fi connection to share files.

1. **From any Home page, tap the Apps icon and then Gallery.**

2. **Tap a folder or category to open it.**

3. **Tap More and then tap Share.**

4. **Select a folder and open it.**

5. **Tap images, and then tap Share.**

    See Figure 12-8.

6. **Select a communication service and then follow the onscreen instructions to share the image by Wi-Fi or Bluetooth.**

You can share images right from the Camera app. When you're reviewing a photo, tap the > icon and choose Share.

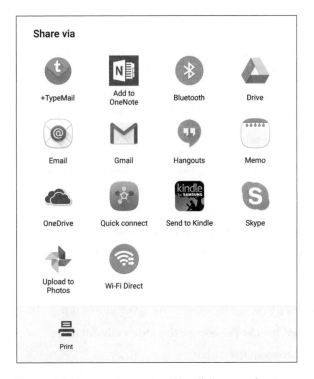

Figure 12-8: You can share or provide a link to any of your images using built-in communication services and most apps you add to your tablet.

Playing Your Videos

Your Gallery also holds videos you've recorded using the built-in cameras of the NOOK. You can put video files into folders or categories just like you do still images. Share them by sending them as email or over a wireless or wired connection. Bear in mind, though, that video files can be quite large; the longer in length, the bigger the file.

Here's how to play a video from the Gallery:

1. **From any Home screen, tap the Apps icon and then tap the Gallery icon.**

2. **Tap a folder or category to open it.**

3. **Tap a video to prepare it for playback.**

4. **Tap the Play icon.**

    To stop playback, tap the Stop icon.

Shearing Videos

The Galaxy Tab S2 NOOK has a basic video editor. You can buy something with a little more oomph as an app from the app stores on your tablet.

If you save the video under a different name from its original, you can keep the full file. This way you can carve up a video into several shorter clips.

To use the tablet's built-in editor, do this:

1. **From any Home screen, tap the Apps icon and then tap the Gallery icon.**

2. **Select a video for playback.**

3. **Tap the screen once to display the editing options.**

4. **Tap Editor and then tap the Trim (scissors) icon.**

   Below your video's large opening scene, you'll see a kind of storyboard of your full video.

5. **Drag the start bracket to where you want your edited video to begin.**

6. **Drag the end bracket to where the video should stop.**

7. **Tap Export to save the video.**

   You can modify the name of the file to save the original and create a second, edited version. You can also reduce the screen resolution of the video to make the file smaller.

If you reduce the screen resolution of a video, it will affect its appearance — not for the better — if you play back the video on a larger screen than the NOOK tablet. On the other hand, if you're planning on sending the file to a device with a smaller screen, like a smartphone, reducing the resolution should have no adverse effects and will save quite a lot of file size.

13

Singing, Dancing, and Noisemaking

*N*ow, I'm not going to try to compare the quality of sound you hear from the tiny speakers on the Tab S2 NOOK — a nevertheless impressive pair of devices about the size of the head of a matchstick — with the sound from a much larger system.

And although the LCD screen of the Tab S2 NOOK is beautifully colorful and quite detailed when you're looking at it from a distance of a foot away, it doesn't match the visual thrills of a 90-inch HD screen or the astounding experience at an IMAX theater.

But the Tab S2 NOOK fits in your back pocket or a small purse. And don't overlook the fact that it can be a *source* for audio and video when you connect it to a larger system. This chapter looks at playing items from your well-honed, tasteful collection.

Starting with the Hardware

Your tablet has internal and external memory, each of which can store files. Since this is, at heart, a computer, those files are *digital* representations of sound and imagery: 0s and 1s that can be converted by the microprocessor into music and movies.

You can get files from almost any source, including the NOOK Shop, Google's Play Music and Movies, Amazon, Apple, YouTube, and other web-based sites.

Or you can *stream* audio and video, which means that the material doesn't reside on your tablet but instead arrives from the Internet across a Wi-Fi connection and is immediately played. Music sources include Pandora and Samsung's own Milk service; many sites provide streaming video of live broadcasting or recorded material.

I discuss Pandora and similar apps online at www.dummies.com/extras/ samsunggalaxytabs.

Speaking of Which . . .

The speakers for the Tab S2 NOOK are on the bottom edge of the tablet. If you place your tablet on its back with the speakers facing you, the sound will be pretty good — not as great as a huge studio monitor, but pretty darn amazing when you consider these little guys are about the size of a match head.

Some users swaddle their tablet in a case, which is very considerate, but do bear in mind that the case might block the speakers as well as the microphone.

Customizing headphones with Adapt Sound

Before I discuss alternatives to the speakers, consider utilities that are part of the Samsung hardware controls and the Android software components. You can use these adjustments to improve — just a little — the depth of the music and certain other effects.

The only way to find out if the app helps your particular pair of ears in your particular listening place is to experiment with the settings. Here's how:

1. **From any Home screen, tap the Apps icon and then tap the Settings icon.**

2. **Tap Sounds and Notifications.**

3. **Tap Sound Quality and Effects.**

   See Figure 13-1.

4. **Tap Adapt Sound and follow the prompts to change some of the settings.**

   You'll hear a clicking noise; you're supposed to wait for a faint beep. The beeps vary in frequency from high to low and shift from ear to ear.

5. **Tap Yes if you can hear the tone.**

In Figure 13-2 you can see my results; as if I needed proof, my old-school (and just plain old) ears are deficient in hearing high frequencies. The adaptation improved the sound quality a smidge.

As I say — Can you hear me now? — experiment with any and all of the settings to find the one best for you. And don't forget that the quality of your headphones and the amount of ambient noise in the room will have an impact on your aural experience.

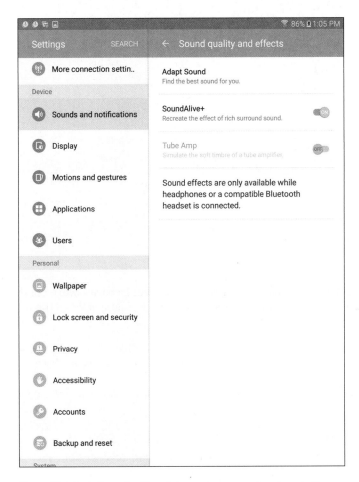

Figure 13-1: Install a pair of headphones by connecting them to the jack on the bottom edge of the tablet and turning on the Adapt Sound utility. Listen for the faint beep and then customize the sound.

SoundAlive+ and Tube Amp

On the same Sound Quality page of settings, use slide switches to turn on one (or both) special adjustments that may improve the quality of sound:

✔ **SoundAlive** + uses some fancy programming to simulate the effect of surround sound, seemingly bending sound so that it doesn't come directly *at* you but also from the side and even behind you. It's a magic trick nicely done. Experiment to see if it improves your experience.

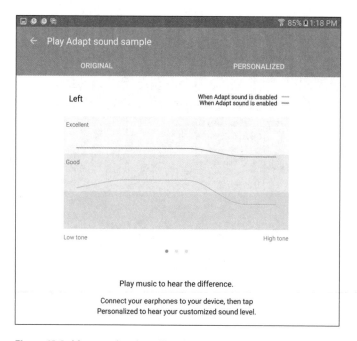

Figure 13-2: After running the utility, the tablet adjusted for the fall-off in high-frequency perception that comes with age (and wisdom).

- ✔ **Tube Amp** is a back-to-the-future utility that claims to soften the sound of digitally derived music (made up of discrete 0s and 1s in a file) to seem closer to the old-fashioned analog sound of a tube amplifier. Again, try it; you might like it, or you might not notice the difference.

An equalizer for ultimate customization

The basic equalizer (confusingly called SoundAlive without the +) has a cousin, the graphic equalizer. You can find these on your music collection's playback panel. I discuss those in a moment in the section on playing music from your tablet.

Alternatives to Built-In Speakers

In addition to the built-in speakers of the Tab S2 NOOK, you have several ways to go outside the box:

- ✔ **Headphones.** The 3.5mm headphone jack on the bottom edge of the tablet (between the speakers) can connect to earphones or a headset, which greatly improves the quality — at least for the one person who can use it. (You can buy a *splitter* so two people can connect headphones to a single tablet, and boy does that ever look geeky. But it works.)

There's a wide variety of quality in headphones. Basic ones use the signal straight out of the tablet, but more advanced (and more expensive) models include a built-in battery-powered amplifier that boosts the signal, especially when it comes to booming bass.

- **Connect to speakers via cable.** You can use the same headphone jack with a cable to connect to a set of larger external speakers; most of these have a built-in amplifier that improves the quality. These need battery or AC power.

- **Connect to a home stereo system via cable.** You can connect a cable to the headphone jack and go from there to a home stereo system, which can significantly boost the output wattage (and add all sorts of adjustment options, including knobs to individually control treble, midrange, and bass signals). My home stereo system includes left and right speakers plus a subwoofer that sits on the floor and produces a bass deep enough to be felt miles away if I were so inclined.

As it happens, my car's stereo can accept audio through a jack on the dashboard; it was necessary to invest in a male-to-male cable with 3.5mm connectors at each end. You can find cables online if you know exactly what you're looking for, or you can visit a home electronics dealer. The cable shouldn't cost more than the price of a candy bar, an internationally accepted means of comparison that I invented.

If you're hooking up to a sound system, the end of the cable that connects to the Tab S2 NOOK must be a 3.5mm stereo plug; there are half a dozen or so possibilities for the design of the plug at the other end, including RCA, quarter-inch, bare wire, and more.

Use your Tab S2 NOOK to take a picture of the connectors on your stereo system. Take the tablet with you to the store when you go shopping for cables.

- **Connect to speakers via Bluetooth.** You can buy *amplified speakers* that communicate with your tablet using Bluetooth radio signals. If you choose this route, I recommend buying a system that includes a subwoofer, which is an additional speaker devoted entirely to producing deep bass tones.

Jamming Out on Your Tab 4 NOOK

In this age of fancy and sometimes cryptic names for utilities and apps (Why is Samsung's streaming music app called Milk?), it's refreshing to come across some software components that tell you the unvarnished truth in their name. Android gets pretty close to that with its elegantly titled Music Player.

You'll find Music Player in the Apps collection or, if you've created a shortcut to it, on one of the Home screens. Tap the icon and prepare to groove. (Why do we say *groove* when we mean *enjoy some music?* Because in ancient times, recorded music came on rotating wax and then acetate disks with *grooves* that contained wiggles that vibrated a needle that converted those markings into sound. Trust me; I was there.)

When you open Music Player, you'll see a screen like the one in Figure 13-3. Tap any of the tabs at the top of the screen to see its contents:

- ✔ Playlists
- ✔ Tracks
- ✔ Albums
- ✔ Artists
- ✔ Folders

The information varies depending on how you got the music on your tablet and where you stored the files.

Pressing Play

You probably know how to play a track. Okay, if you insist: To play a song, tap any tab or playlist. Then tap the name of a song or artist. Playback is almost instantaneous. No need to wait for the needle to find the right groove, or a CD player to find the chosen track.

- ✔ You'll see the name of the current track near the bottom of the screen. If you bought the track from certain music services, or if the NOOK or another computer device has gone out on the Internet to find information about the music, you may see an image of the artist or the album cover.

- ✔ Along the right edge of the Music Player control at the bottom is a volume control, presented as a vertical gauge. The higher up the gauge, the higher the volume. You can adjust the volume by tapping the Volume icon, or by pressing the Volume+ or Volume – key on the side of the tablet.

- ✔ Near the bottom of the screen is a horizontal bar that shows you how far along you are in the current track. At the left side of the bar you'll see how many minutes and seconds have elapsed; at the right end of the bar you can see the total length of the track.

  You can touch and hold the current playback position and drag it back to an earlier part of the music, or drag it forward to advance.

- ✔ You can probably handle it from here:

  - Tap Play to begin the music; tap again to pause the track.
  - Tap the Rewind icon to move to the previous song in your collection.

- Tap the Fast Forward icon to skip from the current track to the next one waiting.

- Tap the Shuffle icon to skip hither and thon through all the tracks in the current playlist. When enabled, the Shuffle icon shows a criss-crossing set of right-facing arrows. Tap it again to turn off Shuffle. When Shuffle is turned off, there's a slash through the arrows.

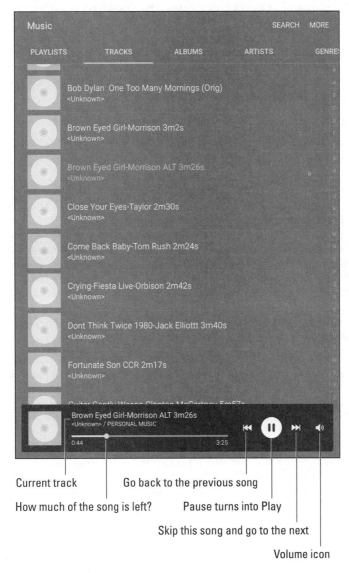

Current track

How much of the song is left?

Go back to the previous song

Pause turns into Play

Skip this song and go to the next

Volume icon

Figure 13-3: This playlist is one I use at the end of the day as I struggle to avoid falling asleep at the keyboard. The tabs at the top of the screen are key to organizing your collection.

Playing favorites or adding to a playlist

To create a subset of your favorite tracks, do this. (If they're not your favorites, why are they occupying space within your tablet?)

1. **With the Music Player displayed, tap the More button at upper right.**

2. **Tap Edit.**

3. **Tap to place a checkmark next to any track you want as a favorite.**

4. **Tap More again.**

5. **Tap Add to Favorites (or Add to Playlist).**

Now when you load the Music Player, you can play just your favorites or just the ones in a particular playlist.

SoundAlive equalizer and settings

With the music playlist displayed, tap the More button in the upper right to see more settings.

Tap SoundAlive to view a set of dials that look more or less the ones you used to see on an old stereo system. See Figure 13-4.

- Touch the blue dot on the upper dial and rotate clockwise to increase the bias of the sound toward treble (away from bass). Experiment with the dial as needed, and remember: Not every song will have the same sound, and different rooms have differing acoustic environments. (A carpeted living room will absorb and muffle sound and benefit from a boost in treble, while a hardwood kitchen floor will sound sharper and may need a turn toward bass.)

- The lower dial is boosts or deemphasizes the midrange of sound, the area where voice (vocals) take root in a song. Try the dial in each direction.

To adjust the sound range graphically, tap the Details button near the top of the screen. Figure 13-5 shows what you'll see.

What you see here is a scale that's neutral in the middle (at 0dB) and adjustable 10dB up or 10dB down for each of seven audio frequency ranges. Let me break that down: 60, at the left end of the scale, means 60 Hertz or 60Hz in technospeak, which is a deep bass sound. At the other end of the scale is 16K, which means 16,000Hz, up around the sound of a dog whistle. The typical adult male's voice is in the range of 85 to 180 Hz, and a typical adult female from 165 to 255 Hz. A young adult can be expected to hear sounds in the range from about 20Hz to 20,000Hz, with the upper limit declining with age.

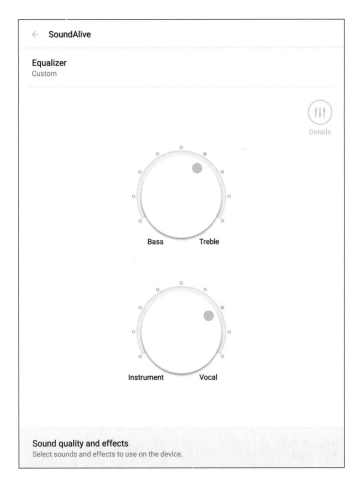

Figure 13-4: Touch and move the blue dot to adjust the bias toward treble or bass, or to emphasize or deemphasize vocals or instrumentals.

And one last definition: the adjustment called dB, meaning *decibel*. (The bel part comes from Alexander Graham Bell, by the way.) It is a logarithmic scale for power, but when it comes to volume the difference between 0 and +10dB is about three times the amplitude. Going the other direction, from 0 to -10dB reduces a particular frequency to one-third the volume.

Touch and drag any or all of the buttons on the graphic equalizer to see the effect, or try one of the presets at the bottom of the screen. There's no right or wrong setting here: Choose the one that sounds the best to you.

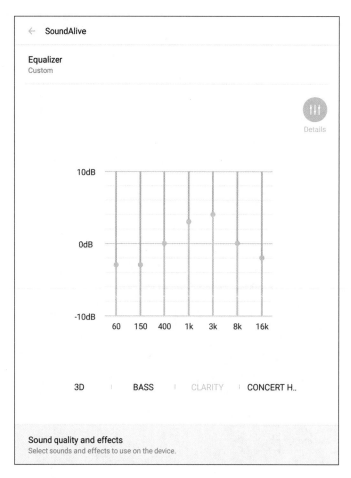

Figure 13-5: The graph shows emphasis or reduction of frequencies ranging from low (bass) at the left to high at the right. You can adjust the settings for each frequency or use presets for music styles.

Play speed

Try this one with your old record player: You can play a track at double speed or half speed. Disappointingly, you cannot, as Joan Baez once sang, "play me backwards."

1. **From the Music Player, touch the More button in the upper-right corner, and then tap Settings.**

2. **Tap Play Speed.**

3. **Move the slider.**

   Move it to the right to play a track at double speed, or all the way to the left to play at half speed.

The magic trick here is that the frequencies of the human voice are electronically almost unchanged, even as the rest of the music is altered. See Figure 13-6.

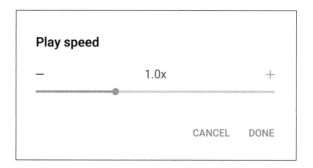

Play speed

—   1.0x   +

CANCEL   DONE

Figure 13-6: The tablet does a pretty good job of maintaining the frequency for the human voice, making this an interesting tool for listening to podcasts. You can also make your own Chipmunks music.

Why would you want to use the Play Speed feature? Suppose you have a lecture in a file or a podcast; you can speed up or slow down the track without changing the voice very much.

Other settings

Tap Music Auto Off in Settings to enable a timer that shuts off the music player after a specified period of time. You can choose from five preset times or select Custom. You can play yourself to sleep or use your music system as a timer while you exercise or eat or whatever you might choose to do.

Turn on Smart Volume to automatically adjust each track to an equal level.

If you press the Home key to go to another app, music keeps playing. A Play icon stays in the notification panel at the top to remind you that the Music Player's active. Swipe down from the top to see a mini control panel for music. Tapping the X closes the Music Player without you having to go back to the app.

How about a nice piece of music to play while you're reading a book? No problem. Unless you tap Pause or reach the end of your playlist, the Music Player will keep singing to you.

Press the Volume key to raise or lower the sound. The end of the switch nearer the Samsung logo on the tablet is + (up); the other end is – (down).

Deleting a song

I almost *never* delete a track of music, because I am a multifaceted guy. As I write these words, I'm listening to a 1966 recording of Grace Slick singing "Sally Go Round the Roses" with her original hippie-dippie group The Great Society. Later, I may feel in the mood for Bob Marley, and tonight as I wrap up a long, long day in your service I may close out the night with Rachmaninoff's "Caprice Bohémien." Into which category would you put that particular mix?

But if you insist on removing a track, here's how:

1. **Open the Music Player app.**

2. **Tap More.**

3. **Tap Edit.**

4. **Tap to place a checkmark next any track you want to delete.**

   If you want to delete a song from your tablet, don't just *remove* it from a playlist. That just takes it out of the list. It doesn't take it off the tablet.

5. **Tap the Delete button that has appeared alongside More at the top of the screen.**

A deleted song is gone. If you have another copy on a computer or another tablet, it won't be deleted from there.

Showing Your Own Movies

We all aspire to be the next Alfred Hitchcock or Martin Scorsese, but I suspect we're all much closer to Ed Wood, who's on most film critics' and fans' list of the worst director ever to have a career in Hollywood. Check out *Glen or Glenda* or *Plan 9 from Outer Space*. Wow, they just don't make them like that anymore. His stuff was so bad it became must-see material.

Of course, I'm sure your productions are very much worthy of an Academy Award if only you could get someone to sit down and watch them. And pay you for the privilege. But one of the beauties of digital cameras is that you don't need tens or hundreds of millions of dollars to produce a picture or a movie. And the magic of digital video means you can point, shoot, and immediately see your work. This chapter deals with video you've made for yourself, using the built-in video camera of the Samsung Galaxy Tab S2 NOOK.

When you buy through the NOOK Shop, the Google Play Store, Amazon, Apple, and most other sources, you play the movie using a simple interface that has Play, Pause, Rewind, and Fast Forward.

Movies that you record with the video camera are stored in the MP4 file format. That's not something you have to bother with, except if you want to import another video from a computer or other source; MP4 is the preferred format, although the tablet should handle *most* videos encoded in 3GP, WMV, AVI, and a few other formats.

I say the tablet *should* be able to work with other formats because it might balk at files that stray even a tiny bit away from certain formats. You can find some conversion utilities on the Internet that are pretty good at fixing certain deficiencies.

Loading a video

Playing a video that you made with your Tab S2 NOOK is exactly this easy: Find the file, tap the Play icon, sit back (not too far), and watch. It's so easy that Samsung and Google have dotted the Home and the App screens with multiple onramps to the movie screen.

The playback screen for a video is remarkably similar to the one for music. See Figure 13-7.

Figure 13-7: I just got back from shooting a quick movie. Just for giggles, I applied the cartoon special effect. Here you can see the Play, Rewind, Fast Forward, and More buttons.

Using the Gallery to play videos

Here's how to start in the Gallery, which has all your photographs and videos:

1. **In the Apps collection, tap the Gallery icon.**

2. **Tap the folder called Camera.**

   Photographs are *thumbnails* (small pictures). Video files look similar, but have a large Play icon on them.

3. **Tap the Play icon.**

   The video enlarges to fill the screen.

4. **Tap it one more time to start the video.**

Using MyFiles to play videos

You can get to videos from the MyFiles app, which is similar to Windows Explorer on a PC and the Finder on a Mac machine.

1. **From any Home screen, tap MyFiles.**

2. **Tap the Videos tab on the left side.**

3. **Tap the filename for any video you see listed in the right panel.**

   See Figure 13-8.

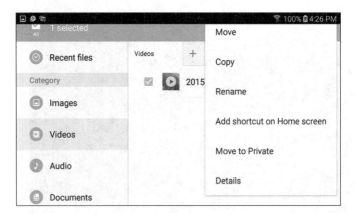

Figure 13-8: You can start videos from MyFiles. If you touch the More button (upper right), you can move, copy, or rename any video file displayed here.

The first time you watch a video from the Gallery, you may be offered a choice of players: the Video Player or Photos. You can choose one and then tap Always to make that a permanent assignment. If you tap Just Once, you see the same message the next time you play a video from the Gallery.

Both Video Player and Photos apps work fine. Both have a basic Trim tool that allows you to choose a starting and ending point for the video. They also have a Details option, which tells you the file's size, resolution, and duration. You can also export your video to a personal computer and use a more full-featured editor to create your own blockbuster.

Video Player has a few extra options, including grayscale, blur, invert (a negative image), sepia, and sharpening of the file. See Figure 13-9.

Using the Video app

With this app, there's no need to choose a folder.

- Tap the video's filename or thumbnail.
- From the Video app, you can tap the Folder icon to look for a specific video.
- Tap the Search (magnifying glass) icon in the Video app and type a search term.

You can play a video from the Camera and Photos apps.

Figure 13-9: I applied a sepia tone to my video tour of the sand-covered lane near my home. The Trim button allows you to cut out and save a section.

Managing your videos

You can cut away unwanted parts of a video at its beginning or end using the Trim tool; I explain how in Chapter 12. But to tell you the truth, and I always do, the apps on your Tab S2 NOOK for video aren't all that helpful for anything other than playing them back.

If you want to do some video editing, including cutting, special effects, and sound, transfer the file to a desktop or personal computer and use the software there.

You can share the file with many services and apps, even while you're watching. Tap the Share icon on the screen or do this:

1. **Tap the Play icon to pause.**

2. **Tap the Menu (three stacked lines) icon.**

3. **Choose Share.**

   Depending on how your tablet is set up and which apps you have, you might be able to send the file by Bluetooth, add it to Dropbox, OneDrive, or another cloud-based storage, or send it as an email or Gmail.

The Play Movies & TV store has current titles (many sold in either *SD,* standard definition, or higher-priced *HD,* high definition). If you're only going to view the video on your Tab 4 NOOK, you might want to buy the SD version; on your tablet's small screen, the difference in resolution may not be noticeable.

You can also rent certain titles at a lower cost. Again, SD and HD versions are available. The amount of time and the conditions of rental can vary from studio to studio, so be sure to read the fine print before tapping Buy. Play Movies & TV has films, individual television shows, and entire seasons for sale or rent.

Also available through the Play Store are games, apps, magazines, and newspapers. Prices for some magazines and newspapers are quite reasonable — well below what you'd pay at a real newsstand. If you can find one.

Payment for items purchased from the Play Store can be by credit or debit card or through PayPal.

Samsung has free apps in the Galaxy Apps panel that appears on the Home screen of your Tab 4 NOOK tablet.

Part V
The Part of Tens

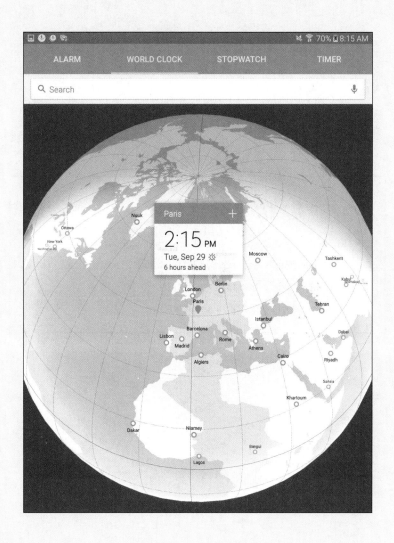

Visit www.dummies.com/cheatsheet/samsunggalaxytabS2nook for ten free apps worth checking out.

In this part . . .

- Make the most of apps that are already on your tablet.
- Try some troubleshooting if your tablet throws a tantrum.
- Back up files to protect against disaster.
- Transfer files to and from your tablet.

14

Ten Worthy Apps

*T*his chapter looks at some of the most useful extra features that come with your tablet, plus a few of my favorite apps you can download and install.

An Alarming Clock

All this technology, all this money, and we're going to look at a clock? Well, yes — but this is a bit more than just a plain old clock. Find the Alarm app in the Apps menu; just look for the imaginative icon of an alarm clock. Tap the icon to display its simple charms.

Your alarm will sound even if your tablet is sleeping (just like you). *Sleeping* means the screen has turned off; if you've shut down the tablet completely, the alarm will sleep right through your wake-up time.

When the alarm sounds, tap Dismiss to turn it off or Snooze to steal a few minutes more. Don't throw your tablet out the window; it could hit someone.

Here's how to manually set an alarm:

1. **Tap the Clock icon.**

2. **If it isn't already selected, tap the Alarm tab at the top of the screen.**

3. **Tap Date and choose the starting date for the alarm.**

4. **Tap Done.**

5. **Tap the upper or lower part of the digital clock display to move the chosen time forward or backward.**

   If you prefer, you can tap Keypad to enter the hour and minutes directly.

6. **Tap AM to change to PM if needed, or the other way around.**

   See Figure 14-1.

7. **Tap Repeat Weekly to display a list of days for recurrence of the alarm.**

8. **Choose Every Day or individual days of the week.**

9. **Tap the left-facing arrow beside Repeat Weekly to return to the main clock screen.**

10. **Tap Options. Here are your choices:**

    - **Volume Control.** Touch and hold the blue dot and move it left to decrease volume or right to increase.

    - **Alarm Tone.** Select from not-very-creative snippets of music — kind of a computer Muzak with names like "Bunny Hopping" and "Drifting Downstream," which sound to me more like lullabies than weekend bugles.

      But here's the real beauty: You can tap+Add Alarm Tone to select one of the tracks in your music collection. I vacillate between *10,000 Maniacs* singing "Who Knows Where the Time Goes?" and Bob Dylan's "One Too Many Mornings." See Figure 14-2.

    - **Snooze.** Get those extra minutes in. The alarm will repeat three times at five-minute intervals.

    - **Smart Alarm.** Tap a checkmark to have the alarm tone or music start at a low volume and increase for the first 60 seconds.

    - **Name.** Keep it professional. It appears onscreen.

11. **Tap Save.**

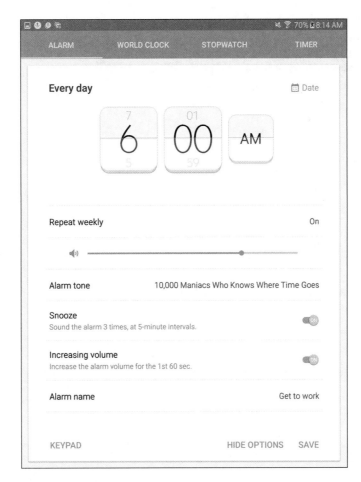

Figure 14-1: Here are the controls for creating your personalized alarm wakeup or reminder.

12. **You're done setting up an alarm, but *you have to set it or it won't trigger.* Tap the icon of an old-fashioned alarm clock to enable it.**

Tap again to disable the alarm. You can delete an alarm by tapping the X in the right corner of its description.

If you use an advanced calendar, you can set reminders for meetings, travel schedules, bill payments — whatever you need. The calendar displays its own reminder and sound at the appointed time.

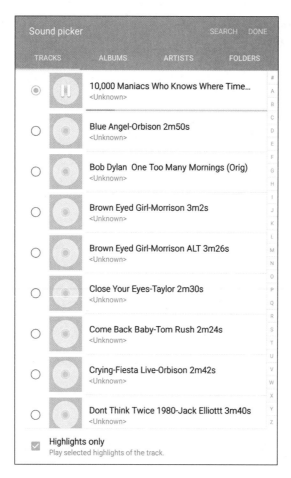

Figure 14-2: You can select your own music for each alarm you create, using tracks stored on your Tab S2 NOOK.

Other goodies in your Clock app

Three other little goodies are worth noting in the Clock app:

- **World Clock.** A very simple, very useful tool for travelers as well as those who have dealings with people in different time zones. Tap the World Clock tab at the top of the clock, and then tap a place on the globe; you can pinch out to expand the view. The result: the current time at the place you have selected. Did you know that Newfoundland, Canada, is half an hour ahead of Eastern Time in North America?

- **Stopwatch.** Do you need to time something? Tap the Stopwatch tab and then tap Start. Tap Stop (I bet you guessed that) to end the timing, or on Lap to record a midway point in an extended timing. Tap Reset to clear the records.

✔ **Timer.** This is a countdown timer. Tell the clock you need reminding in 3 minutes, 27 seconds and it will do just that. In fact, if you really want to plan ahead, you can set a timer to go off in 99 days, 59 minutes, and 59 seconds.

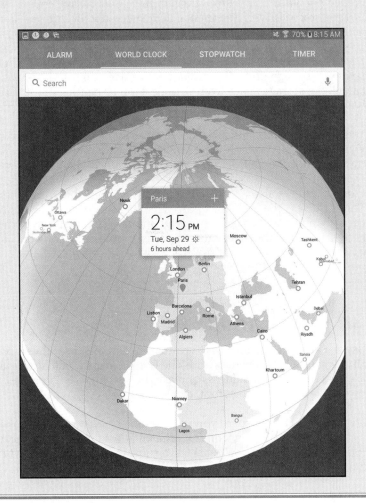

Get Offa My Cloud

The Tab S2 NOOK comes with two free cloud-based storage options: OneDrive (from Microsoft) and Drive (from Google). You can also add Dropbox by downloading its app from the Play Store.

Each of these cloud-based boxes are valuable if you use your tablet as an adjunct to a desktop computer, or want access to files while you travel with your NOOK.

For example, I make copies of my works in progress, as well as important reference documents, and store them in the cloud. (I save copies on OneDrive or Dropbox or Drive.) And then, if I unexpectedly need to use something when I'm traveling, I sign in to the storage and download the file.

Each cloud service, as well as others that are out there, works in a similar fashion. You sign up for an account with a username and password, and then can fill the storage space from your desktop or laptop computer or from your tablet.

You can also set up cloud storage to store copies of all photos you take with your tablet; you can later delete them from your tablet to save space and then download them from the cloud to your desktop or laptop computer.

Cloud service is also a way to make your files available to another user. That's the way the very book you're reading was produced. As I completed each chapter and its associated art, I uploaded the material to the cloud, and then shared those files with my trusty, politically correct, and all-around good-to-work-with editor Tonya Cupp, who downloaded them to her computer and did her thing.

Checking Your Latitude

Use the Maps app to search for restaurants, hotels, hospitals, and just about anything else in this wide world. The Google Maps app figures out where you are; you can enter an address and ask the system to tell you how to get there by vehicle, public transit, foot, or bicycle.

If you want to know where you are, you must turn on the GPS. You can do so by tapping the Location icon from the pull-down notifications panel at the top of your screen. If you're asked to allow the system to use Wi-Fi systems to fine-tune its ability to find itself, do that. See Figure 14-3.

You need an active Wi-Fi connection to see a Google map of where you are and to plot a course. If you connect to the Internet using Wi-Fi and get the necessary map, you can go off Wi-Fi and still see the last map displayed, which will be some help.

The Google Maps app doesn't follow the same layout as most of the Android, Samsung, or NOOK screens. Keep these tips in mind:

Menu icon

Transportation mode

Tap to go back to your current location

Figure 14-3: I began working on this book while at the dock in Monte Carlo, Monaco. See, look. That's one of the ships in the company fleet in this satellite image.

- ✓ The Menu icon is in the upper-left corner. Before you head out on the road, spend some time checking out the help and tips and tricks sections.

- ✓ Tapping the tiny compass rose icon (lower right) takes you back to your current location from anywhere else you may have virtually traveled.

- ✓ Save maps to your tablet for when you're not connected to the Internet.

NOOK! Take a Memo

The Memo app is a multipurpose tool you can use to record audio notes for your own or to send to others. I say *multipurpose* because the memos can include text you enter (or dictate), images from your Gallery, and task assignments you create for yourself.

To take a memo:

1. **Tap the + icon in the lower-right corner of the screen.**

2. **Enter a title for the memo.**

3. **Tap in the body of the memo and type your memo.**

   You can also use the dictation feature by tapping the microphone icon on the keyboard.

4. **Tap one of the options at the top:**

   • **Category.** Assign a category to the memo to make it easy to sort.

   • **Image.** Insert an image from the Gallery on your tablet.

   • **Voice.** Record a memo that will be stored as an audio file.

   • **Tasks.** Start a bullet list of things that need to be done.

5. **When you're done, tap Save in the upper right.**

Now, with the memo stored within your tablet, you can tap it (there's even a Favorite star if you want to make it easy to find) and then tap More in the upper-right corner. There you can share the memo using any of the communication services installed on your tablet. See Figure 14-4.

Popcorn, Soda Pop, and Movies

If you already have a Netflix account for your TV, you can access it from your Tab S2 NOOK. So, too, are streaming video services from the likes of Amazon and from most cable television providers. Comcast, for example, has Xfinity TV Go. Check the Play Store for various movie apps. If not, you can set up an account right here to stream television series, current movies, and classics. (At the moment, you can't get popcorn and soda streamed to your tablet via Wi-Fi.)

One key point: Make sure you have a strong, fast Wi-Fi signal for streaming video. A weak, slow signal will remind some of you of the days before cable, when a distant broadcast channel looked like it was being broadcast through a snowstorm. Swipe down from the top to see the strength in the notification panel.

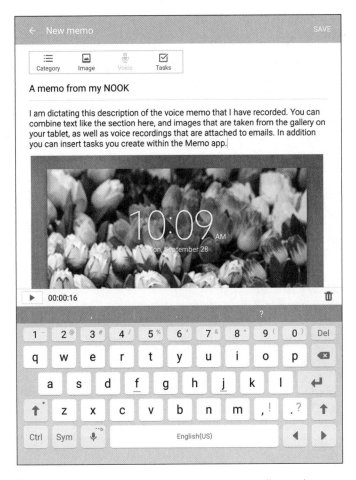

Figure 14-4: I dictated the words, added a voice recording, and inserted an image from the Gallery of my tablet before sending the whole package off as an email. What a world!

Talking to Your Tab S2 NOOK

How about teaching your tablet to respond to your questions? The Tab S2 NOOK has two personal audio servants (a term I just made up; feel free to use it any time you want).

The Google system is the more full-featured, hobbled mostly by its uninspired name: Voice Search. It can answer questions like the one I asked: "How do I get from here to the Steamship Authority terminal on Nantucket?"

You start by displaying the Google search bar on the Home screen. To turn on the Voice Search, say, "OK Google." It beeps to tell you it's listening.

Think about what's going on here: First of all, the tablet had to be able to listen to my voice and recognize the words. Then it had to consult the GPS system to find out where "here" was. And then it looked up the location for the Steamship Authority terminal, which is our local ferry line. Finally, it calculated the best route to get there, offering me driving, public transit, walking, and bicycle options. That's pretty cool, don't you think? See Figure 14-5.

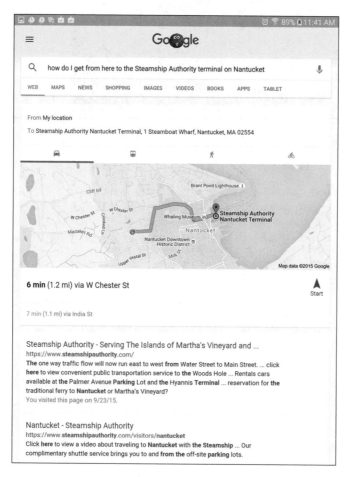

Figure 14-5: Voice Search can combine the Google search engine with Google Maps. I asked for the routing to the ferry terminal.

You can also use Voice Search to issue a command.

I'm a pretty regular guy. I get up early and go right to work, and I like to have my lunch at precisely 12 noon. (Muenster cheese on a sourdough bread with a bowl of fresh popcorn most every day. 18 minutes later, I'm back to work.) So, a moment ago, I said to my tablet: "OK Google." After the beep I continued, "Set an alarm for 12 noon today." And it did, and the sandwich was as good as ever.

What else can you do with Google Voice? Ask about the weather at your location (or anywhere in the world). Pose a Google search question. Launch an app. ("Launch the camera, please.")

The future is just about now; wait, let me ask Google Voice if that is true. "Is the future now?" Hmm. . .it told me about an album of that name by a hip-hop musical group called Phixion. I did not know that previously.

Pandora in the Box

Quite simply, Pandora is a personal DJ dedicated to catering to your every specific musical whim. Even better, the more you use it, the better it gets.

Pandora, available for free from the Play Store, begins by asking you to name a favorite singer or songwriter or song. Chances are quite good the service will respond by playing exactly what you want. But then it gets better: Its computer algorithm (aided by a staff of serious music lovers) considers what makes that first song special and then seeks out others that are similar.

Like the Caesars, you get to give a thumbs up or thumbs down to suggestions. The more feedback you give, the better the system gets at figuring out your taste in music. If you like Paul Simon, you'll probably like James Taylor and you may not know how much in common both have with the Everly Brothers and selected songs by Elvis. Or Bob Dylan to Pete Seeger and Woodie Guthrie with side trips to Robert Johnson, Muddy Waters, and The Rolling Stones.

Pandora is a relative old-timer in the world of the Internet, rising out of the Music Genome Project that began in 2000. Over the years a team of musicians and music lovers has been sitting around and listening to recordings old and new, popular and obscure. The experts rate each song for as many as 400 attributes: its musical DNA, or *genome,* if you like. The details include style, instrumentation, rhythm, tempo, harmony, the subject of its lyrics, the type of singer, and the secret sauce that makes a song a hit or a flop (for me, but possibly not for you).

As a user, you get to create and fine-tune your own stations. You're allowed 100 channels and you can pick just one to play, rotate through them all, or ask the computer to shuffle from channel to channel at random. See Figure 14-6.

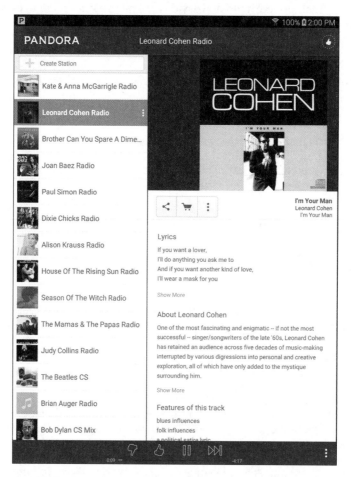

Figure 14-6: Pandora is my companion. On the left you can see some of my eclectic music channels; at right is the track currently playing: "I'm Your Man" by the astounding poet-musician/musician-poet Leonard Cohen.

My Pandora mix includes more than a dozen stations that reflect my musical tastes (mostly frozen in the swinging Sixties). I've got a station, called "House of the Rising Sun," that's based around that seminal bluesy song and I enjoy seeing how old and new artists are related to it. The same goes for a station called "Season of the Witch," which branches off the 1966 song by Donovan and has since been covered by dozens of artists including British jazz-blues-rock singer Julie Driscoll when she sang with Brian Auger and his band.

The free version is interrupted every few songs by short commercials; for a monthly fee you can subscribe to an adless Pandora. If you use the same account on the Samsung Galaxy Tab S2 as you do on your smartphone and personal computer (and I don't know why you wouldn't), all your preferences and channels travel with you.

Samsung has its own version of this sort of personalized music channel, with the oddly named Milk service. You'll find it preinstalled on the Tab S2 NOOK. Try Pandora, or Milk, or both.

What Was That Song? Shazam!

What is that song? And who's the singer?

I'm a pretty serious music lover, from way back when. "Oh yeah," you say? I was at Woodstock, and I hung around Greenwich Village in the times of Dylan and Baez and Havens. But enough about me: This app, Shazam, is like mother's milk for audiophiles.

This is one of those apps where you want to grab a non-techie by the lapels and say, "You've got to see this!"

Shazam is a musicologist in your pocket. Tap its icon, point your NOOK toward the sound (stereo speakers, the background music in a bar, or the fuzzy noise in an elevator) and give it a few seconds. And then Shazam — the name of the song, the name of the artist, and often a bit of the lyrics and a biography of the writer or singer, and (if you want) the opportunity to buy the track or concert tickets or other swag. See Figure 14-7.

I call this magic, but of course there is technology behind it. Shazam captures a snippet of sound (it's called *tagging* the music) and sends it over the Internet to its computer center. There it compares an "acoustic fingerprint" of the music you sent to a huge collection of fingerprints it has on file. Apparently the company is able to identify most songs by comparing a small group of peak intensity frequencies; no matter how complex a song is, it can be encoded at the Shazam end and the little snippet you send matched to it.

Occasionally, if the sound quality isn't great or if the music is very obscure, it may take two or three tries before a match is made. And very rarely, the magic doesn't happen; I tried as hard as I could to find obscure music and Shazam was only stumped a few times. I suspect it was because the music I was playing wasn't from a released version but instead some sort of outtake or amateur recording.

The app even keeps a record of the tracks you've tracked. Shazam is free; you can get a copy from the Play Store.

Figure 14-7: Within seconds, Shazam figured out that I was listening to "Don't Think Twice, It's All Right," by Ramblin' Jack Elliott, who traveled with Woodie Guthrie, influenced Phil Ochs and Bob Dylan, and is on my ready-at-all-times favorites list.

My Daily Planner

The Galaxy Tab S2 NOOK comes with a quite adequate online calendar cleverly named Calendar. It works, and it integrates with Google calendars and Outlook calendars.

My personal preference is a third-party calendar app called Sunrise, which you can get for free from the Play Store. I say third-party, but it's a large party: Microsoft, which purchased the company in 2015 and has made a very good product even better. See Figure 14-8.

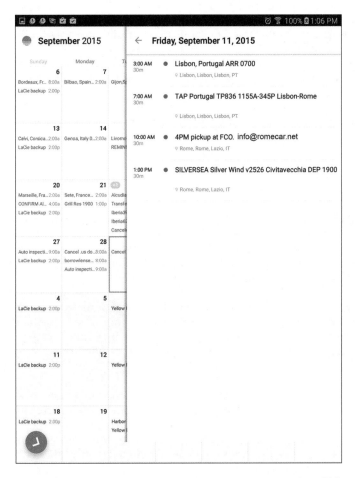

Figure 14-8: I'm lost without my calendar . . . and my email and my GPS and my Internet connection. They all come together in Sunrise, available from the Play Store.

Sunrise allows you to connect with Google Calendar, the iCloud calendar from Apple, and with Exchange Server for Microsoft enterprises. And the list of apps and other services it can work with continues to grow, now including Foursquare, TripIt, and Evernote, amongst others.

It also works with another of my faves, Wunderlist, an online to-do or shopping list that can be shared and updated by multiple users. (You have not truly experienced the digital age until you've gone shopping with your significant other, each of you armed with a shared shopping list on your phone or tablet; it becomes a race to the checkout line with no excuses accepted for failing to buy arugula.)

Sunrise has also added its own cousin, called Meet, an app that lets authorized users select available time slots on multiple calendars for meetings and other assignations.

If you use the same Google account or Outlook account on your tablet and your smartphone and your laptop, they'll be synced. You can change your calendar on any device, but *syncing* depends on an Internet connection. If you're not online at the moment, then the device syncs the first chance it gets.

A Certain TypeMail

Your Galaxy Tab S2 NOOK comes with the factory-standard email client, the one with the clever name Email. It works well and there's nothing bad I can say about it: You can set it up to use accounts on services such as Gmail, Outlook, AOL, various cable Internet providers, and just about all other comers. It just doesn't, well, *sparkle with excitement.*

I know, I'm heading deep into geekery here, but for many of us, our email client is the app with which we have the most intimate, longstanding relationship. And so, when my eye was caught by a third-party product originally called Blue Mail, and then (for reasons beyond my ken) renamed as TypeMail.

The name aside, it is to me the most polished Android email manager, working as well as any other product and adding some neat features including the ability to read or delete *clusters* of mail from the same sender, track back-and-forth *conversations* with a single sender, and apply all sorts of other organizational features to the stacks of mail that come to your tablet. It's available for free from the Play Store.

15

Ten Galaxy Tips and Tricks

*T*his chapter gives you lots of tricks to put up your sleeve.

Extending Your Warranty for Free

Many credit cards offer added protection for devices that you've bought with those pieces of magic plastic. For example, American Express Extended Warranty automatically doubles the warranty protection for most devices — including tablets — for as much as one year. There are similar programs offered by some issuers of MasterCard or Visa cards. Some credit cards even offer free coverage for theft or accidental damage during the first few weeks or months of ownership. What's in your wallet?

Contact customer service for any credit cards you own to see if this is included, and find out exactly the terms of coverage.

My recommendation: Always use credit cards with warranty protection when you buy electronic devices. Keep records of purchase dates; the credit card company should be able to assist you with this.

Using Your Tablet as a Backup Device

The Galaxy Tab S2 will work with a variety of file types: jpg images, MP4 videos, WMA or MP3 audio files, and EPUB or PDF files for NOOK books and Adobe Acrobat files.

But here's a tip for travelers and others who need access to unusual types of files: Even if the Tab S2 NOOK won't work with a particular file type, you can still use your tablet as a storage place. Connect your tablet to a desktop or laptop PC with the USB cable and drag and drop files into a folder on the Tab S2 NOOK.

Yes, you'll probably see a warning message from the NOOK saying that the file type won't work on the tablet. Ignore it and store the files anyway. And then if you ever need them, connect your tablet to a computer and move them the other direction.

I do this all the time as one of several sets of copies of speeches, presentations, and other materials I need to take with me.

Glimpsing Your Office on the NOOK

The Samsung Galaxy Tab S2 NOOK is a marvel of technology, wedded to a solid and capable operating system, and able to run some very impressive apps. But it isn't a fully featured desktop or laptop computer. Someday, I expect, that step of convergence will arrive: a holographic projection of a full-sized screen, a wireless real keyboard, and completely uncompromised software programs. We're *almost* there: I'm not the only one who can envision the necessary next steps.

With this edition of the Galaxy Tab, Samsung delivers a tablet version of Microsoft Office with versions of Word, Excel, and PowerPoint.

Why didn't I include Microsoft Office in Chapter 14? Well, I could have (which would have made the Part of Tens into a Part of Elevens), but I held back because I'm not yet willing to think of a tablet as a direct replacement for a desktop or laptop computer.

Don't get me wrong: Word, Excel, or PowerPoint on your tablet are amazing pieces of work. You can create a document, spreadsheet, or simple presentation on your tablet, and you can download (by USB cable, by Wi-Fi Direct, or by email) an existing file from one of these programs and perform some basic editing on them.

But, at least for me, we're not quite *there* yet. I could have written this book using Word on the Galaxy Tab S2 that's sitting in front of me, but it was much easier to use all the features of my desktop computer. The same goes for managing the chapter structure of the book, something I do on an Excel spreadsheet that's running on the second screen attached to my desktop PC.

And as far as PowerPoint, which is a great tool for many of us, I have loaded my presentations for an upcoming speaking engagement onto the Galaxy Tab S2 and they look *marvelous,* but on the tablet they don't include special visual and audio effects or any embedded audio or video. And I can't (yet) output the presentation in high definition and audio and video to a projector in a theater.

Someday, I expect all of this will be possible. But, for the moment, I include Microsoft Office on the tablet in this chapter of tricks and tips.

Herewith my tip: Upload copies of your important Office files to your tablet to allow you to edit, notate, rehearse, and admire.

Transferring from One Device to Another

Many of us are the sort to always want the latest and greatest hardware. But one reason to resist that urge is the prospect of not being able to bring to the new device all the apps, as well as photos, videos, and music you have acquired along the way.

Samsung makes it relatively painless with a software utility called Smart Switch. One part installs as an app on smartphones or tablets and the other on a PC or Apple computer, which serves as the intermediate stop in a mostly automated process that can use a USB cable or wireless transfer. You can get the tablet app from the Play Store and (if necessary) a utility to install on a desktop or laptop computer at www.samsung.com/smartswitch.

The software can work from most current Android-based tablets or smart-phones (including the Samsung Galaxy Tab S2 NOOK and most Samsung Galaxy phones). Android-to-Android transfers require that the Smart Switch Mobile app be installed on both the old and new devices.

If you're upgrading from an Apple iOS device including iPads and iPhones, the Smart Switch Mobile app needs only to be installed on the Android device — in this case on your new Galaxy Tab S2 NOOK.

 You can get a free copy of the Smart Switch apps from Samsung. From your tablet, load an Internet browser, search for Samsung Smart Switch and download it to your device. You can also find the app in the Play Store or the Samsung Galaxy store. See Figure 15-1.

Transferring files from an iOS device

You can transfer the contents of your iOS devices by using either of these methods:

  ✔ Via iCloud using either Wi-Fi or over the Internet. Visit the Samsung support page for the Smart Switch app to learn which types of files can be transferred from your iOS device using this method.

Figure 15-1: The Smart Switch app is available from the Play Store, and from Samsung's website.

➤ By connecting the iOS device directly to your Tab S2 NOOK using a Micro USB-to-USB adapter in combination with an Apple 30-pin or Lightning-to-USB cable that came with your device.

Transferring files from an Android device

You can transfer the contents of older Android devices, including the Samsung Galaxy Tab 4 NOOK and many other tablets and phones, by using one of these methods:

- By syncing your old device to your new Galaxy device using Wi-Fi Direct. Bring the devices within about four inches of each other to *pair* them, open Smart Switch Mobile on both devices, and select the data you want to transfer.

- By manually pairing the two devices for Wi-Fi Direct. A code is created on the sending device, and when entered on the receiving device, the two devices are connected manually.

- By transferring the content from your old device to an SDHC card and then transferring the card to the new device.

Transferring apps from device to device

The Smart Switch Mobile app smartly scans all apps you have downloaded or purchased and installed on your older device. Then it presents you with a pair of lists:

- The first tells you which of the apps on your older device pairs up with a current version available from the Google Play store. You can download and install any that you want; in some instances you can install a new version of an app you previously purchased for free.

- The second informs you of any apps for which there isn't an exact match and offers suggestions for possible substitutes.

Taking a Screenshot

Everything you see on the screen of your Tab S2 NOOK is based on a "map" of the page constructed in the almost infinitesimally small recesses of the memory chips of the device. There's an instruction for each of the nearly three million individual dots (320 pixels per square inch). That's a huge amount of information, but something that is easily managed by a modern computer or tablet.

The fact that the screen is created based on the memory map means that it is very easy to convert that image into a file; it's called a *screenshot* or *capture*.

You can capture a Web page, or a page of a book or publication, or anything else. Now, for the record, I will point out that the fact you can capture a screen doesn't give you the right to violate copyright. However, as long as the captures you make are only for your own personal use, the law is on your side.

There are two ways to make a screen capture. They both end up with the same result: an image, at full resolution, of everything you can see on your tablet. It's stored in the Gallery in a folder called Screenshots.

Display on the screen whatever you want to capture. Then do either of these procedures:

- ✒ Press the Home button and the Power button at the same time for three seconds. Listen for the electronic reproduction of the sound of a camera shutter.

- ✒ Place your hand at the left or right side of the screen with your pinkie and side of your hand touching the screen and your thumb pointed up. Now sweep across the display while maintaining contact with the screen. You'll hear the camera shutter sound.

Images you capture this way can be viewed within the Gallery, shared with other users over email or by Wi-Fi connection, and adjusted using photo editing programs.

Staking Your Power Vampire In the Heart

What can you do when your tablet seems to drink too deeply of the cup of electrons within?

- ✒ Turn down screen brightness using the slider at the top of the notification panel; the lamp that illuminates the screen is one of the largest users of battery power.

- ✒ Set the automatic sleep mode to 2 minutes or 5 minutes.

- ✒ Turn off Wi-Fi, Bluetooth, and location services if you don't need them.

- ✒ Get in the habit of pressing the Power/Lock key anytime you walk away from the tablet for a few minutes.

- ✒ Turn on Power-Saving Mode.

Adding Apps from Strange Places

To be absolutely safe, Samsung and Barnes & Noble and Google individually and collectively advise you not to add, install, or use an app that comes from someone other than them. That is probably good advice, assuming we believe that the makers and marketers of our Tab S2 NOOK truly know what's good for it (and us).

That said, there are some apps floating around in the digital universe that come from other sources. Some of them may not be the highest quality, and some of them may be malware or spyware or other forms of evil. But some just might be fine pieces of work that exist outside of the official world of the NOOK.

Consider yourself warned.

Say now that you come across an app from an unofficial source and really do want to install it on your device. To do that, you need to take down — permanently or temporarily — one of the fences erected by Samsung. Here's how:

1. **From any Home screen, tap the Apps icon, and then tap the Settings icon.**

2. **Tap Lock Screen and Security.**

3. **Tap Unknown Sources.**

   This opens the door to installation of apps from . . . unknown sources, or at least not from Samsung, Google, or Barnes & Noble.

You can (and probably should) re-enable the block against foreign apps after installing and testing any app you get in this way. In fact, I recommend installing only *one* such unknown source app at a time and use your tablet for a few hours to see if it misbehaves before adding a second or third new app. Doing it that way should allow you to figure out the source of problems easier.

Taming a Misbehaving NOOK

The Samsung line of tablets is pretty mature; the hardware is in its fourth or fifth generation, and the Android operating system is in a similar state of advanced evolution. Leaving aside problems caused by accidents — drops, dunks, and other physical disasters — I suggest there are three broad categories of possible issues for a NOOK: It won't turn on, it won't turn off, or it won't behave.

NOOK won't turn on

Is the battery completely empty? Use the AC adapter and give your Tab S2 NOOK at least an hour's time to gulp down some electrons; the AC adapter is considerably faster than using the USB cable in connection to a laptop or desktop computer.

If the device still fails to turn on after a recharge, it's time to call in the troops: Call the NOOK center at 800-843-2665, use the online chat from www. nook.com, or visit a Barnes & Noble store, which promises lifetime support for your device.

Note that you can't replace the battery in your Tab S2 NOOK; it requires disassembly of the case. If your NOOK is still within its warranty period and isn't holding a charge properly, get help from B&N. Samsung may also be able to help. Visit their website or call 800-726-7864 if you think you're dealing with a hardware problem not of your own making.

You may be able to purchase an extended warranty for your tablet, something that may or may not make economic sense. In this chapter, I also tell you how you may be able to add a year to your warranty for free.

NOOK won't turn off

Try the following:

1. **Unplug the USB cable from the AC adapter (if it's attached to your tablet).**
2. **Remove any device connected to the headphone jack.**
3. **Press and hold the Power/Lock key for 15 to 20 seconds.**
4. **If the tablet turns off: Wait a few seconds, turn it on, and check its operation.**
5. **Try turning it off in the usual manner.**

Seeking Safe Mode

Most apps work as advertised. Some don't. I discuss the Application Manager in Chapter 15, which allows you to stop, disable, or remove most apps.

One way to see if one of your added apps is causing problems is to reboot your tablet into the somewhat secret Safe Mode. See Figure 15-2.

 Try to work backward from the most recent app you installed or updated. What's changed since the last time the tablet was working properly? It may take a while, but uninstall one app at a time and restart the tablet each time. You can't uninstall apps that came preloaded on your tablet.

Here's how to turn on your tablet in Safe Mode:

1. **Turn off your Tab S2 NOOK.**
2. **Press and hold the Power/Lock key for one or two seconds to turn it on.**
3. **When the Samsung logo displays, press and hold the Volume – (down) key until you see the lock screen.**
4. **Let go of the Volume key.**

   The unlock screen shows up, and you'll see the words "Safe Mode" in the lower left portion of the display.

   Note that any apps you may have installed on or moved to the SD card are marked with an SD icon and are disabled.
5. **Test your Tab S2 NOOK.**

   If all seems well, your next step is to figure out which app is causing the problem.

Figure 15-2: A temporary foray into Safe Mode may help exclude misbehaving apps.

Bad app. Bad app!

Quick story: I took my fancy smartphone into a company store run by my cellular provider to ask about a problem I was having. A nice young man there brought my phone to his desk and plugged in a connector to a computer. He then loaded an app on my phone which ran diagnostics. "Nothing wrong with your phone," he said. But when I continued on my way home, I could watch the battery level draining, like water down the drain. When I called the company (on another phone) we determined that the *app* their own representative had loaded onto my phone wasn't authorized and was chewing through electrons like a teenager at an all-you-can-eat buffet. I removed the app.

Safe Mode is turned off when you shut down and restart your tablet. Here's a quick route to that:

1. **Press and hold the Power/Lock key for one or two seconds.**
2. **Tap Restart.**

Doing a soft reset

A *soft reset* tells the device to forget any recent commands or data. It doesn't erase any of your books, documents, or configuration settings and it may leave some data in the memory cache of your device; I deal with that in a moment in a section about the Android System Recovery command.

To soft reset, do this:

1. **Press and hold the Power/Lock key for 10 seconds, then release the key.**

   Wait a few seconds.

2. **Press the Power/Lock key again for 3 seconds to turn on your Tab S2 NOOK tablet.**

   If the reset doesn't fix the problem, do nothing else. Do not pass Go. Call NOOK customer care for assistance.

Visiting Android System Recovery

Deeply hidden — and not mentioned in the NOOK manual or the Samsung manual or in that email you keep getting from Nigeria declaring you the winner of a gazillion dollars tax-free or an invisibility cloak (your choice) — is a secret control panel for Android. Please, please, be careful here. For most users, there's only one option you'll want to try here: clearing the system cache, which may solve some problems you encounter with your tablet such as system crashes or freezes.

Now, if you want, go ahead and look at this screen. But *please* read all of the instructions fully and don't make any sudden movements because you could end up making things much worse. Ready? Really? Okay, this is going to take a bit of finger gymnastics:

1. **Turn off your tablet and let it catch its breath for a second or two.**

   Crack your knuckles and stretch your fingers. Take a deep breath. Look up at the ceiling and spot a few cobwebs that need clearing.

   In other words, think about what you're about to do and follow these instructions carefully.

2. **Place the tablet on its back on a soft surface, in a safe location where it won't easily fall.**

3. **Press and hold the Volume up key and the Home key at the bottom of the tablet.**

4. **While still holding those two button, press and hold the Power key.**

5. **When you see the Android System Recovery screen appear, let go of all three keys.**

   A few seconds later you you're in the deep, dark recesses of the Android system recovery screen. The highlighted line on the screen says Reboot System Now.

6. ***Read this carefully:* Use the Volume key to move the highlight bar. Go down four steps, to Wipe Cache Partition.**

   Don't go anywhere else. (Especially stay away from Wipe Data/Factory Reset.)

7. **With Wipe Cache Partition highlighted, press the Power/Lock key.**

   The little Android guy on the screen will hop, and a message reports that the cache has been *wiped,* which means cleared away.

8. **Make sure that Reboot System Now is highlighted. Check again, please.**

9. **Press the Power/Lock key to restart your tablet.**

   Welcome to the super-secret Android geek club.

Performing a Factory Reset

Beyond here lie dragons. If you really, truly want to (or need to), you can perform a factory reset that takes your Tab S2 NOOK back to the condition it was in when first you pushed its power key. Gone will be any updates, registrations, configurations, downloaded apps, and any other files you installed; the original Samsung and Android setup files remain.

You might consider performing the dire act known as a factory reset for two reasons:

- ✔ All other attempts at fixing an operating system or app problem have failed and you're willing to start over. Completely.

- ✔ You want to sell or give your Samsung Galaxy Tab S2 NOOK to someone and you want to remove all traces of passwords, account names, photos, and anything else you've added to the device.

A *factory reset* deletes all your settings, including your NOOK account, Google account, Samsung account, and any others you have registered. It also *permanently* removes all files, including books, movies, music, text, and photos. That's what it means by factory reset: The tablet will go back, as closely as possible, to the pristine state it was in when it arrived.

Here are the steps:

1. **From any Home screen, tap the Apps icon and then the Settings icon.**

2. **Tap Backup and Restore.**

3. **Tap Factory Data Reset.**

   Really? Are you sure?

4. **Confirm your intentions.**

5. **Tap Reset Device.**

   This should work properly to wipe out all apps, personal files, settings, and other changes you have made to the system since you first got it. In this procedure you're working within the shell, or skin, that Samsung has placed over top of the Android operating system that lies beneath. See Figure 15-3.

Go to Super-Secret Developer Mode

Developer Options has settings usually reserved for people who are writing apps or developing software. You probably don't want to go there. Understood?

If you do enable the option, you'll be able to work with utilities on a personal computer to develop an app. In certain very unusual cases, you may want to enable this mode to connect with a non-standard piece of hardware or software. It won't disable or harm your Tab S2 NOOK, or so I am told by Android experts. And you can turn it on or off, but you won't be able to remove the option from settings once you allow it to appear. I'm only telling you this because I promised to deliver some secrets. But you probably don't want to go there.

If you turn on Developer Options, there's no easy going back. The Developer Options panel is always on the General tab. As long as you keep Developer Options in the Off position, no changes will be made to your operating system.

The only way to remove the Developer Options panel is to perform a factory reset. Warning! Warning! Proceed at your own risk. Here's how to load the mode:

1. **From any Home page, pull down the notifications panel and tap the Settings icon (or get to the Settings icon from the app that appears on one of the Home screens).**

2. **In the left panel, scroll up until you see the System group. Then tap About Device.**

3. **In the right panel, find Build Number.**

4. **Tap Build Number not once, not twice, but seven times.**

   Seven as in seven dwarves, seven brides for seven brothers, seven sleepers.

   Follow the instructions you see on the screen to enable or disable this new super-secret option. But maybe you don't want to go there.

If you suspect there's a problem with the Samsung shell, or if you want to really scrape away all evidence of previous use, you can go to the Android System Recovery Page and perform a hard reset there. Once again, all will be lost except for the Android operating system itself. I discussed the Android System Recovery Page just a moment ago; re-read it and proceed carefully if necessary.

Figure 15-3: This is permanent.

Index

E

About the Author

Corey Sandler has lived a life (thus far) that is the envy of everyone he sees in the mirror when he occasionally shaves. He holds degrees in journalism and psychology from Syracuse University back in the days when writers pecked away on typewriters and publishers hired squadrons of monks to hand-letter and illustrate parchment books. Well, at least the first part is true.

As an undergraduate and graduate student, strictly for fun, he also took courses to learn how to program a gigantic IBM mainframe computer, and in doing so he developed (and then promptly forgot about) the concept of Windows, Facebook, Google, and Amazon.

And so, instead, he went on to work for daily newspapers in Ohio and New York, covering local and then national politics before joining The Associated Press as a newsman.

When the first personal computers were introduced, Corey managed to temporarily switch off the portion of his brain devoted to presidential politics, the Great American Novel, and his unrealized dream of hitting for the cycle in his debut in Major League Baseball as a switch-hitting, switch-throwing second baseman and occasional spot starting pitcher, and returned to his interest in computers. He became the first Executive Editor of *PC Magazine* in 1983 and wrote about and directed the coverage of the birth of the personal computer industry, the Internet, and microwaveable pizza. (Sorry about that last one. It still doesn't quite live up to expectations.)

More than 25 years ago he decided to try his hand at books. Since then he has written more than 200 titles on computers . . . and travel, business, and sports.

When he began writing about computers, the devices came with ten-pound "technical manuals" typed by engineers and programmers. Today, tablets and other technology often come with no instruction books at all; not that they unneeded, but it seems manufacturers have decided not to even bother.

That's a good thing — at least for those of us who make a nice living translating mysterious onscreen menus and hidden features into language readers can actually use. We call them *books*.

Corey lives with his lovely wife on the lovely island of Nantucket, 30 miles off the coast of Cape Cod in Massachusetts. Their two children, no longer troublesome laptops, have begun their own lives on the mainland. About half the year, Corey travels the world as a destination and special interest lecturer for one of the most luxurious cruise lines in the world. (Someone has to do it.) You can vicariously travel along by reading his blog at www.coreysandler.com.

Dedication

For my daughter Tessa and new son-in-law Chad, embarking on their life of happiness together . . . and kind enough to schedule their wedding for two days after the deadline for this book.

Author's Acknowledgments

I would like once again thank fellow traveler (metaphorically speaking) Tonya Maddox Cupp, who polished my prose with professionalism and nonpareil good humor. And Katie Mohr of Wiley, my faithful patron. Once again, they are my publishing all-stars.

Publisher's Acknowledgments

Senior Acquisitions Editor: Katie Mohr

Project Editor: Tonya Maddox Cupp

Sr. Editorial Assistant: Cherie Case

Production Editor: Siddique Shaik

Project Manager: Mary Corder

Cover Image: tbd